FROM OUR OWN CORRESPONDENT

CONTENTS

v

CONTENTS

CONTENTS

CONTENTS

CONTENTS

CONTENTS

CONTENTS

CONTENTS

CONTENTS

Acknowledgements

The editor would like to thank Judith Hart, the production assistant on *From Our Own Correspondent*, for tirelessly and efficiently carrying out the massive amount of research required for this project. His gratitude is also extended to Penny Jackson, whose contribution to this volume included tracking down the photographs of the correspondents. Many thanks also go to Mike Popham, editor of the World Service edition of *From Our Own Correspondent*, for his help and encouragement. The editor is grateful also to Geoff Spink for his assistance, Donna MacEachern-Price for her valuable contribution and Jeff Walden at the BBC Written Archives Centre.

Misha Glenny

Time to slip off your shoes and settle in a comfy chair with a cup of tea or a glass of whisky. Lean back and wait for the reassuring voice from BBC continuity, 'And now *From Our Own Correspondent*, introduced this week by . . .' A thirty-minute programme of observation, analysis, exotica, crisis, humour and the weird from around the world.

Despite the outrageous, momentous and tragic events recorded by BBC correspondents on *FOOC* (as we all call it), the programme orders and explains the world outside for the audiences of Radio 4 and the World Service like no other.

So how does *FOOC* fashion a comprehensible picture of global baffledom into its taut half-hour format? Surely it is the measured voice of the correspondent, blending his or her authority with wit and composure? Of course, the correspondent will adjust tone and speed. The assassination of Kennedy, the bombing of Cambodia or the massacres in Rwanda demand a sobriety completely inappropriate to a story about Michael Jackson's pet monkey or the naming of Monsignor Sin as Cardinal of the Philippines.

But common to all is a sense that people who know what they are talking about are sitting down and telling the audience a tale without hesitation or rush. It is almost as if the correspondent were sitting in the armchair opposite. Or, in the case of the crackly phone line (whose demise in the face of digital technology

I personally regret), you may assume that he or she is sitting in a well-appointed hotel room with at least a minimum of creature comforts. Here, however, there is a good chance that you would be as wrong as you possibly could be.

For behind the correspondent's voice there often lies several days of logistical gymnastics which would challenge even the most disciplined military unit.

Let us assume that our correspondent is, like me, entirely dependent on the laptop computer for writing. All around, the battle for Jajce in central Bosnia is raging. The town's electricity supply has been cut and the computer's battery pack has dried up. So the craftsman's most essential tool is out of commission.

Hunkered down in a cellar, the correspondent now tries to balance a torch uneasily on a pile of charred books in order to see the painfully slow handwritten scrawl emerge. Food stocks are very low — a few dry biscuits and a couple of cans of Coke — so additional cigarettes provide compensation, provoking an unwanted headache. Suffering simultaneously from sensory deprivation and overkill, the mind begins to wander aimlessly: images of a warm bed, a fine Indian restaurant in Brick Lane, sharing a joke with close friends — it spies and settles on anything associated with casual relaxation — anywhere but here, far away from here. A shell explodes nearby and discipline returns. The *FOOC* shall be written.

Long before the scrappy notes are completed, our correspondent is pondering ways to tackle the most terrifying challenge of all — finding a working telephone. Unlike colleagues from the huge news organizations, Reuters or the Associated Press, some BBC correspondents do not haul around portable satellite telephones. Nor indeed are these devices likely to offer lines of suitable sound quality. The only option is to leave battered Jajce and head for Banja Luka, a Serb stronghold in northern Bosnia.

Dashing through the back of the town, the correspondent stumbles upon a piece of luck. Under such circumstances, he or she will always have at least one break which is almost as valuable as the computer. Indeed, if not blessed by the gods of coincidence and fortune, the budding journalist should not even entertain any aspirations to become a BBC correspondent.

On this occasion, our worker-ant has just come upon a European Community monitor driving back to Banja Luka. The gun-toting guardians of the roadblocks *en route* are suspicious of a journalist travelling with one of the EC monitors, who themselves are considered spies. But a mixture of bluff and misunderstanding overcomes these barriers.

Finally at the hotel (the deadline clock still ticking inexorably), a five-minute break for composure. The good news: there is a telephone and it is working. The bad news: there are no international lines, you can only dial as far as Belgrade. But again, the gods order a reprieve. The correspondent catches a friend at home in Belgrade who knows how to record onto a cassette from a phone line:

'I'm really sorry – I'm just on my way out to dinner and can't stop.'

'Look, I know this is dreadfully inconvenient but the piece is due to run in two hours' time. Please can you tape it and then send it down the line to London.'

A pained pause. All journalists in difficult situations have to rely on the sacrificial goodwill of their colleagues, even those working for the competition.

'Oh, God, I suppose so. But you really owe me for this one.'

'Thank you. Thank you. Thank you. Thank you. I'll call again in five minutes after I've set things up here.'

'Six minutes and I'm out to dinner.'

Filing for radio does not involve just talking into the mouth-piece. First, correspondents have to explain to the grumpy receptionist that they must dismantle the hotel's telephone to install the 'mutterbox', a curious little device which acts as an amplifier while also squeezing your voice into those frequencies which nestle sweetly inside a radio.

Hands shaking, pouring with sweat, dropping screwdrivers and crocodile-clips, the correspondent smiles weakly at the receptionist who is visibly unimpressed. Then comes the twenty-five minutes of recording and re-recording. And this is the heart of the matter. For regardless of our hero's physical or mental state, he or she must always be ready to shift into the commanding style of the BBC. Calm, considered, reflective – always on the outside, never involved in the events. It is a great job but it requires enormous strength and determination.

The producer in London will offer thanks, occasionally effusive but invariably genuine. The producer is the unseen, unheard pivot of *From Our Own Correspondent*. The seamless way in which a programme subtly changes mood and intensity is all the work of the producer. It requires careful thought and organization to produce a successful *FOOC* and not everybody can bring the requisite skills to the job. But the only time the audience will notice these is when they are absent. With a bad producer, the show sounds disjointed and uneven. Not even the most talented presenters and correspondents can compensate for the destruction which a bad producer can wreak. In my experience, however, the BBC has been very lucky with its producers.

But of course at the heart of each *FOOC* is our own correspondent. Talk to any of them who have worked over the last four decades and they will all say the same thing: '*FOOC* is a programme for which I will take time and particular care. This is the one chance I have to write.' It may appear strange but as journalists, radio correspondents often feel as though their wings are clipped. A piece for the six o'clock news lasts between forty-five seconds and one minute fifteen (the latter if you are on a very big story) which means that you may say nothing but the bare minimum. If you are producing a feature, your own sentiments are invariably, and correctly, drowned by sound effects and other voices. It is only through *FOOC* that the BBC correspondents are able to communicate directly and personally with their audience. Not only does this mean that it is our most treasured half-hour of the week, it also means that the contributions are of a consistently excellent standard. This volume contains the *crème de la crème* from four decades. Savour it!

*'This is the BBC Home Service.
From Our Own Correspondent. We are broadcasting now the first
of a new series of programmes in which BBC correspondents will
deal with current affairs as seen from their own posts in various
parts of the world . . .'*

1955–1965

POST-WAR REFUGEES

Edmund Nunns

NEW YORK, OCTOBER 1955

Ten years after the end of the Second World War, the continent of Europe was still awash with refugees, many living in camps in atrocious conditions.

I have been spending a good deal of the past week with the Social Committee of the United Nations Assembly listening to its debate on the problem of refugees. I remember well, as many of us do, the sight of the vast numbers of trudging, homeless people in many parts of Europe during the war and just after it, people who, in one way or another, had been uprooted from their own countries and could not or would not return to them. But that was nine or ten years ago, and it came as a shock last week to learn that there are still three hundred and fifty thousand refugees not permanently settled, living, as one delegate put it, always on the edge of despair. And of those, seventy thousand are in camps in Europe in conditions of squalor and overcrowding. The amazing thing is that so many of them are still able-bodied.

The Social Committee began by hearing a report from the United Nations High Commissioner for Refugees, Dr van Heuven Goedhart. Inevitably the report was rather dry and official and very full of statistics, but you could feel the intense human sympathy in the High Commissioner himself that drives him along on what is an onerous and, at times, a thankless task. The refugees in camps are not the only problems he has to cope with;

there are what are classified as the 'difficult ones'; that is, people who are physically or mentally infirm and have to have constant attention. And also those who are beyond the age when they can embark on a new career. There are fifteen thousand of these and efforts are being made to find vacancies for them in homes or institutions where they can be looked after.

Then there are more than a thousand refugee seamen who either have not got adequate papers or none at all, and so have to stay on board ship because there is no shore they can legally set foot on.

I had a talk with Dr van Heuven Goedhart during the week and he told me about these cases. One was a Latvian who was in a refugee camp in Germany but was determined to begin life again; he made his way to Hamburg and signed on as a seaman on a little ship flying the Panamanian flag. He knew that he would not be able to go ashore without papers and he stuck on this ship for three years. When finally he did take a chance and went ashore in a foreign port he was immediately arrested.

He spent four months in prison with the local authorities not knowing what to do with him and no one else even aware of his existence. Dr van Heuven Goedhart heard about him through another man who had been in the same gaol, and persuaded another government to give the Latvian temporary sponsorship. So the man was let out of prison and provided with papers which entitled him to move freely around the world.

The High Commissioner is hoping that a conference of experts which is to meet shortly will work out a way of providing an international document for all of those seamen.

The main emphasis of the new programme is on clearing the camps. There are two hundred of these, in Germany, Austria, Italy and Greece. They consist, mostly, of groups of wooden huts, many dilapidated, with numerous families crowded in each hut with only a blanket hung between them to give a semblance of privacy. The High Commissioner did a tour of them this summer and he kept referring to the smell that permeated the camps caused by cooking, eating and living in the same quarters combined with inadequate sanitation. Most of the inhabitants have been there since the war ended and many are bringing up children who know of no other existence.

If the chance of a job arises in the country a refugee is in, the first thing that has to be done is to set him on his feet and help him over the initial period of his new life. Housing is the biggest problem – often an expensive one. In Germany a loan bank has been started to enable refugees to buy land or small businesses. The loans are guaranteed by the High Commissioner and, so far, out of twelve hundred that have been made, all but eighty have turned out successfully. So a similar scheme is to be started in Austria.

Resettlement of refugees in countries other than their own is often less expensive, for the receiving country covers much of the cost. The other possibility for the refugees in camps is to be repatriated to their country of origin. Actually, pretty well all of them who want to go home have done so by now, but the Soviet Union and other East European governments have been making new amnesty offers in an effort to persuade some more to return. And their representatives on the Social Committee tabled a resolution saying that information about these amnesty offers should be spread among the refugees, who at the same time, are to be protected from what the resolution calls 'hostile propaganda'. The British and other delegates are opposing this, saying it would mean that the refugees would be subjected to a one-way traffic of information, which would itself be tantamount to propaganda.

A Western resolution, sponsored by nine countries including Britain and the United States, calls on the High Commissioner to continue working on his present lines, and urges other countries to contribute to his fund. The fund has so far not had adequate support and you can understand the eagerness of the High Commissioner that his work should not be held up for lack of money.

COMIC HAT DIPLOMACY

Gerald Priestland

Delhi, December 1955

The Soviet leaders, Marshal Bulganin and Mr Kruschev, were on the final stages of their visit to India and Burma when our correspondent sent this assessment of their tour.

A few days ago, I was sitting in the pantry of the Presidential Palace in Rangoon, eating a cold pheasant leg and waiting for Mr Kruschev to make his speech in the banquet hall next door. Almost every night there was a speech or the threat of one. In any case, there could be no bed before midnight and it was up again at four or five in the morning for a dawn take-off so as to reach the next stop in advance of the fast Russian aircraft.

After nearly three weeks of this I was glad to stop, but they have been weeks so full of interest that I cannot regret a moment of them. They have provided, as they must have done for the Russian party too, a dazzling scrapbook of recollections. Here are just a few of my own. The Bakhra Gorge, carved and blasted by the dam builders until its own Mother Nature would scarcely recognize it. The sound of eighty thousand children in a stadium at Bombay – like the sea heard from a high cliff. The contrast between the green and red of the south Indian landscape and the tawny monotony of the north. The princely splendour that still pervades Mysore. The cool green heights of Ooty. The terrifying crowds in Calcutta and, in Burma, the young Buddhist monks in their orange robes, the fantastic regatta on Imle Lake, the pagodas of Mandalay, the captivating Burmese girls and the incessant tintinnabulation of Burmese music.

Of course, Marshal Bulganin and Mr Kruschev have themselves provided scores of these snapshots. Smothered in flowers, wearing Boy Scout scarves, turbans or Gandhi caps, hugging children, riding elephants, always ready to oblige the cameras. It has been said frequently that they make a perfect team, that the Marshal is the straight man and the Party Secretary the comic. This view of them accounts for much of their popularity over here, but to some of us who have literally been rubbing shoulders with them during the tour it seems an interpretation which could be misleading and dangerous. One of Mr Kruschev's most cleverly worded speeches was delivered with a comic hat on his head. He knew very well how funny it looked, but from the Western point of view what he said was far from amusing.

I do not propose to repeat all the points which the two Russian leaders made in their many speeches. By and large, there was, in fact, only one speech, with Marshal Bulganin reading a conventional, relatively subdued version of it and Mr Kruschev delivering it impromptu and with far greater aggressiveness. The main line of the argument was that Russia, like India and Burma, had been a backward and exploited country, that like them she had been persecuted by the West, that like them, she wanted peace and hated colonialism – that, in fact, only Russia could really understand Asia and be her firm and faithful ally. The colonialists, it was argued, were still colonialists at heart. They might pretend to help Asia, but really they wanted to hold her down. Russia, on the other hand, respected Asia's independence and was prepared to give her all kinds of technical aid, train her specialists and intellectuals and offer increased trade.

The five principles of co-existence were a *sine qua non* of every speech. In fairness, I suppose one should add Mr Kruschev's

9

twinkling assurance that he was not trying to disseminate propaganda. But whatever he meant by propaganda, one could hardly say that his speeches were tolerant of the West. Words like 'peace' and 'colonialism', which require perhaps more definition than they are usually given in India, but which Indians accept as needing little examination, were used in a context which gave them an entirely pro-Russian, anti-Western significance.

It might be worthwhile, at this point, to mention the controversy which has arisen over what the Russians really said on certain occasions, particularly the remarks attributed to Mr Kruschev by Western correspondents at Rangoon and later denied by the Soviet Press. It has been suggested that the fault may have lain with the interpreters, who on all important occasions worked in English. Now, of the two Russian men selected for this job, one, a former correspondent of the official Soviet News Agency at the United Nations, regularly translated for Mr Kruschev. Mr Kruschev was translated into English sentence by sentence. The translations were a bit clumsy, and on two occasions turned out to be positively wrong in important details, but the substance was there. Always, there were two interpreters present, and only once did they announce a correction. After the conversation in Rangoon, between Mr Kruschev and the Burmese Ambassador to Moscow, the Western and Burmese correspondents who were there taking notes, sent their dispatches immediately. The Soviet version was compiled two days later as a counterblast. This version entirely omitted certain passages, and attributed others to the Burmese Ambassador. The Ambassador has since refused to comment.

What makes the affair even more extraordinary is Mr Kruschev's subsequent behaviour. Having invited the Western correspondents to attend his next speech he announced, not that they had misreported him, but that, as he put it, they had not been quite satisfied with his speeches. They were, he said, going to be even less satisfied with this one, and he proceeded to launch an attack on British colonial policy which was far more objectionable than the one attributed to him in Rangoon. It left correspondents even less inclined to believe they had misreported him and wondering why so much trouble had been taken to deny what was almost immediately surpassed.

But what will be the effect of this tour upon the Indians and Burmese and their respective governments? In each case the decisive factor will be the lead given by their Prime Ministers, and both have repeatedly said they do not intend to abandon their policy of non-alignment. Since the Russian tour began, Mr Nehru has twice referred in public to the need for restraining one's language if one really wants peace, and has made some impressive remarks about the value of the Commonwealth. Many Indians and Burmese of the Western-educated upper class have been shocked by the use the Russian leaders have made of the platforms offered them here. At the same time, while the Indian and Burmese governments are embarrassed by some of the speeches, they seem prepared to make allowances. One Indian official expressed the view to me that nothing should be done to upset the Russians, and that the Americans were the people who most needed restraining. Another Indian said he very much hoped that the Russian leaders would go to London, because, as he put it, it would throw doubts on India's neutrality if she were the only democratic country they visited.

As for the common people, it would probably be wrong to attach too much importance to the enthusiasm of the crowds, and again wrong to sneer at the organized nature of their welcome. Both countries felt that after the reception Russia had given to their own Prime Ministers, they could not do less. There is, moreover, a very ancient tradition here of seeking the presence of distinguished visitors and turning the occasion into a public carnival. The Indians in particular have been flattered by the visit, and delighted to hear they have powerful new friends. A lot will depend on how the visit is followed up, and on what use is made of the goodwill created.

Millions of Indians are now getting their first education in democratic politics, and part of this has been to teach even the tiniest child to shout, 'Indians and Russians are brothers.' Whether they will get the opportunity to shout the same of the British or Americans remains to be seen.

LUNCHING WITH DR NHLAPE

Patrick Smith

SOUTH AFRICA, MARCH 1956

Dr Jacob Nhlape, the Zulu editor of an African newspaper, was the first African journalist ever to be granted facilities in Parliament. He was not allowed in the Press gallery and he had to report proceedings from a small corner bay normally reserved for non-European visitors. Our correspondent sought out his opinions.

A few of my foreign correspondent colleagues and I recently took Dr Nhlape to lunch. This itself needed a little thought, for the main hotels in Cape Town are for Europeans only. We did, however, find a pleasant Indian restaurant in District 6, the notoriously tough coloured quarter of the city, where all guests, whatever their colour, are welcomed with biting hot curry. Doctor Nhlape is a stocky Zulu, whose large stomach adds to his dignity. A few white touches in his wiry hair are the only indication of his fifty-two years. Originally a schoolmaster, a product of the long-established Presbyterian Mission at Lovedale in the eastern Cape, he has a ready smile, a superlative flow of English and can draw on his experiences in America, Europe and the Middle East to help him assess developments in his own country today.

He was critical of the African National Congress, that is the largest non-European political organization in the Union, of which he has been a member for many years, and was particularly worried about the growing Indian influence within it. He was, it perhaps goes without saying, extremely critical also of the present National Party Government with what he called its 'foolish policy of apartheid' – adding, however, that if the opposition United Party were returned to power they would not give his fellow Africans more opportunities than they had at present.

We asked him what in his opinion was the gravest injustice done to the Africans in South Africa. His reply came very quickly. 'There are more than nine million of us, we form the vast majority of the Union's population, yet we have no direct say in anything. There are some good people working in the Ministry of Native Affairs, but their policy is all wrong. We want more land for ourselves; we want more schools and the freedom to choose our own type of education. And we want to see an end to the colour bar. But we are patient and we know all this will inevitably fall to us in time.

'We are against the present system of migratory labour,' he went on, 'migratory labour to the mines, where the Africans are but a cheap means of extracting the gold, uranium and diamonds from the earth. They have to leave their wives and families behind, and when they are ill they are dismissed and sent home to die. That is all wrong. I suppose,' he added, 'that as long as the present apartheid policy prevails, there is little chance of our getting what we want unless we are prepared to take part in economic and labour boycotts, and that will not be easy. A war might hurry on the process because in that event we should not, perhaps, feel very loyal to the government. But we are a patient people and are prepared to wait. Who knows? One day South Africa may have to adopt a policy of partnership as the government is doing in Rhodesia.'

Well, all this was uttered quietly in a reasoned tone of voice. 'No,' he added, in answer to another question, 'No, I do not think racial conditions are so bad that they can be said to have passed the point of no return. We Africans want to cooperate with the Europeans, but there are practically no opportunities for doing so under the present regime.'

The lunch ended and we came out into the sunshine and shook the hand of our guest in farewell. With a smile he said, 'They say that charity begins at home, but I find it begins abroad. You are the first Europeans in the Union ever to have invited me to a meal in a public place.' And with that remark, the heavily built Zulu ambled off to catch his bus.

AMERICAN MOONSHINE

Douglas Willis

WASHINGTON, MAY 1956

Moonshine, an illicitly distilled spirit, usually whiskey, was enjoying a record popularity – despite the efforts of the Federal Treasury, the Bureau of Internal Revenue and the sheriffs.

Serious drinkers in the United States, particularly those who travel, need to be as expert in their knowledge of licensing laws and elementary geography as their fellows in Britain, who know the opening and closing hours of the various London licensing districts, all major cities and most rural areas. They also know when the pubs shut and the clubs open, the times when trains with restaurant cars leave mainline stations and the sailing schedules of river steamers from Westminster Bridge.

Here in Washington, it is illegal to stand up and drink. Across the river in Virginia, only beer and wine may be consumed in public; it is illegal to carry a bottle of spirits from Washington into the state of Maryland which surrounds the city on three sides. The sale of spirits in Oklahoma and Mississippi is prohibited. In Texas you can only drink spirits in a bar if you take your own bottle in with you.

There are, particularly in the deep South, the traditional home of bourbon whiskey, Old Fashioneds and Mint Juleps, a surprising number of counties where the sale of liquor, as it is called, is strictly illegal. Such a place is Tuscaloosa, Alabama, where a professor at the State University there, asked over a glass of bourbon why the county remained officially dry in a sea of whiskey, replied, 'We hold occasional referendums but between the Church and the bootleggers we're licked.'

American drinkers are also plagued by the cost of spirits made, as in Britain, much more expensive by the Bureau of Internal Revenue, and, in dry areas, the profits of the bootleggers. Enter then the moonshiner to their rescue, hotly pursued by sheriffs, state revenue officers and agents of the Federal Treasury. But the man who makes the spirits illegally and sells them without burden of tax is usually one jump ahead.

The *Wall Street Journal*, in a special survey, estimates that moonshining is enjoying its biggest boom since Prohibition, and it is causing the federal and state governments to lose perhaps a thousand million dollars a year in evaded taxation. One out of every four gallons of hard liquor produced in the United States last year was moonshine – also known to its patrons as 'Corn Squeezings', 'White Lightning', 'Pop's Skull', 'Bumble Bee's Stew' and 'Mountain Dew'.

The state of North Carolina and its legal distillers of bourbon whiskey became so concerned at the amount of moonshine whiskey that was being bought and drunk in the state that it introduced its own brand of legal one hundred per cent proof moonshine, called it 'White Lightning' and proudly labelled it, 'Less than one month old'. At first it sold at a monthly rate of two thousand five hundred cases to those who had developed a taste for moonshine, but carrying a small tax, it was still more expensive than the illegal variety and sales fell to three hundred cases a month. An official gave another reason – moonshiners just cannot tolerate buying liquor in shops.

In a recent twelve-month period, agents of the United States Treasury's Alcohol Tax Division seized fourteen thousand five hundred illegal stills and most were found in fourteen Southern states, usually hidden away in isolated pinewoods. Most of the moonshiners now use bottled gas rather than wood fuel, which sends up tell-tale smoke. Revenue agents often detect a still from several miles away by the pungent smell of fermenting mash. The biggest profits from the sale of moonshine, says the *Wall Street Journal*, are made by retailers who receive from fourteen to eighteen dollars a gallon for spirits that cost two dollars to make. Sometimes the retailers increase their profits by thinning the product with such liquids as prune juice, paint thinner, or embalming fluid.

Most of the illegal stills are simple affairs calling for nothing more than a barrel for fermenting mash, an empty petrol tin and some copper tubing running to a disconnected car radiator. With this and yeast and water the moonshiner is in business. The finished product, made in about ten days or less, is said by experts to taste nothing like legal whiskey. 'But,' said one, 'you'd be surprised how many persons tell us they prefer moonshine because it burns all the way down.'

There are several reasons for the popularity of moonshine in the Southern states. They include a high ratio of poorer people who appreciate its cheapness; the fact that more than forty per cent of the South's population live in dry counties; and because the Southern pine forests offer ample secrecy and water supplies, while the warm, humid climate speeds up fermentation and allows work to proceed all the year round.

ROCKING AT THE DIXIE PIG

Douglas Willis

WASHINGTON, SEPTEMBER 1956

Rock and roll was sweeping all before it in its conquest of youth culture in the United States and around the world.

The Dixie Pig is a one-storey establishment, built on the lines of a prefabricated warehouse, and it stands in a parking lot amid the litter of empty beer cans on the outskirts of Washington. Motorists passing by on the highway are left in no doubt that it is there as, apart from an illuminated pig on its roof, a loudspeaker carries its thunderous message for a hundred yards around.

The Dixie Pig is one of the District of Columbia's two more notable rock and roll establishments, and here, wearing a look of enquiry but without benefit of earplugs, I found myself the other night. The purpose of my mission: to determine the effects of rock and roll on its devoted followers and, what was more, to try to determine its effect on me.

It is a style of music that for a time captivated adolescents because it was a change from jive, bebop and boogie-woogie. It is hillbilly music with a downbeat. It came, as all jazz, from the South, where the Negro bands called it rhythm and blues but rarely play it now because it limits their free-swinging style. It made an unknown white hillbilly band – Bill Haley and his Comets – famous, but their popularity is beginning to wane now that a young man named Elvis Presley has appeared on the tortured scene.

Ten million of his records are expected to be sold this year, even more than you might have guessed while trying to elude the sound of his voice. Rock and roll is said to evoke a physical response from its listeners. Its beating pulse forces extraordinary gyrations from those who dance to it. Mr Presley, when he sings in public, gives full vent to his feelings, and a policeman is said to have commented, 'If he did that in the street, I would arrest him.'

Fascinated adolescents have become rowdy in half a dozen cities; one or two authorities have banned the music; people have been injured in brawls. But it must be pointed out that these disorders have been negligible in a country where dance music has infinite variations and where the vast majority of adolescents can take new fads like rock and roll in their stride.

Now return with me, if you will, to the Dixie Pig. Nothing much was happening. Friday night is the big night and bottles of beer are vibrating to the music of the band, a five-piece ensemble known as Bobbie Boyd's Jazz Bombers. Mr Boyd stood at his piano – rock and roll pianists never, never sit – his long arms dangling, beating the keys with sledgehammer force in a simian and revengeful way. The trumpet player sucked and chewed his trumpet, the saxophone player perspired and clapped his hands while the saxophone dangled from a cord around his neck. A muscular guitarist plucked and thumped while the drummer kept up his unrelenting regular downbeat syncopation. All five twitched, shook, wriggled, jumped and bobbed up and down like puppets on a string and occasionally joined together in shuddering harmony to deliver lyrics in hillbilly idiom.

However, this was getting me no nearer to finding out what effect rock and roll has on American adolescents. I had seen what it had done to Mr Boyd and his Jazz Bombers, but not what it was doing to the youth of Washington. Therefore, another journey appeared to be necessary. So now, late at night, I drove to within five blocks of the navy yard in Washington and there at

Guy's Dance Hall and Café I found Pete Dennis and his four Dynatones, one of whom was suffering from a cold in the head and sneezed as he called out at intervals the strange words, 'Loose as a goose; as crazy as a loon.' This appeared to be advice to the couples crowding a small dance floor – sturdy young men with crew-cut hair and young and lissom women with tight velvet pants and ponytail hairstyles. The band paused only for twenty minute breaks ordained by the local branch of the Musicians' Union. The rest of the time, without giving the dancers more than a minute's rest, the band produced a noise like artillery gunfire with accompanying lightning effects like those made by an old-time cinema pianist during the big storm scene.

There were shouts of, 'Go, go!' The drummer beat out a pounding rhythm that excited the senses and sent the dancers into convulsions, so that a girl in horn-rimmed glasses held on to them with one hand while she clutched a Filipino gentleman in a red and white shirt round the neck, and was at times whirled completely over his shoulders, though still managing to hang on to her glasses.

All the dancers, notwithstanding their efforts, were detached, deadpan, bearing faraway expressions as they shook, shimmied and rocked and rolled. Yet when they left the floor, breathing heavily, their vivacity returned. Most sat with the same bottle of beer for the hour I was there. They all seemed to be enjoying themselves in a remarkably athletic way. There was no disturbance nor hint of it. Some were married, some were not. If they were unduly excited they were no more so than the ultrasophisticated night club correspondent of the *Washington Daily News* who had recommended me to visit the establishment. 'Each time I go,' he said, 'I go home and vibrate for two hours.'

Sociologists, psychiatrists, leaders of the Church and of education have analysed and debated the effects of rock and roll on youngsters. Some feel that it is a symptom of a condition that might produce delinquency; but others feel it has no more influence on morals or behaviour than the Charleston.

HUNGARY INVADED

Peter Raleigh

VIENNA, NOVEMBER 1956

Budapest was bombed and occupied by Russian troops with tanks but foreign correspondents were unable to get their stories out. News organizations had to rely on the refugees streaming over the frontier into Austria to tell them what was going on inside Hungary.

It is a little difficult to report from Vienna at the end of a week such as this with detachment. It seems sometimes like waiting outside the hospital ward in which a friend lies desperately ill and fighting for life. The doors are closed, the news is meagre and the outlook grave. And I think I can say that this feeling is shared by nearly all Austrians. I exclude the few Austrian Communists who had to bow down to considerable popular hatred this week.

We have had to wait, fearing the worst and moved by the sight of thousands upon thousands of men, women and children tramping across the frontier to safety, or waiting patiently in the tall rooms of some camp, their homes and friends behind them and a difficult new life ahead.

As the fighting flickered and coursed through an isolated Hungary this week, Vienna has been inevitably awash with rumour and contradictory reports. For it is a week since Western correspondents in Budapest, among them the BBC special correspondent, Ivor Jones, who would otherwise be talking to you, filed their last reports to Vienna and the outside world. Most of these correspondents we know to be in safety in the legations of various countries in Budapest. It is a week since the Russians marched on Budapest and sent their armour running through the streets. It is a week since the last moving appeal from the Hungarian Prime Minister, Imre Nagy, for help from the United Nations, from the great powers. Then silence came down on the true state of things in Hungary, and fact and fiction mingled together have trickled at intervals through this curtain.

Inevitably, many of the reports reaching Vienna are exaggerated, perhaps false. But through these mists of uncertainty you can still see the outlines of the almost unbelievable fight for freedom which the people of a small country, badly armed and badly fed, have made against an overwhelming military strength. Last Sunday, few observers gave the Hungarian Resistance Movement more than a day or two. The Russians themselves were soon asserting over Moscow Radio that resistance had been crushed, but it was not so. Day by day, at least some reports of fighting came into Vienna – fighting in the narrow streets of the old part of Budapest; in the main industrial districts; fighting from Nationalist strongpoints in the bigger buildings. Men of the Resistance have been bombed at least once. They have faced attacks by tanks, but they have held out. Reports of fighting have come from outside Budapest, for example from the neighbourhood of the uranium mines near Pécs in the south. One refugee told me, by the way, that these uranium mines had only just been got ready for production – a production destined, he said, wholly for the Russians. Reports of fighting have come from north-western Hungary, from the Györ area, where the Nationalists had one of their main military headquarters.

That the unequal battle could last so long as it has seems to afford proof of the stories of incredible gallantry reaching Vienna – stories of gallantry to the point of death on the part of young boys, sometimes armed, as in the days of the first uprising three weeks ago, with little more than bottles of petrol with primitive fuses. One story, which may or may not be true, tells of a Russian tank unit which was attacked by three boys with bottles of petrol.

One by one the boys were shot down. And then the Russian tank commander surrendered — surrendered because, he said, such gallantry showed that he was meeting a genuine resistance of the Hungarian people.

But for that one report of a Russian being moved to surrender, there are others which speak of the complete ruthlessness and disregard for life shown by the Russian soldiers. When the Russians offered an amnesty recently and some few Hungarians accepted it, they were shot at once. The loss of life cannot be gauged. The most conservative figures I have heard mentioned three thousand dead and seven thousand wounded, and casualties are thought to be in fact far higher. And all this week the International Red Cross units have been unable to get from Austria into Hungary to carry out their neutral, humanitarian task. If and when they do get into Hungary, the Red Cross teams will take with them food as much as medical supplies, for they will find starvation and hunger and devastation, a land without much transport or fuel. For three weeks there has been a general strike in Hungary. Radio Budapest has told of districts without electricity; shops looted; houses burned down; queues for food. There have been urgent appeals to workers to return to work, threats, and promises of bonus pay, but the latest reports say that few of the workers are yet at work.

If in this last week the International Red Cross has been unable to help those inside Hungary, it has done much to help the Austrians care for the seventeen thousand refugees who have arrived here. I have seen these refugees in so many places, crossing the frontier — sometimes with a small paper parcel, sometimes without one — in clothes that make one realize that at a given moment they had dropped what they were doing and come over, just as they were, to safety. A man who came over the border on a motor bicycle was lucky; he still had on his old leather jacket. I have seen the faded yellow buses provided by the Austrians driving the refugees to the reception camps. I have seen the battered barracks where those children, luckily few, who are all alone in the world, were being cared for. I have seen the peeling army cadet school at Traiskirchen, the main reception camp, where hundreds stood, pallid and weary in a greasy November rain, exchanging news or standing silent looking into space. I have seen the families lying on the straw-filled mattresses, holding their children. Sometimes the children were crying in these strange surroundings.

I have heard doctors talk of the tiny children, weak and thin for want of food when they arrived; of the older people whose hearts could hardly stand the strain of their scramble to safety. Some of the refugees I have talked to were bitter. 'You can't fight tanks with bare hands.' 'Why don't you send us arms as well as penicillin?' 'Why did Suez have to happen now so that we were forgotten?' Others are content to have found refuge, saying, 'I've been waiting to escape the Communists for years.' And then they may talk about what they want to do next, but often they will ask for news of what is happening in Hungary, and then they are clearly thinking of their friends or relatives and the sad prospects before them.

PORT SAID BOMBARDED

Hardiman Scott

PORT SAID, NOVEMBER 1956

In a bloody operation, British troops seized control of the Suez Canal Zone after bombarding the centre of Port Said.

This is the story of a battered city of confusion, struggling, it seems, against, a feeling of inertia to get going again, to become normal. If it is a little depressing, I am sorry, but it is true. Once again the Union Jack flies from what used to be the Admiralty mast on the harbour at Port Said. And not far away the statue of Ferdinand de Lesseps, the man who built the Suez Canal, looks out upon the countless ships that lie in the harbour and offshore. And the harbour itself is a frantic scene of vessels unloading stores and food.

Behind de Lesseps is the shell-shocked, rocket-hit town. No bombs were dropped on Port Said, and there were strict instructions that no naval guns larger than those on a destroyer were to fire on the town; but the Egyptians who saw wave after wave of aircraft sweeping in cannot distinguish between bombs and rockets. They think we have bombed Port Said. Well, the sight is very much the same. It is true that in the heart of the town the damage is light, but there are whole sections of it which look like the East End of London during the Blitz, and some blocks near the beaches are razed. There is only rubble. Many of the glistening white luxury flats are gaping open where the rockets have torn into them. People left them in a hurry. Even their clothes are hanging in the wardrobe, the beds unmade, the pyjamas lying in a huddle where they had been taken off, wedding photographs on the sideboard, a child's toy gun on the floor. On the bedside table a book is open where someone had put it down meaning to pick it up again. I could not help wondering if they ever would.

Along the beaches were numerous bathing chalets – only the foundations remain; and immediately behind them, concrete buildings have been reduced to piles of rubble. All this devastation was far more than I had expected to see from the communiqués I had read in Nicosia.

And the loss of civilian life has been put officially at one hundred. This cannot be right. I have seen more bodies myself. I drove past a cemetery where fighting had taken place, and there was body piled upon body like so many sacks in a granary – Egyptian troops and civilians. I could not count them. And then I went to the civilian hospital – it is a white, modern building, and I was shown round by a doctor wearing a green smock. He showed me children who would not live, and he kept muttering to me, 'We had no defence; no protection.' I saw the operating theatre, a rocket had gone right into it. Although this is a modern hospital, there were dust and flies everywhere, flies settling on the bloodstained sheets and on the bandages of the wounded. And here I am not going to tell you everything that I saw, but the children with their stomach wounds were the most gruesome sights.

And now the people are beginning to come out of their houses; some of them I watched leading Commandos to stores of weapons and ammunition. The guns were Russian. But it is not true to say that this is Russian aid supplied especially for the battle. They were, in fact, the armaments which Egypt has been buying from Russia for some time.

Egyptians wander about the streets, walking in the roadways; they stand and stare at you, and when you speak to them, they give the impression of being frightened, and out of their fright they put on a smile of excessive friendliness. Perhaps they are just dazed. I have talked with some who speak English, and with Maltese, and with a few Englishmen; all of them were surprised at the ferociousness of the attack. One Maltese man and his Italian wife and their young children stayed the whole time in the basement of one of the modern blocks of flats near the beaches. They were the only people to remain in the building. It has great holes rent in it. But they survived; and he told me he thought the Egyptian fighters were fanatical, that they had been misled, and when they realized it they ran away.

And the Allied forces went on, almost unstopped, down twenty-two miles of the Canal into the scrubby, dusty brown desert glimmering with a haze of heat, and there they stopped at the time of the ceasefire. I have seen them dug in, and the fellows – some of them reservists – are making the best of it, and they have begun to get mail from home.

ESCAPE FROM BUDAPEST

Ivor Jones

VIENNA, NOVEMBER 1956

The foreign correspondents, including the BBC's Ivor Jones, who had been trapped for several days as fighting raged in Budapest, finally managed to flee to safety.

Reporters are notorious individualists but, five days after the Russian attack started, we in Budapest found ourselves almost spontaneously working together. We had to get out to tell our story. There were no normal communications, and we thought that the bigger our convoy, the better our chance would be. So early in the morning of Friday the ninth, we began to form up outside the American Legation.

It was an amazing collection of cars – more than thirty of them – some barely roadworthy, some elegant enough for a glossy advertisement, but nearly all plastered with the flag of some Western nation. We set off. We had no papers allowing us to go. Some of us had not even got visas allowing us to be in Hungary. But we set off. There was still some firing going on.

We crossed the Danube by what seemed the easiest bridge. There were Russian tanks at either end, but the sentries let us pass. Beyond, in the suburbs, the debris of fighting was as heavy as in the city centre. Wrecked Hungarian guns lay beside the road; walls and the sides of houses had been shot away.

About ten miles out we reached a big barracks held by the Russians. We were stopped at a checkpoint outside it. There was already one tank there and some Tommy-gunners. Another tank came up and I spent most of the next few hours looking down its gun barrel, which seemed to be trained directly on my car. Our spokesman sought out the barracks commander, a Russian colonel. He was correct, almost affable. He said that, unfortunately, he had no authority to let us pass and, since we had no documents . . . we urged him to do something about it; to ring the Foreign Ministry, to do anything. He said he would try, but nothing happened.

We sat and watched Soviet troops coming and going and, with them, small groups of AVH men – Hungarian security police. I had met men who had been obscenely tortured by them. Others showed me perjured documents and bogus confessions from the AVH files. Well, when the Russians arrived the remnants of the AVH came out of hiding. And there some of them were, outside these barracks. It was not a comforting thought for those of us whose passports were not in order.

We stayed until mid-afternoon and then went back to Budapest, to the Foreign Ministry. We stood in the hall there, a frustrated rabble, calling for the Minister, for senior officials, for anybody. The Minister appeared – at least I think it was the Minister. He said yes, he thought he could arrange for us to have a safe conduct pass to the Austrian border. We settled down again to wait while permanent officials came and went. They were quite friendly. It turned out that we were to be given a document in Hungarian and Russian and signed by the Deputy Prime Minister of Hungary – but not, unfortunately, until the next morning.

Next morning we were back at the Ministry. The documents finally arrived. But by this time we had learned that the Russians were not willing to accept these pieces of paper, even though they were signed by one of their puppet ministers. He is probably well used to such humiliations.

So we started all over again by going round to the Soviet headquarters, the Kommandatura. This is housed in a curious pink rococo mansion surrounded by tanks, armoured cars and troop-carriers. We stood around in the hall, an immensely tall room painted white and decorated with plaster roses. At the corners of the walls were coy statues of naked girls. And everywhere were tough-faced, square-built Russians armed with pistols and Tommy-guns. Around the edge of the room, halfway up, ran a gallery from which Soviet secret police in plain clothes looked down on us.

Finally we got a sort of assurance that we would be given passes. But not until tomorrow. Next morning we actually did get them. They were blurred and untidy and I do not know what magic formula was written on them, but they got us past the Russian checkpoints, about a dozen of them, between Budapest and the frontier. Anyway, we reached the border.

As we crossed, there was some small-arms fire in the distance. We were told that it was AVH men firing at Hungarian refugees – some of the millions who were less fortunate than ourselves.

CYPRUS CURFEW

Ronald Robson

Archbishop Makarios, the exiled leader of the Greek Cypriot community, rejected a British peace plan and Cyprus was again under curfew as violence flared between the island's Greeks and Turks. More than forty people were killed in July alone.

What will the members of the average family in Britain be doing at a quarter to seven tonight? It depends, I suppose, on the average British weather, on the income group, but largely on personal inclination. Some may be thinking of going to the cinema, or spending an evening with friends at home or at the local pub; some boys and girls might just be returning to an anxious mother later than they had promised from a cycle ride.

To a Cypriot, all or any of these possibilities would arouse envy. For what happens in Cyprus tonight and every night at a quarter to seven? In main towns, the air-raid siren howls; it sounds when the hot sun dips to the horizon, and as the light fades it seems to suck with it not only the colour from the landscape, but from the very people of Cyprus themselves. From the first wail of the siren, all but those with special permission to be outside on duty have just fifteen minutes to reach home, there to remain indoors until dawn – for this is curfew time. In the villages, there is no house curfew, but it is forbidden to leave the village. There are many anxious mothers but not because their younger offspring are late home from a bicycle ride – nobody under the age of twenty-seven is allowed to ride a bicycle, known in the past as a popular vehicle to help the bomb-thrower escape down twisting narrow streets. During curfew, no traffic at all is allowed on the roads except for security forces vehicles and a few others. In towns at night, there is no cinema open; not even a coffee-house – that institution which is even dearer to the Cypriots than the local pub is to Englishmen. If visitors to a house are caught by the curfew, they cannot go home, so guests are the exception in the evening. But in areas where Greeks and Turks live close together, there is often that unwelcome guest – fear.

With the uneasy night over, what happens in the average day? In the present situation, Greeks and Turks try to keep clear of each other's area in towns, but in Nicosia, for example, where law courts and administrative buildings are in the Turkish quarter, Greek staff must enter; at first they refused, but now they are convoyed in and out. The other day a trial was held up for two hours because fifteen witnesses refused to attend until provided with an escort. Even shopping has its problems; Turks are boycotting Greek shops and merchandise, but most of the shops and shopkeepers – the people of commerce – are Greeks so marketing can be difficult. On the Greek side, EOKA has commanded a boycott of certain foreign goods, which means mainly British goods. For example, British cigarettes are supposed to be banned. Actually, they still sell openly in many places; but for some reason, other bans are more effective, for instance, on dresses and materials, and I was told only today that a well-known shop is, for this reason, having a sale and closing down.

That is what we find in towns. Villagers are less dependent on shops for their simpler needs, but they have their own problems. In Greek and Turkish villages, which lie close together, or in those villages shared by Greeks and Turks, careful watch is kept to see how many of the menfolk of the other side have gone out to the fields – a sufficient reserve must remain behind in case of trouble, even if the land suffers. Men sleep with axes, knives or sticks handy, prepared for the alarm. Few men visit the towns now, even for important business; Greeks at least, I know, are forming conciliation committees in the villages; instead of going to law, they now settle disputes amongst themselves, so the Greek barristers feel the drought. Other professional men are similarly affected.

Some Turks are leaving their homes to travel quite long distances to live in tents nearer their own kind, but I have heard of at least one mixed village where Turks and Greeks have come together. They have agreed that neither side should attack the other; and more, if, say Turks from outside should attack Turk property in the village, then the Turks of the village will pay for the damage. The Greeks have agreed to meet the bill should damage be caused by any of their expatriates from outside. Maybe in this example there is a spark of hope for this island where, in recent weeks, old shepherds and young children have been killed simply because of the accident of being born into one community or the other.

CUBA'S REVOLUTIONARIES

Christopher Serpell

HAVANA, JANUARY 1959

As the rebel leader Fidel Castro proclaimed a new government for Cuba, our correspondent met some of the other people behind the revolution.

Before Castro reached the capital, in the days when a beard and flowing hair and hollow cheeks still set a man apart as a revolutionary hero, there were three key points in Havana, three centres of power: one of them was a huge military camp, an area like Aldershot, which had been handed over to Camillo Cienfuegos, the leader's chief of military staff. It was he, aged only twenty-seven, who had been in command in the final desperate battle. The second centre was the Cabanas military barracks overlooking the harbour and the old Spanish part of the town and this had been occupied by Castro's other principal lieutenant, Ernesto Guevara, aged thirty, and known affectionately to his command by the simple nickname of 'Che' – perhaps because that was how he pronounced the word 'que' with his Argentine accent. And the third centre was the university, perched on a hill in the fashionable suburb where one skyscraper after another has rocketed up to the blue sky – the university which had been closed for nearly three years by a students' strike but was still the home of the revolutionary directory, a movement born out of the students' defiance of the dictator, Batista.

Visiting Cienfuegos and Guevara was like visiting the temporary headquarters of two condottieri chieftains of the Rinascimento. Cienfuegos held court on the first floor of a barrack building; Guevara, in the orange stucco villa of some dead Batista colonel. But each of them had an antechamber full of henchmen, courtiers and supplicants, all contributing to a continuous uproar in the staccato Cuban-Spanish which has exactly the same rhythm as the samba. Every minute more people press in – a deputation of patriotic mothers, a committee of the Chamber of Commerce, a television camera crew, a bevy of tightly sweatered sweethearts and then a roaring bearded veteran clasping his firearm as if it were some religious symbol and embracing old friends last seen in battle.

Cienfuegos came out into his antechamber to hold court while I was there, and sat on a horsehair couch between his aged father and mother who held him possessively while the pop-eyed cameramen crouched before him like adoring angels in a holy picture.

And indeed Cienfuegos himself, with his grave, austere face, his candid eyes, his straight reddish beard and the thick hair escaping beneath the halo of his sombrero, might well have been one of the saints militant, perhaps St George. He answered all questions courteously, clearly and firmly; he listened with gentle interest to hours of fervent oratory. He won all hearts. And beside his couch, and later on outside his office door, there stood like a watchdog his page and bodyguard – a fourteen-year-old boy dressed rather like Buffalo Bill and with the raven locks, the high cheekbones and the opaque but shining eyes of the true Carib Indian; always he held his gun at the ready and always, even when his legs were wavering with weariness, he watched suspiciously those who approached his master.

Guevara, the soldier of fortune from Argentina, was a fascinating contrast: a man of this world, but of equal charm. His lean, mobile face is dominated by his brilliant eyes: his long dark locks pour down over his shoulders from a black beret. He enjoys meeting foreigners and matching wits. Pessimists in the United States have accused him of being the Communist 'Trojan horse' inside the Castro movement. But this, he said to me, was an ineptitude of the State Department, due to the fact that he had at one time shared in the opposition to the Mexican government. He said flatly he was not a Communist. 'But I refuse,' he added, 'to have my politics dictated by anti-Communism.' He agreed that he could be called a 'Latin-American internationalist', and he said he was against accepting United States aid because he thought it might involve accepting a measure of United States sovereignty.

As for Cuba, he said he wanted for the country a more diversified agriculture which would be less dependent on the price of sugar, and also a reformed system of land tenure which would give the peasant permanent ownership of his farm.

Beside these two formidable individuals, the committee of rather studious young men running the revolutionary directory seemed somewhat pathetic and ineffectual. Their saint is Marta Ximenez, the young widow of a boy leader who was shot to death by the Batista police for plotting the assassination of the dictator. Marta is youthful, slender and dignified; but she has had her own hair-raising career of escapes and disguises inside the resistance movement, and now all she wants, she confided to me, was to retire into obscurity and to look after her 'muchachito', the little boy born to her after her husband's death. But both she and her friends in the university, who between them recruited a powerful and semi-independent revolutionary movement, are deeply worried about the future. They were ignored by Castro when he nominated his provisional government; they are anxious now for free elections at the earliest possible moment, and they dread another government in which the ruling party is identified with the army. They are the intellectual theorists of the revolution, and because they are a committee they lack, perhaps, the heroic glamour; but they too have had their heroic past, and they still have their loyal following. They demand – and deserve – a place in the new Cuba.

IMPRISONED

Lionel Fleming

KATANGA, JANUARY 1963

The breakaway Congo state of Katanga, led by Moise Tshombe, was within days of surrendering its independence when our correspondent was detained in frightening circumstances.

I think it must be that the soldiers, defeated, resentful and suspicious, demanded our arrest as spies. The immigration officer himself had been courteous, if a trifle cool, as he examined our passports and filled in details on a form. Everything pointed to the granting of our entry permits. At last he rose to his feet, gathered up his papers and our passports and said: 'Follow me.' We fell in behind him, and then I noticed that two Katangese soldiers, armed with Tommy-guns, had fallen in behind us. We laughed a little about this, still imagining that there would be only some final formality in the building we were approaching. I said, 'Anyone would think we were under arrest.' In fact we were. We were hustled into a shed and told to sit on the floor while four soldiers covered us with Tommy-guns. The two African car drivers – I had come in one car, the two Americans in another – were summoned. We were told to pay them off.

To me, this was the first awful moment, for the implications were clear. We argued; if we were not to be allowed into Katanga, we said, that was fair enough; in that case we would go back to Rhodesia with the drivers. The only response to this was the demand for the car keys, and while some went off to unload our luggage, others relieved us of our wrist watches and currency, spectacles too – spectacles are a status symbol among Africans.

The drivers were sent off, and the trouble then began. The shed was only half-walled. What I mean is that it had a kind of balustrade and pillars supporting a roof. The result was that a crowd of Katangese soldiers aimed their guns at us and yelled abuse. They egged on the guards, who beat us in the face and made as if to club us with their rifle butts. I was terrified of being lynched. And then, to my utter relief, I saw Peter Younghusband of the *Daily Mail* walking by, giving just a half-glance into our shed.

I seriously think we might have been dead men if it had not been for Peter; for he set the machinery going that got us out. John Monks of the *Daily Express* joined in too. I will not go into all that now, except to say that Peter's efforts led to his being pushed in with us and manhandled too before they let him go. When he had gone, the trouble continued. 'Who is the Irishman?' they shouted. 'Which are the Americans?' To each we tried to answer. To each, because there was a pointed rifle in front of the question; we said again and again that we were journalists and not spies. But it was quite useless; they were not disposed to listen.

The half-wall of the shed meant that everyone could peer in on us. African women with blank, uncomprehending faces and babies on their backs; little boys who jumped gleefully up and down and made gestures indicating that they would slit our throats; soldiers with guns and slightly glazed eyes who shouted, 'Murderer!' It was difficult to know how to look back, whether to attempt to smile or remain absolutely deadpan. On the whole, the latter seemed best. It was like being on the wrong side of the bars in the zoo on August Bank Holiday.

In the end we were told to get up and get into a field car. This was the second bad moment, walking through the crowd. It only needed one man to start kicking and the rest would follow suit. But they held back, and we were driven off amid screams of 'Kill them!'

There were two possibilities now. The immigration post was well inside Katanga, so it might be that they were driving us back to dump us on the Rhodesian frontier; or they could be taking us into the bush to shoot us. The mood had changed; the guards were quiet and even allowed us to smoke – but you could put two interpretations on that.

The third and worst moment came as the car swung away from the main road and into a bush track. The guards then took our ties and coats and our few remaining possessions. It was at this point that we felt we were finished. I have often wondered how one would react to that kind of thing. My two friends agree with me that, while we had been very frightened up to then, we were now almost unmoved. We were even able to joke in undertones about the grand story that we ought to be sending to our offices. But we got away. While we waited in another hut for the climax, in a mood now almost approaching boredom, Younghusband and Monks had secured our release, and the end came in apologies, handshakes and cries of '*Au revoir*.' *Au revoir*? Well, perhaps.

DAY TRIP TO THE EAST

Charles Wheeler

BERLIN, JUNE 1963

*A drive out from the divided city provided an insight into life in East
Germany and a view of the ferry boat which few were allowed to use.*

One of the snags about living in West Berlin has always been the
impossibility of a day in the country, away from the crowd. Often
I have gazed at a map and envied the pre-war Berlin correspondent who could get into his car and drive due north to the lakes
or the forests, or better still, to the Baltic coast where he could
put his car on a ferry and be in Copenhagen by tea-time. Now,
since the war, high politics have ruled out this kind of trip. Allied
nationals here have had to conform to Allied rules, and the
strictest of all is that you may not ask the East German government
for a travel permit lest this should imply diplomatic recognition.
Instead, to get out of Berlin, you either fly or drive down the
autobahn to Helmstedt, a long and boring journey, and often in
the wrong direction. However, recently the Allies stopped treat-
ing correspondents as officials. We lost some diplomatic privileges,
but we won the private citizen's right to apply to the East
Germans for permission to drive through the territory they
control. So, the other day, I took the family to the seaside, using
a road out of West Berlin that had always brought us up short at
the barbed-wire border only twenty minutes from our front door.

Entry was easy: four passport checks, but no queue of cars, and then the open road ahead.

The East German interior surprised us. After East Berlin, surely the saddest of all capitals, one expects the surrounding country to be similar; but it has a rather special charm. There is hardly any traffic. One meets occasional cars and trucks, but for the most part it is like moving back in time to the days of haycarts and windmills and fat female peasants weeding on their knees in the fields, and like returning to the pre-branded goods age. Think of driving a hundred miles without seeing a single advertisement for petrol, beer, detergent, anything. It is restful and it blunts one's critical sense. But this is restored by the towns. There are no big towns on the road to the coast – certainly none to justify the kind of effort the Communist government puts into what it calls 'projects', and the small towns simply do not find a place in the Plan. The consequence is decay. Imagine any little market town in England in which the local council has made no repairs since the middle of the last war, in which nobody has repaired a pavement or painted a lamp-post, no more in fact than cart away the rubbish; in which all the little corner shops and the pubs have been taken over by the State, the names rubbed out and a single word printed in their places, FOOD, HOTEL – nothing else. These small towns are worse than dreary – they are lifeless, and one begins to understand why so many inhabitants have chosen to leave everything behind and become refugees; and why those who have stayed have lost interest, not only in doing what the State requires of them, but in their personal surroundings. At a guess, I should say that nine householders out of ten no longer put flowers in their gardens.

It was a relief to reach the coast. The little Baltic port of Rostock has become a showplace and it has a high position in the Plan. It was always a pleasant place, and in repairing its war damage the authorities have avoided those dreadful yellow tiles that disfigure East Berlin and have used good red brick instead. They have enlarged the docks and they hope to capture

Czechoslovakia's transit trade from West German and Polish ports.

As you drive into Rostock, a big hoarding proclaims that this is the 'Gateway to the World'. Well, pehaps one day it will be – but for the people of Rostock this must be the bad joke of all time, for the gate is shut and guarded by youngsters in bell-bottom trousers and armed with Tommy-guns. At the water-front, we found the latest pride and joy of the East German regime: the motorship *Warnemuende*, the most up-to-date of train and motor-car ferries brought into service three weeks ago on the short sea-route between Rostock and Gedser in Denmark, a truly imposing vessel with accommodation for complete trains, a hundred cars and fifteen hundred passengers, a dining saloon for four hundred, a smoking room with dance floor, a cafeteria, a crèche, bars, shops and great teams of pursers, porters, stewards and nursemaids, lined up to care for the happy trippers – everything, in fact, except happy trippers. We sailed for Denmark on that sunny Friday morning with half-a-dozen fellow passengers, three cars and five empty railway wagons. She made the return trip, we heard later, with one passenger, no cars or trains. No East German has ever sailed in the *Warnemuende* apart from the officials who went on her maiden voyage and her crew, who are not allowed ashore in Denmark. The *Warnemuende*'s prede-cessor on the Gedser run, a Danish ferry, used to be allowed to take East Germans just for the trip; they were not allowed to land in Denmark. But there were too many ugly scenes, with passen-gers leaping over the rail and swimming for it, and plain-clothes People's Policemen splashing after them in pursuit. So now East German holidaymakers and dockyard workers wave to the *War-nemuende* from a distance, closely watched by seven naval ratings spaced along the quayside and armed with sub-machine-guns. The People's own motorship is for foreigners only, and the People's chance of ever seeing Denmark, just across the water, is rather smaller than the prospect of a visit to Peking.

TOPLITZ TREASURE

Ian McDougall

Vienna, October 1963

Official preparations were being made to salvage a number of cases which were submerged in an Austrian lake by the Nazis during the last days of the war.

Lake Toplitz, fifty miles east of Salzburg and deep in the heart of the mountains that were to have been the Nazis' last stronghold, is one of the smallest lakes in Austria, but also one of the deepest. In the last days of the war, SS troops drove up to the lake and sank in it a number of metal and wooden boxes, perhaps as many as sixty. Some of these boxes contained gold bars, others contained forged Bank of England notes made by prisoners in concentration camps and intended to undermine the British economy, while yet others contained secret documents. The boxes with the gold bars are probably now deeply buried in mud and hard to get at. The forged notes, some of which have already been brought up and destroyed, can have little more than curiosity value even when found. The secret documents, however, are dynamite in all but the most literal sense. They are believed – by those who have every reason to care – to include in the first place lists of names of highly placed SS officials; many of them hold lists of code numbers which give access to bank accounts, now blocked in wartime neutral countries, notably Switzerland and Sweden. These accounts were opened by the Nazis in a number of devious ways which included the allocation to each account of code figures,

44

known only to three persons. None of these three could touch
the account without the agreement of the other two. Where the
three men knew each other, this would be easy, but in a large
number of instances the three men were strangers to each other,
and the only remaining clue to their identities lies in a list on the
floor of Lake Toplitz.

From what I have said it will be clear, I hope, that whereas
there are in the world today a number of former SS men who
want to get at the boxes in Lake Toplitz at almost any price, so as
later to get their hands on the gold and fabulous sums in blocked
accounts, there are also a number of other former SS men, perhaps
now in safe, comfortable circumstances, who have no interest in
the money side of the matter, but are equally determined that
their past records and tasks, as described in other documents on
the floor of the lake, shall never see the light of day and be used
to blackmail them. This is the stuff of which rough in-fighting is
made, and where silence and mystery remains.

In 1959, a West German magazine financed a diving operation
in Lake Toplitz, during which one of the boxes containing
documents was brought to the surface. On the next day, the
diving operation was called off without explanation, and without
the magazine publishing anything about the contents of the box.
Later applications to dive, made by a group of people with clearly
Nazi backgrounds, were turned down by the Austrian authorities
on the grounds that diving in the lake was dangerous and that it
would not be in the public interest anyway. Later still, an actual
ban on diving was imposed on all-comers, irrespective of their
affiliations. Shortly after the ban came into effect, however, an
illegal attempt was in fact made in the dead of night by a group of
Germans, during which a young diver disappeared. Whether he
was drowned and, if so, whether accidentally or by foul play, or
whether, as his father tends to believe, he may have made a
successful dive and then disappeared partly to enjoy the proceeds,
and partly to avoid military service, is merely one of the latest
mysteries to merge with the mists and gloomy precipices sur-

rounding the lake. But the disappearance has at least produced one clear result, which is that the Austrian Ministry of the Interior has at last decided to act, and to combine a search for the missing boy with a salvage operation aimed at retrieving the sunken boxes. Already, soundings are being taken of the lake bottom. The rest of the job will not be easy in view of the large quantity of mud which when stirred up obscures a diver's vision, and because of the dangerous accumulation of weeds and rotted tree stumps under the surface.

The whole Toplitz story does of course have an adventurous fascination about it, simply because it is quite literally a search for hidden treasure. But it is also an adventure with high rewards or penalties in it for an unknown number of tough, desperate or avaricious men who, in their younger days, were the scourge of Europe. And the air will be pleasanter to breathe when the mystery of Lake Toplitz is at last officially laid to rest.

DEATH OF A PRESIDENT

Anthony Wigan, host

A day after President John F. Kennedy was shot dead in Dallas on 22 November 1963 a special edition of From Our Own Correspondent *was broadcast from the BBC studios in New York. It was hosted by our correspondent there, Anthony Wigan, and included the voices of the new President of the United States and of members of the public.*

WIGAN: It is dark here in New York and across the country from coast to coast. When the new day breaks it will be the beginning of a new era for this great country, perhaps for the whole world. Who can tell now what it will be like? There are perhaps some pointers and here is our Washington correspondent, Douglas Stuart, to outline them for you.

STUART: President Johnson has two immediate tasks before him. Shot into the White House by the bullet of an assassin, he must now brief himself swiftly on the military, economic and political factors affecting the policies of the United States at home and abroad. Having done this, he must choose the men who will help him carry out his policies. It must not be assumed that he will necessarily ask all the men who formed President Kennedy's cabinet to serve under him, nor can it be assumed that all members of the Kennedy administration will wish to serve in the

47

Johnson administration. True as this is of the cabinet, all of whose members are the personal appointments of the President in office, it is even more true of the White House officials. These form the personal staff of the President and it is reasonable to suppose that President Johnson will want his own new Secretary, his own advisers on domestic and foreign affairs and on military and strategic matters.

More even than his public utterances, political observers in Washington will watch the new President's appointments as a measure of his future political intentions. Will he, for example, retain Mr Rusk as Secretary of State? Will he dispense with the services of the so-called Kennedy egg-heads, the professors from Harvard and Yale who gave the late President's administration its special intellectual flavour, a flavour incidentally not greatly to the taste of many Americans? And perhaps most important of all, will Mr Johnson ask Mr Robert Kennedy, the dead President's brother, to continue to serve as United States Attorney-General? If he does it will be widely interpreted as underlining President Johnson's determination to maintain the executive's drive towards giving Negroes equal rights. If he does not, the nation will see in the change of the Department of Justice a change in the policies of the White House towards the racial problem in the North as well as in the South. The Negro community already sees President Kennedy's assassination as the martyrdom of a man as dedicated to their cause as was President Lincoln ninety-eight years ago. And the man who has sought to put into effect President Kennedy's racial policies was his brother Robert. In the field of foreign affairs President Johnson is likely to stress the continuity of his policies with those of President Kennedy. He may even reiterate the famous passage of President Kennedy's inauguration speech: 'Never fear to negotiate, but never negotiate out of fear.' And the new President will certainly be at pains to set at rest any fears or doubts regarding the firmness of future American policy that may be raised by the allies of the United States around the globe. But, and this is a very big but, Mr Johnson has become President of the United States at the beginning of an election year and elections are not won on foreign policy issues.

His job will be to get himself re-elected President and to take his party with him to victory in Congress and in the state legislatures. This means that Mr Johnson's thoughts will tend to dwell on domestic rather than on foreign policy issues. There can be no doubt that this, in any case, is how his mind works. He has the reputation of a skilful and ingenious politician. He faces a divided party and a divided nation, torn apart racially and politically on the issues of Conservatism versus Liberalism.

The assassin's bullet which killed President Kennedy did more than murder a man. It killed an idea and a dream, symbolized in the 1960 election phrases 'Get America moving again' and 'The New Frontier'. For the first time since the days of President Truman, a grass-roots politician is back in the White House. He may surprise America and indeed the world.

WIGAN: Now let's go back to a moment only twelve hours ago – to Fifth Avenue in New York City and to St Patrick's Cathedral. The church's great bell was spreading the news to shocked and saddened people as they went back to their offices after lunch. Malcolm Davis was interviewing passers-by for the BBC.

DAVIS: I'm talking to people now outside St Patrick's Cathedral. How do you feel about the President's death?

VOICES: Very badly ... I don't know ... Everyone's crying ... It's a terrible shock and I think it was the work of a fanatic ... I'm sure it was one of those hate groups which are so prevalent in Dallas ... It will be a terrible thing for the country.

DAVIS: One of the ironic twists to this extremely horrible situation is that you can probably hear in the background the bells ringing celebrating the bringing in of Christmas and there's a

Santa Claus here on Fifth Avenue. He's calling for alms and for food to celebrate the forthcoming season. He represents the Volunteers of America. Would you like to say something to the British Broadcasting Corporation about how you feel about this?

VOICE: Well, it's shocking. I think it's something that the American people don't want to have on their consciences. It's something that we should all be ashamed of as American citizens. I think it was because Kennedy went deep into discrimination – that was the cause of it. I think that he should have taken it a little bit slower, it truly is sad that there is discrimination, but Kennedy went a little bit too far and a little bit too fast.

DAVIS: I have next to me another gentleman. This gentleman is from – I would imagine you are, sir, if I may say to our audience, a Negro American. Do you feel that this is the result of President Kennedy's policies on integration?

VOICE: Well, first I must say I'm a citizen of the United States and secondly, I'm an Afro-American. I think that this is a very grave and very deep-rooted situation which reflects seriously as to our position both internally and externally. This savagery expressed by American people cannot be contained and cannot be condoned. As to whether or not Kennedy went too far, no one can ever go too far with regard to human liberty. But colour is incidental, and its significance has nothing to do with the right of a human being who is born of a woman and who dies like everybody else.

I think Kennedy did what he thought what was right as a human being and again I would repeat that the colour has nothing to do with the right and wrong. We live in a country dedicated to freedom, to equality, and I say this – that we've got to go the farthest possible way to internally securing American rights, American freedom and American liberty. I say America has to rededicate and re-educate our people as one regardless of our colour, as to the firm principles, for the love of mankind, the Christian philosophy which we preach and which we stand for. This is a horrible, horrible thing that can now never be erased and I say that unless the hearts and minds of all Americans are sufficiently cleaned and pledged to accept human values and to accept the Christian doctrine, America as a country will be lost.

WIGAN: Those interviews give a good clue to the first reaction of New Yorkers, probably of people all across America. They are shocked and angered, scarcely believing what they hear but already inclined to blame the great divisive force of segregation and the President's part in trying to tear it down for a tragedy which had happened while he was actually engaged in trying to repair his political fortunes in the South. Now there is a reason to believe that another cause altogether lay behind the President's assassination, as our correspondent Peter Watson will tell you from Dallas, Texas.

WATSON: After the murder, the weapon with which it had been done, the 6.5 millimetre Italian rifle with a telescopic sight, was found under a staircase in a nearby warehouse in Dallas. Forty-five minutes later, after a description of the suspected killer had been broadcast over the police networks, Police Officer Tippit was driving alone along a street two miles away. Witnesses saw him stop, get out and approach a man coming from the opposite direction on foot. The man pulled out a .38 calibre pistol and shot Police Officer Tippit through the head, chest and stomach. He then fled into the nearby Texas Cinema, where he again tried to shoot it out when police closed in on him, but on this occasion, his gun jammed and he was overpowered. This man was Lee Harvey Oswald, who was immediately taken to police headquarters, charged with the murder of Police Officer Tippit and later with the assassination of the President.

This much is known about Oswald. He is twenty-four years

old, slim, dark, with a markedly pointed chin. He's married and has two children. He worked at the warehouse from which the President was shot and he has a curious history of connection with the Soviet Union and Cuba. Oswald is a Texan-born from Fort Worth, the President's last port of call before Dallas, and he served for a short while in the United States Marines. Four years ago he went to Russia, some reports say he in fact defected to Russia, but after eighteen months he was returned to the United States at government expense. It's since then that he seems to have become involved in pro-Castro Cuban affairs and is said to have been Chairman of an organization called The Fair Play for Cuba Committee.

Oswald was charged after ten hours of questioning at the heavily pillared and porticoed Police Headquarters in downtown Dallas. As reporters and cameramen crowded the pale green corridor outside a glass door marked HOMICIDE AND ROBBERY, detectives came from the basement laboratories with hand-prints and the results of a paraffin test. This test, it was later said, showed that Oswald had, at some time in the day, fired a gun, though they couldn't say what kind of gun or when. At no time has he made any sort of confession.

As for Dallas, the brightly lit streets are rather empty, but still brightly lit, except for one small shop full of children's toys which is dark and bears a neatly printed notice: CLOSED IN MEMORY OF JOHN F. KENNEDY.

WIGAN: The United States was without a President for hardly an hour. The Vice-President went straight from the hospital to the presidential plane and he took the oath in its forward compartment with his wife and Mrs Kennedy looking on. This is NBC's description of the scene.

REPORTER: At the oath-taking aboard the plane, Air Force One, President Johnson put his hand on the Bible, his left hand, and he swore, as we are all familiar with the oath, to faithfully execute the duties of President and to defend the Constitution. And the oath, as we've noted, was administered by a United States District Judge, the first woman ever to administer the oath to the President of the United States.

WIGAN: Two hours later the new President was back in Washington, and there he made his first public statement.

JOHNSON: For me it is a deep personal tragedy. I know that the world shares the sorrow that Mrs Kennedy and her family bear. I will do my best. That is all I can do. I ask for your help and God's.

WIGAN: And now for news of what has happened in the nation's capital since then. Here is BBC correspondent Leonard Parkin.

PARKIN: Well, a rather dazed President Johnson began straight-away to see members of the late President Kennedy's Administration. The first man he saw was Mr McNamara, the Secretary of Defense, to get an early briefing on the presidential responsibilities in the military field. Then he saw the Congressional leaders from Capitol Hill, and according to the reports, they promised him bipartisan support, support from the Democratic and Republican sides during these critical days of his leadership. This morning he's seeing Mr Dean Rusk, the Secretary of State.

It has been noticed here with great appreciation that President Johnson, who was big enough to swallow his feelings and give President Kennedy his loyal support in spite of having been defeated by him for the Presidential nomination, immediately tonight made another gesture of deference. He conducted his first formal interviews with members of the administration and Congress, not in President Kennedy's own office in the White House, but in his own suite of offices nearby. And nor did he stay the night at the White House.

Well now, during tonight the body of President Kennedy is being taken from a naval hospital in nearby Maryland to the White House. Mrs Kennedy is staying at the hospital where she's been under the care of a doctor. Today the President's body will lie in repose in the East Room of the White House, flanked by two white candles, as members of the President's family, of his cabinet, of Congress and of the Diplomatic Corps pay their last respects. And tomorrow the body will be taken to the Capitol where it will lie in state in the Rotunda until Monday morning, and the public will file past the catafalque. The funeral service will take place on Monday at St Matthew's Catholic Cathedral. And the President's family has asked specially that no flowers shall be sent, but that any money which would have been spent should be donated to charity.

THOMPSON: This is E. R. Thompson speaking now from Washington. I've been out in the streets of the capital tonight and I must say that as yet there are very few visible signs of mourning. The White House lights still glitter in long rows down the great processional avenues, and the long lines of motor traffic move in steady order and the electric signs flash crimson and green.

But there is a focal point of restlessness round the White House. There under the floodlights a sparse, uneasy crowd moves continually, and the television cameras wait, and the passing cars slow down to give the occupants a glimpse of the white façade and the gardens and the police manning the gates. You can park and look, but you must not linger. When I left, the cavalcade bearing the President's body from the naval hospital to its temporary resting place in the West Wing of the White House was still awaited.

A young man of whom I asked the way, asked me in turn whether I was English. 'I've been thinking about this thing,' he said, 'we've had several Presidents shot in our history. You don't seem to have had that. I wonder why? Maybe we put too much seriousness into politics.' He was polite, gentle, puzzled and anxious. Earlier I spoke about the President's death to a Negro taxi driver. 'When I first heard I just couldn't talk about it,' he said. Then he went on to speak simply about his feelings for John F. Kennedy. This was a man who fought for the rights of the poor, the little people. 'In losing that man,' he said, 'we lost a father and a brother. That man's going to be missed by a lot of people in this country and other countries.' It was impossible to listen to this Negro without feeling the presence of genuine grief.

Well, the early editions of the newspapers, of course, have been coming in, and here's Leonard Parkin to say something about the first edition of the *Washington Post*.

PARKIN: Well, the *Post* – it's a liberally minded paper – devotes the major portion of a two-column leader to an appreciation of the late President. And it says of him, 'Nothing will wholly eclipse the national memory of a cheerful, courageous, imaginative and inspired young President.' And then, under the title of THE ROAD AHEAD, the *Washington Post* leader goes on to assess the fitness of former Vice-President Lyndon Johnson to assume the highest office. It judges him to be better qualified than was Harry Truman when he was thrust into succession on the death of Roosevelt. It calls on the country to rally behind the new President and to, 'purge from our national life the sordid hate that destroyed his predecessor'. And now from Washington, back to New York.

WIGAN: Of the New York papers, the *New York Times* devotes twelve of its sixty pages to the assassination, and a full page to the many reports from all over the world of the reactions of the world's statesmen to the news. The sports and entertainment pages are full of news of cancellations, including the annual football match between the President's University, Harvard, and its principal rival, Yale, which should have been played today. Theatres and cinemas closed and radio and television are without commercials and without, too, their regular programmes of entertainment until after the funeral. The *Times* reports the fall on the stock market as the worst since Black Monday in May 1962 – stocks fell an average of 21 points before the exchanges across the country closed, when the President's death was confirmed.

The *Times* prints two columns of editorials. The first, between black mourning lines, is a tribute to the man himself, 'The personal loss,' it says, 'is deep and crushing, the loss to the nation and the world is historic and overpowering. He represented vitality and energy, the intelligence and enthusiasm, the courage and the hope of these United States in the middle of the twentieth century. No madman's bullets can stop the inexorable march of human rights, no murder however tragic can make it falter. The light of reason was momentarily extinguished with the crack of a rifle shot in Dallas yesterday but that light is, in reality, inextinguishable.'

Most of the papers recall that the President was here in New York just two weeks ago when he dispensed with all the formality of a motorcade with outriders and screaming sirens. His car entered and left the city as any other motorist would, stopping at traffic lights and giving precedence to pedestrians on turns.

An ominous note is sounded by the *Herald Tribune*'s columnists. One recalls some recent words of the late President, 'I think it is a very dangerous, untidy world, I think we will have to live with it.' And his comment is that only Vice-President Truman of all the country's Vice-Presidents who took office because of the death of a President, only Mr Truman inherited a more dangerous and untidy world than the one President Johnson now surveys. Another columnist says bleakly, 'Premier Kruschev is not a man to let an opportunity slip and opportunity for him is any chance to catch us here in the West off balance.'

Lincoln has been much in people's thoughts these past few hours. One man, asked for his thoughts on the death of the President, said, 'Well, it only happens to great people. They shot Lincoln the same way. That's the way it is, that's all, just great people.' And here is another individual, part of the great American crowd outside St Patrick's, talking to Malcolm Davis:

VOICE: I would like to say that when I heard the news I went to church and I went to pray for forgiveness for my sins, because I feel that I am as guilty as the assassin because I have been apathetic and I have left the responsibility of international peace and of local racial integration to our leaders and not taken enough of the burden upon myself, and I hope to do penance for it.

WIGAN: Emotional, distressed, confused, horrified and even repentant. Those are the ways in which individual Americans have reacted to the news of yesterday. Soon tomorrow will begin here and America will look forward again with the remembrance perhaps of the great inaugural speech made not three years ago in a spirit of both hope and determination: 'Let the word go forth from this time and place to friend and foe alike that the torch has passed to a new generation of Americans.' That is how it began and it ended with those words: 'Ask not what your country can do for you, ask rather what you can do for your country.'

A DHOW TO ZANZIBAR

Angus McDermid

DAR ES SALAAM, JANUARY 1964

Nationalists overthrew the Sultan's regime on the island of Zanzibar and proclaimed a people's republic. Our correspondent got there as quickly as he could.

There was nothing for it but a dhow, and the best dhows, they said, were forty-five miles down the coast from Dar es Salaam at the old German capital of Bagamoyo, twenty-five miles across the strait from Zanzibar. It was dark when we got there. The breakers tumbled into the shore; the palm trees curved over the sand. This was not one of the luxury dhows that take tourists up the east coast of Africa, nor was it one of the ocean-going cargo variety. This was the humblest kind, say forty feet long, built of rough-hewn timber, bolted together, much of it salvaged driftwood – and no deck, but for a few square feet at the stern, where the helmsman perched and the skipper stood in a kind of cockpit. His main duty seemed to be to empty out the bilgewater in a biscuit tin, which needed doing every two or three minutes. The four of us had to fend for ourselves, if possible to keep out of the boiling sun. The estimated time for the voyage was three hours but it took that time to catch the right wind and tide; but at last the sail was changed, all three of the crew hauling it over, and the passengers and sacks of mud ballast changed with it. It was the first of many, many such changes, but at last we were on the right tack for Zanzibar.

The sea grew choppier, the sky grew dark. We were clearly not going to get into Zanzibar that night, and the crew were perhaps fearful of their reception. So we cruised round through the night uncomfortably clinging to the rigging. A doze and a sudden awakening as the boat lurched; the crew cooking a fish in the early hours; the helmsman singing little songs about Muslim heroes; the skipper performing his morning devotions at dawn. Finally we hoisted the Tanganyika pennant; then a police launch with a young man with a revolver at the bows hailed us, and we were soon ashore surrounded by gunmen in scraps of uniform and civil defence helmets.

We had been nineteen hours on the dhow, without lifebelts, navigation lights, radio of course, and virtually no food or water, but we had made it. The young man took us straight to see the President. The President was cordial enough, but had other things quite clearly on his mind. He was in the radio station, by now the revolutionary headquarters, a fantastic place, piled high with looted furniture, clothing and fifty sewing machines laid out neatly on the grass. People with guns, people shouting, pushing, crying, and outside, thousands of Arabs being interrogated, being marched away with hands raised, excited teenagers and bearded old men.

But how to record all this? How to tell the world? There were no radio communications, but the cable office was working hard and for a while it was easy to drive round the town in a taxi – provided by the revolutionaries with an armed guard, but costing us ten pounds a day, the guard included. Then some more reporters came in by dhow, and spy mania set in.

The telephone to Dar es Salaam was cut off; and while the suspected journalist spies were being expelled, we others were confined to the hotel, where the splendid Scots proprietress cooked and baked and coped; where a tall African said, 'Welcome to Zanzibar, I am a plain-clothes detective,' and where a young revolutionary, when not in solemn conclave with the Chinese News Agency man, spouted Karl Marx, or spoke in Russian to the three other Communist journalists.

Then there was the censor. He was in fact the young man with a Leningrad badge in his lapel who had welcomed us off the dhow. The cable office had two armed guards at the door; the censor had another one at his side, and on his desk was a revolver and a hand grenade. He weighed every phrase of our cables carefully but, alas, inconsistently. 'Did he say this?' he asked incredulously about a statement which a government press officer had made. Well, it may have been coincidence, but the press officer did not show up for his next conference that afternoon.

One correspondent piloted his own plane in and the guards greeted him with the words, 'You can't possibly be a pilot and a journalist, there's no such thing.' Well, Zanzibar, like the Congo, will be a place for journalists to reminisce about.

But the moment came, as seemed inevitable, when the censor refused to accept my messages – 'After,' as he put it, 'what the Field Marshal said about the BBC last night.' So there it was, no telephones, no cabling, it was a good time to leave. There was a plane. I took it. Next morning at Dar es Salaam airport, I was told quietly, 'There are spies all around us.' And that night the Tanganyikan army mutinied.

ANOTHER VICTIM

Erik de Mauny

MOSCOW, JUNE 1964

In the Stalin era even Red Army generals were not immune to the early morning knock on the door.

At two o'clock in the morning of 22 October 1938, General Aleksandr Vasilievich Gorbatov, a Red Army cavalry commander of long service and many decorations, was awoken in his Moscow hotel bedroom by a knock on the door. He thought it was a telegram from his wife. Instead, three men in military uniform marched into the room, and while one set about removing the medal ribbons and badges of rank from the general's tunic, another abruptly informed him that he was under arrest. General Gorbatov had become just one more among the thousands of officers to fall victim to Stalin's great purge of the Red Army in the wake of the secret trial and execution of Marshal Tukhachevsky.

General Gorbatov was luckier than many others. At least he survived to fight another day and subsequently to write his memoirs. During the past three months, substantial sections of these memoirs have been published in the magazine *Novy Mir*. They present one of the most striking indictments yet to appear of the enormities of the Stalin regime.

General Gorbatov's strength is that he is a simple man, although also a very brave one. He writes without art or embellishment, with a plain directness of narrative style that can be compared to Defoe in *The Journal of the Plague Year*. And of course, what General Gorbatov is describing was a sort of plague, a contagion of lying, denunciation and false confessions. That sort of contagion leaves deep traces, and the effort to throw them off is not yet over.

But what makes General Gorbatov's case especially interesting is that by origin and upbringing he was almost the typical Soviet citizen. By that I mean that although he had advantages of character he had none of birth or fortune. He was one of ten children born into a miserably poor peasant family in Central Russia, and therefore could feel no nostalgia for the world before the Revolution. To find such a man arraigned as 'an enemy of the people' is to be shown a dislocation of reality that only a madman could achieve. The general himself certainly saw it in this light, and during the long months of imprisonment and exile no question tormented him more than these: Can our leaders really believe that so many Soviet citizens would turn to treason and espionage for the imperialist powers? And if that is the case, then what bases remain for Soviet power to stand on? The pain in these questions still comes through, even if at the time there were more direct physical torments to be endured.

General Gorbatov's crime, such as it was, arose from nothing more than personal loyalty. Some months before his own arrest another cavalry commander, General Grigoriev, who was also a close personal friend, was detained, tried and sentenced. General Gorbatov was intrepid enough to speak in his defence at a Communist Party meeting. The 2 a.m. knock on the door was the inevitable sequel. Stripped of rank, he was taken to a cell in the Lyubyanka, the Security Police headquarters in the centre of Moscow, and to a first realization of what he was up against. Of his seven cell companions, not one had withstood the process of interrogation. All, under torture, had signed fabricated confessions and falsely denounced former colleagues. General Gorbatov is sparing of physical details, although at one point he does mention being carried back to the cell bloody and exhausted, and of another interrogation he says, 'Then I began to want to die.'

But the interrogators got nothing out of him. Later, in a regular prison, crowded with seventy men into a room built for twenty-five, he again found that he was the only one who had not signed a false confession. His sentence, incidentally, was one of fifteen years' imprisonment with an additional five years' deprivation of civil rights. In the event he was under detention for two and a half years, spending most of that time in the cold wilderness of the Kolyma region, and in the months of slow travel there and back by goods wagon and ship.

In his narrative one is struck almost as much by the small senseless cruelties as by the big intentional ones. His wife, frantic with anxiety after his disappearance, goes to enquire after him at the NKVD headquarters in Moscow. There she is told to pursue her search at a number of the city prisons, and given a list naming every gaol except the one he was actually in. General Gorbatov was tormented by similar anxieties for his wife who had already seen her father and brother arrested as alleged enemies of the people. At the same time, even in their Siberian exile, the purged officers were well aware of the Nazi threat gathering in Europe, and General Gorbatov, a simple patriot, who through everything stuck to his Communist faith, was more and more consumed with fear for the Red Army itself after the loss of so many of its most experienced leaders. These fears were not without foundation.

In March 1941 he was finally rehabilitated, and posted as deputy commander of an infantry corps. Three months later the German invasion began and in the early fighting around Vitebsk General Gorbatov saw how the ill-trained Soviet front lines broke in disarray, and abandoned their positions. Their demoralization was only one of the many aspects of Stalin's legacy from which the Soviet Union has since struggled to free itself.

FUNERAL TRAIN

Gerald Priestland

ALLAHABAD, JUNE 1964

The death of the President of India led to a train journey which would never be forgotten.

'You must be mad to go on that train,' they said. 'Why spend twenty-four hours in a cattle truck when you can fly there in just over one hour?'

Well, that train was the funeral special taking the major remains of Mr Nehru for immersion in the holy Ganges at Allahabad. I am glad I went on it, not because it was not uncomfortable – it was – but because it reminded me what India is really about. As we rumbled across the sandy flatness of the north Indian plain, bleached and corroded by the sun, people came down to the side of the line to have '*antim darshan*' – to pay their final respects – and to be vouchsafed vision of the sacred relics in their copper globe. This was the heartland of Mr Nehru's Congress Party, and they came down from villages that one could see were still untouched by the first, second or third Five Year Plan. They stood among fields where peacocks strutted in flocks as evening gathered, they packed on to the platforms of country stations to bathe in the reputation of a man whose constant urgings to become scientific, secular and socialist they must have considered far above and beyond them. Such advice was for the learned, for them there remained the spiritual emanations from his ashes.

In the Press coaches it was suffocating. Officialdom did its best. There were free issues of explosive fizzy lemonade; in every compartment there were earthenware crocks of drinking water; sweepers crawled on all fours mopping up the dust that swirled in; and at one stop great blocks of ice were dragged aboard in galvanized baths and set under the ceiling fans, so that the blast they circulated would become a little less searing.

At every stop it was like the rush hour on the London Underground turned inside out. Those lounging on the seats inside stared with wonder through securely barred windows at the shoal of humanity pressed against the outside. Once the Indian reporters in my compartment told the curious peasants who peered back at us that a French correspondent was President Nasser of Egypt. The peasants replied that they were grateful for the honour his Excellency was doing them. They meant it, and I am glad the Frenchman gave dignity to a bad joke by bowing in reply.

It was impossible to get on to the platform to make one's way to the white funeral coach where the urn was displayed on its floodlit pedestal. But at Kanpur, I managed to climb out on to the roof of my coach and stumble along the top of the train, jumping the gaps until I reached it. It was one of the most enthralling sensations of my life, one that invaded every physical sense. I squatted there, wedged between the roof of the station and the roof of the coach. Below the crowd surged to and fro like a heavy sea against a cliff, uttering a continuous wordless roar – they were men, all of them men, not a woman in sight. I was battered by the sound, stifled by the heat that rose up with a strange mixed aroma of sweat, spices and flowers, the flowers they had brought to toss before the urn. I was rocked by the beating of thousands upon the side of the heavy coach.

It was like observing the very bloodstream of India, hot and throbbing – every head a human corpuscle.

Then on through the night, with every now and again a chant of 'Chacha Nehru amar hai' – 'Uncle Nehru is immortal' – swelling up and tapering off from the trackside. The final scenes at the confluence of the Ganges, the Jumna and the invisible Sarasvati River, the holiest of Hindu ends for this agnostic Westernized leader, hammered it all home, the unalterable Indianness of India. As one Indian pointed out to me, it was inevitable that Mr Nehru, despite his wishes, should have had a religious funeral. The New Delhi electric crematorium still is not operational after eight years' work on it, and the priests are the only people who know how to set about a cremation.

And so Hinduism took its wandering son back to its bosom, with the Indian Army amphibians handling the transport, and the Indian Air Force scoring one direct hit and two near misses with showers of rose petals. On shore, a million people joined in the public holiday. There was hardly a wet eye to be seen, the weird triangular banners of the holy men fluttered over their encampment on the sandbanks like a goblin army ready to invade the nation.

THE BEATLES INVASION

Leonard Parkin

NEW YORK, OCTOBER 1964

American parents who had only just learned to accept Elvis Presley now had to come to terms with their youngsters' newest heroes.

On the Monday following the national holiday of Labor Day, the United States goes back to school. Girls in thick white cotton socks, which make them look as though they are wearing soccer players' shin pads, will be standing at bus stops with arms full of books. Stragglers on the way to kindergarten for the first time will be losing their Mickey Mouse lunch boxes as usual. And school-boys in their teens, far too many of them looking rubber-cheeked and overweight in tight jeans and gabardine jackets, will once again offer us the opportunity to remark that there is nothing inherently noble or attractive about a human skull without much hair on it. Crew cuts, madly enough, are still with us, although I did read with hope that in some parts of this continent longer hair for teenagers is now a sign of status and responsibility. Whether this is due in any way to the actively volcanic popularity of the Beatles is difficult to say, although nothing could be more responsible in this country of private enterprise and profit than the way the Beatles are rocking their way round the world making money.

It is no exaggeration to say that America's teenagers are

Beatle-mad. The end of Beatlemania is nowhere in sight, and they are still absolutely 'fab' and the zany, articulate world of the American teenager is engulfing the boys from Liverpool with hysterical cries of 'gear' and screams of everlasting love. Teenagers matter in this country; they do not speak only when spoken to, and they are seldom seen and not heard. Their lives revolve round school and the extensive school social life, dances and dating and coffee shops and driving licences and poor complexions and pimples and clothes and crushes and slang – the latest these days, 'I'm a Beatle maniac, what's your excuse?' An 'overseer' is a strict parent; the classroom is the 'slave cave'; and in the west, they are raving over popcorn, currycorn, pizzacorn, nutcorn, applecorn, chillicorn and cherrycorn. Round their necks they wear 'steady bells' ringing attention to the name that is engraved on them. It is a wacky teenage world, all right.

One teenage magazine asks for readers' solutions to the following problem. 'You, like millions of other teenage girls, just love the Beatles, but your boyfriend doesn't. He wants you to stop liking the Beatles altogether. What would you do? Would you obey your boyfriend and give up the Beatles? Would you disobey him and hope that he changes his mind? Or would you talk to him and explain that you'll try to mellow and calm down a bit in your attitude. How would you solve this problem?'

Wherever the Beatles go, there will be youngsters there to scream, while their parents, who used to swoon and scream for the young Frank Sinatra, console themselves that it did not do them any harm, and that Frankie has become a respected actor in addition to his singing. Parents here, like parents in most countries, tend to think of the Beatles as something slightly mad but quite wholesome and amusing. The first question any Englishman in this country is asked, either by a child or by an adult, is bound to be about the Beatles, simply because when an American meets an Englishman, the Beatles are the first thing that comes to mind.

But among the thousands that go out to scream for John, George, Paul and Ringo, there will be youngsters troubled by disloyalty. Not the girl with the hundred and four pictures of the Beatles on her wall in Los Angeles – she is all right, she has made her decision. It is the Elvis lover who has the problem – Elvis Presley with the swivelling hips, who is king to millions. And there are still girls and boys who are prepared to say that he is still about the best all-round human being America has ever seen. But since 1956, when overnight he became the most talked-about entertainer in America and sold ten million records, Elvis has gradually grown away from the music that made him famous. He is not so much in the public eye these days but he is still the one and only Elvis Presley, and he is still here and wanted after eight years. The serious teenage question here is – can the Beatles last as long?

One Massachusetts girl of fifteen has no doubts at all; the last stanza of her winning poem in a magazine competition said: 'So now what can I say when you ask how I feel, it's fab, it's gear and it makes my head reel, it takes me and shakes me and then makes me cry. I love those four Beatles, I will till I die.'

REPORTING THE HORRORS OF WAR

Daniel Counihan

SAIGON, APRIL 1965

Our correspondent was asked how he was able to separate his private and professional feelings when reporting on something utterly horrible.

Twenty-one years lie between the two most horrible things I have seen as a reporter; and curiously, on each occasion I was covering the story with an elderly correspondent – American as it happens – who was good for my morale. The first time was in Italy just after the Allies captured Rome. In Rome, not long before, thirty German SS men had marched down a street and been killed by an Italian partisan bomb. The Germans cordoned off the entire area, and arrested every man, woman and child in it; they wanted ten for one, so they had to go outside the cordon. When they had made up the number they took all the captives to some caves – the Fosse Ardeatine – and shot them one by one in the back of the head; they then sealed the caves. One of my first assignments after we got to Rome was to write an eyewitness account of their uncovering.

I have no doubt it is easy enough to imagine, without my describing anything, how horrifying this was. All the senses were affronted. There was the sound of women wailing, the sight of innocent people who had died horribly and been half-buried for some time, and then there was the smell. For years, I have recollected with a feeling of shame that I walked about among all this, seriously taking little notes, and trying to reconstruct in my mind from the appalling evidence on and in the ground the exact circumstances of the massacre. I then went to a nearby telephone and gave my story to the office in Rome, and immediately after this I was very sick indeed.

Sam Acheson of the *Dallas Morning News* – God bless him – was waiting his turn at the phone; he pretended not to notice that I had been sick but mumbled kindly, 'Nice story, boy,' and went on calmly to dictate his own piece. A little later, as we walked to the jeep we were sharing, I was sick again and this time he said, 'Never mind, boy, you will see a lot worse than that in this racket.'

As a fact, though inevitably most reporters see some pretty ghastly things from time to time, I have never seen anything quite as bad as the Fosse Ardeatine since.

But a week or so ago, I saw something that was nearly as bad – a small battlefield here in Vietnam left much as it was at the moment the battle ended. Some Vietcong had tried to capture a strongly fortified camp; they were mown down by machine-guns, blasted by land mines, left where they fell, impaled in the deep barbed-wire entanglements, crouched behind scant cover where they had crept to die or lying half in and half out of the water in nearby swampy ground. And inside the camp, there were more dead; these had been collected with what decency was possible at that time and in that place, shrouded and loaded into lorries to be taken away.

Once again, I found myself walking around and taking little notes and I stood in an emplacement to record an explanation of the scene for the television cameras. I remembered very vividly that day long ago outside Rome and asked myself again why I was not becoming victim to proper human shock. I said to myself, as I have tried to convince myself before, people killed violently do not look quite real – it is like a scene in a film. This, however, as any number of soldiers can tell you, is a lie. I suppose I was just being a reporter and, by habit, professional needs took over. I was relieved when a young Vietnamese officer showed me a wallet he had taken from one of the dead North Vietnamese boys. It held a recent photograph of the boy holding a new bicycle that he looked proud to own. There was the inevitable picture of a girl. On a few leaves of a cheap pocket diary there were some sums and some simple equations – he had been trying to teach himself elementary mathematics. Looking at that, I felt better; that is to say, I felt glad to feel much worse. And I suppose I must have been showing how I felt as we got into the aircraft to go back to Saigon.

There again beside me was an elderly American reporter; he watched me and then called my attention to what was opposite us in the plane. A rough oblong box painted light red was taking back to Saigon a man killed in the battle. On top of it were little bowls containing religious offerings, which had to be removed for the steep take-off. Next to the coffin sat some of the man's relatives, completing a family grouping of which you felt the reality – it was not just a box and some people. And at the centre of it all was a small baby that the young widow was suckling. My American friend said, 'I'm going to write my piece around that.' And, of course, he was quite right, that little vignette of life and continuity, closely linked with what we had just seen, did symbolize what makes it possible for the human mind to tolerate the horror of death in war without utter loss of hope and with a little less shame.

ELEMENTARY RIGHTS

Charles Wheeler

Mississippi, August 1965

Thousands of black Americans became eligible to vote under the new Civil Rights Act but, particularly in the South, life for many remained difficult.

Outside the Sheriff's office, a recruiting poster for the Ku Klux Klan. Next to it a drinking fountain, curtly marked WHITE. The door opens and there appears a tall figure in a Texan hat and cowboy boots, with a star on his chest and a pistol in an open holster, and a face that is vaguely familiar.

No, it is not a film, it is last Wednesday – at the County Court House in Philadelphia, Mississippi, and the man in the doorway is Deputy Sheriff Price, who with his chief, Sheriff Rainey, and seventeen other citizens faced charges in connection with last summer's murder of three young civil rights workers, two of them white New Yorkers and the third a local Negro.

You probably remember the case – the three were arrested by Price for speeding, were held in the local gaol until night-time and then, according to Price, were released.

Forty-four days later, after a search by hundreds of federal agents and troops, their bodies were found eighteen feet below the surface of a newly constructed dam.

Price, Rainey and the rest are on bail pending the resumption of their trial before a federal court on charges of conspiring to deny the three victims their civil rights by killing them. And there, for the present, the matter rests.

In the meantime, life in Philadelphia goes on much as before. I called on the deputy sheriff. 'I wonder who killed those men,' he said, and grinned. He and his chief still run the town. A local doctor, who suggested they be suspended from their law enforcement duties until the trial is over, lost too many patients and has moved his practice to another county.

I went to see the mayor. 'I never hear anybody talking about that case,' he said.

'Do the Negroes talk about it?' I asked.

'Oh, we never have trouble with the niggers here,' he said, 'not now.'

Which is, broadly speaking, true. Philadelphia is not part of what is called 'the black belt' in Mississippi. In this town the whites heavily outnumber the Negroes, who are among the poorest in the state. Even getting the vote will not enable the community on its own to elect another sheriff, or even force the local council to give some of the jobs it controls to the Negroes – jobs like postmen and garbage collectors. Not in Philadelphia.

Yet even this sad little backwater is not quite as backward as it was last summer. For others have come to the town to replace the three who were shot and the local Negroes are starting to respond to their leadership, beginning to win their first elementary rights.

In the heart of the Negro quarter in Philadelphia, in a shabby wooden house across the road from the local civil rights headquarters, there lives a certain Mrs Jones. She is a widow in her late sixties with nine children, all of them living in the North. And from all of them she gets letters. But because Mrs Jones is black, her letters are not delivered. If she thinks there may be a letter for her, she has to walk a mile to the post office and ask. Or rather she and the rest of her community did have to walk. It was the civil rights people who suggested that something might be done. Money was collected and Mrs Jones flew to Washington. She took a bus to the Department of Justice and there she told the story of the non-delivery of the Negro community's mail.

This was a year ago and the federal machine moved slowly. But last month the Negroes got their postal delivery and outside each house there is now a brand new letter-box perched on a pole.

And this is not their only gain. For as long as anybody in Philadelphia can remember, the Negro community has been subjected to an unofficial, but strictly enforced, curfew. The sheriff, or one of his men, would chase any Negro off the streets after dark. The present sheriff and his deputy went further. They used to patrol the Negro area by car and when they saw a Negro after dusk, on his own veranda, they would order him, or her, inside the house. Until last summer. Soon after the discovery of the three bodies in the dam, Sheriff Rainey and Deputy Sheriff Price stopped patrolling the Negro area after dark. They have not been back at night for months now; and in their own quarter, at least, Mrs Jones and her friends can cross the road to spend an evening with a neighbour, and if it is a hot evening, they can gossip on the porch if they like. It is an elementary right, but it is a start.

DODGING THE DRAFT

Gerald Priestland

WASHINGTON, SEPTEMBER 1965

More and more young Americans were being conscripted into the armed forces as the war in Vietnam intensified.

The body of a young American soldier had been flown home from Vietnam for burial in the family tomb in New York. On the morning of the funeral the telephone rang and the soldier's brother, a lawyer, answered. The caller asked to speak to the dead man's mother. 'I just wanted to tell her,' he said, 'how glad I am her son was killed. I am a card-carrying member of the Communist Party and he was trying to oppress the Vietnamese people.' That, at least, is what the lawyer told a Congressional committee which is trying to draft a bill to punish what appears to be a nationwide outbreak of calls like this. An increasing number of American mothers are receiving them these days. Sixty-eight men were killed in one two-week period recently, and for every son dead there were five wounded. Casualties are a part of any war, but in this one there are factors which make them harder to bear. Vietnam is still an undeclared war, likely to remain so. To many parents it must seem an irrelevant one. And because it is still a part-time war, and the apparatus of censorship and propaganda is not fully applied, newspapers and magazines show harrowing images of suffering: Marines hit, wounded and dying; soldiers

76

whimpering in their comrades' arms; children sobbing at the dockside as their fathers cast off for the front, quite apart from the pictures of the martyrdom of the Vietnamese peasantry. For a people which can be so proudly jingoist in principle, Americans are showing very little enthusiasm for getting at the enemy in practice.

Few of the young men who face the possibility of conscription today will actually go to war. Half of them will be eliminated for physical or psychological reasons, and another quarter will get into deferred categories. Those who are called up are needed mainly to fill the gaps at home or in Europe. But by most accounts, there has been an undignified scramble to dodge the adventure and vocational training offered by the recruiting posters. When it was announced that the exemption for married men would cease after midnight on August 26, teenagers queued up all day outside the high-speed marriage chapels of Nevada. Now that it has been hinted that this will avail them nothing by next spring unless they happen to have children, one can foresee a rush to fulfil that condition too. A draft board chairman in Chicago told reporters, 'Everybody's fighting to stay out. They bring their parents, their bosses, their lawyers; they run out and get married to somebody they shouldn't; they go back to college; they bring in phoney certificates from the doctors. Everybody's got an angle.'

Without having to embark on a pacifist or more cynical argument, it is still possible to make some excuse for the draft dodgers. American conscription has been so selective for so long that the odds against being called have been heavy. Only dumb oxes get called, has been the assumption. But the jump from an intake of three thousand over the nation in February to thirty-three thousand next month has touched a lot of people who had thought they would be immune, and are now shocked, angry or insulted. Casualties among those already in the field are a rather different matter. I have nowhere seen or heard it suggested yet that they are unreasonable. Even American aircraft losses over the North – which now exceed eighty-five – are not thought excessive. The Pentagon's cost-effectiveness formula has not yet presumed to attach a value to human life. But since pickets charged at the Battle of Gettysburg, the whole American attitude to war has been to substitute machine power for manpower wherever possible. Up against a stubborn pocket of resistance the US Army does not go in with cold steel. It sends for the US Air Force which arrives with bullet-proof seats, armoured vests and helicopters to rescue any pilot shot down.

In spite of this economy of life, I believe that somewhere along the scale there is a price beyond which the American voter will not go, and it will be a price much lower than that paid in Korea. Casualties and call-ups are just the sort of thing to send the voter running to his congressman. And this can have more effect on the White House than all the teach-ins of the past summer. But I submit the danger is less that America will hasten to appease the Communists than that she will hurry to obliterate them.

WAITING FOR UDI

Ronald Robson

SALISBURY, NOVEMBER 1965

Correspondents in Rhodesia were speculating about if or when there would be an announcement that the country would unilaterally declare independence.

The small daughter of an acquaintance here in Salisbury was asked by her father a few weeks ago, 'And what did you learn at school today, darling?' She smiled brightly, wriggled a bit, drew in a big breath and said in her little girlish voice, 'S. M. I. T. H. spells sincerity.' For some reason I recalled this when Mr Ian Smith left his cabinet office on the evening of Friday, 5 November. He had declared a state of emergency only a few hours earlier. In fact, the announcement came just half an hour after I had spoken to him that morning. And at that point he gave no sign that anything was about to happen.

Later, though, he denied that the state of emergency had anything to do with a unilateral declaration of independence. He said, in effect, 'If we want to declare a state of emergency for a UDI we'll do it, and it will be straightforward.' Asked if a UDI was any closer, he said, 'No.' Well, of course, perhaps it was a situation akin to a Chancellor being asked if the pound was about to be devalued, and answering, 'No,' when he knew very well that devaluation was to take place very soon. But Mr Smith's remarks did not ring with the celebrated sincerity.

Thus began a week of swift-moving developments of tension,

79

speculation and sometimes drama. On the Saturday I spent the morning working for television in an African township, partly to show that the situation had seldom been so peaceful, and that we could discover no signs that a state of emergency was warranted. After my middle of the day circuit to London, I spent a short time at a Sunday cricket game being played at the home of a Salisbury journalist. Nobody has relaxed much since. That night we awaited the reply from Mr Wilson – the one which proposed that Rhodesia's chief justice visit London and that the two premiers meet in Malta. From then until Wednesday night we spent hours practically camping on Mr Smith's doorstep.

Rhodesia's chief justice did fly to London – a faint spark of hope, but not much. Mr Smith obviously did not approve. We had weighed up the first orders under the emergency regulations. If I had used the phrase, 'And this brings a UDI a step nearer,' every time there was a crisis point in Salisbury, nobody would believe me now. On Tuesday the ninth, however, I felt con- strained to broadcast a piece listing the discernible apparent preparations over the past year and ending, 'If ever Rhodesia really seemed to be on the brink of taking independence, it looks like it now.' On Wednesday night, with my feet killing me, I was one of those who waited in the street for the longest session yet outside Mr Smith's office. Shirt-sleeved cabinet ministers threw open the windows of the cabinet room for air. We could hear laughter. Some correspondents even called up to the window, 'What's happening?' At one stage a policeman moved us, because, he said, some people had been listening below the window. Mr Smith told me that night, 'Just tell your blokes in London that I want an answer.'

Sweating in my little studio on the late circuit on that tropical night, I said the picture did not look too bright, but, optimist to the last, I added, 'But with a man like Mr Ian Smith, one never knows.'

The next day, everyone's all-Rhodesian boy, fighting influ- enza, sounding not triumphant but infinitely weary, made his broadcast proclamation of UDI. Within an hour, floods of carefully prepared printed material about the new independence, possibly months of work, came into our hands. I finished my last circuit, being interviewed from London, at after midnight our time in the hot little studio. As I switched off the microphone and reached for my jacket with one hand, I scribbled deliberately on the pad in front of me with the other, *S. M. I. T. H. spells sincerity — or does it?!*

1966–1975

CHINA'S RED GUARDS

Anthony Lawrence

HONG KONG, SEPTEMBER 1966

The Chinese leader Mao Tse Tung founded the Red Guards to take action against foreign and bourgeois influences.

For many of the four million Chinese here in Hong Kong, present events on the mainland defy understanding. People are worried and puzzled. When I asked a rather patriotic left-wing Chinese man about the situation he said, 'I simply don't know. When I pick up the Communist papers I just don't know what I'm going to read next. It is as if Mao Tse Tung is destroying the Chinese Communist Party along with his own image. It's very depressing.'

In some cases, of course, developments are being exaggerated. But it does seem true that a kind of reign of terror has been underway. These young students with their red arm–bands, gongs and drums have been moving from city to city in their thousands, out to destroy everything that suggests old customs, old ways of thought, or traces of foreign or Chinese bourgeois capitalism. What it has meant in practice is that remaining churches and temples, and even historical Buddhist monuments, have been damaged or plastered over with slogans; foreign cemeteries have been closed; aged nuns harshly treated and expelled. Then there has been the campaign against foreign hairstyles, pointed shoes, tight slacks, with people being marched off to the barber to be cropped, or sent home barefoot. But it has gone much further than this. Anyone who looks as if he enjoys a higher standard of living than the peasant worker or soldier may be in for trouble. People receiving money from overseas, something the government has always encouraged up to now, have had their houses ransacked and women have had their heads shaved and been spat upon. In Canton, domestic service has been forbidden. Anyone with a bank account may find it frozen.

All this represents the latest phase of a movement that goes back years. It reflects the personality of one of the greatest statesmen of our time, Mao Tse Tung, and the limitations of his experience. He has always, from the beginning, been the revolutionary who believes in the violent pressure of mass campaigns. He has said all along that it is the power of the people, more than any kind of equipment, that can move mountains and win wars.

But in recent years he seems to have come up against the kind of criticism which, when a man is very famous and is growing old, is very hard to bear – the criticism that goes against one's cherished theories but is nevertheless based on statistics and facts of what the land can produce, what materials and finance are essential for national progress. And this criticism has not come from foreigners who know nothing of the Chinese spirit; it has come from Party comrades who have been through as much as Mao himself, men with impeccable records of Communist loyalty.

Some criticized him for the big losses incurred in the Great Leap Forward movement of 1958 and the three bad years that followed. But they never convinced him he was wrong. He stuck to his revolutionary approach – an army organized on guerrilla lines, education combined with labour, Communist rectitude placed before technical ability. Through persisting in these early ideas, Mao has become more isolated. He does not want discussion and argument; he wants praise, recognition from people he can trust. Defence Minister Lin Piao is the man who has praised Mao the most. Lin is now the number two man in China. Men who have shown more dignity, more aloofness towards the deification of Mao, have slipped lower in the Communist hierarchy. Mao's own wife, never before regarded as a political talent, emerges to a new high position in this Cultural Revolution. The reason? Mao feels at least he can trust her, whereas he does not feel so sure about some of the other comrades, or about the normal party machinery. The new creation, the Red Guards, replacing the Communist Youth League, by-passing normal channels, may well become more important still.

Most of what the Red Guards have done so far, renaming of streets and stores, hounding of overseas Chinese, anti-foreign moves, could all have been done through normal channels, by party orders. But instead there is the mass campaign, noise, crowds, slogans and a climate of fear.

However, something seems to have gone wrong with this Red Guards' campaign. There is resistance – some from old-time revolutionaries who are not going to be bullied by teenagers. Some say the army is only partly with the Red Guards. Mao himself recently came out with a sixteen-point directive telling the Red Guards they must use reason in their campaign and not force. Now there is another appeal – to keep away from the countryside, in order to leave the peasants alone to get on with the harvest. Because, in all the uncertainty arising from this strange campaign of anti-bourgeois agitation, one thing is sure: China's economy is suffering. Remittances from Chinese abroad are being held up, production and trade are being interrupted.

When will it end? That depends on Mao Tse Tung. He still thinks he can attain this hundred per cent revolutionary Communist China. It is his ideal – the creation, with the aid of terrorism if necessary, of a new type of human being. For those commonsense Chinese Communists who believe in material progress on conventional lines, it is a nightmare situation.

FLORENCE FLOODS

Ian McDougall

ITALY, NOVEMBER 1966

After a period of heavy rain the River Arno burst its banks causing widespread damage to the city of Florence and to hundreds of its works of art.

The poet Dante, himself a Florentine, might have felt at home in the city hall in the past couple of weeks: the candlelight flickering in great vaulted rooms, the weird processions of muttering townsfolk groping through the corridors in single file in search of an official to complain to, the piles of fresh stores and old debris littering the feet of masterpieces sculpted by Michelangelo – there was something in the grand manner showing through it all, not exactly an Inferno but possibly a Purgatory. Of Paradise, there is in Florence no trace whatsoever.

Most disasters in my experience get exaggerated in the telling but I do not think this one has been. With fewer than fifty people dead, and under a thousand of Florence's tens of thousands of art treasures damaged, the statistics of the story perhaps fail to overwhelm at first hearing. It is only when one splashes through the mud-laden streets of one third of the city, the most ancient and beautiful third, that the facts sink in. These are: that Florence is not going to look the same for a very long time indeed; that in the meantime, thirty thousand people have had their homes or offices severely damaged without any prospect of insurance compensation and that tens of thousands more have begun to realize that to switch on an electric light, to drink from a tap or to pull a lavatory chain are among the priceless heritage of civilized mankind. Dante would have made more of this point, I feel sure, but I do not know where he would have placed the distinguished elderly Italian gentleman, dressed as if for a day's grouse-shooting, who rushed up to me out of the blue with the remark in impeccable English, 'We're lovely people, we Florentines, but we're just a lot of damned artists. What we need now is bureaucrats.' He was referring, as it eventually turned out, to a theory he held that the entire city could be supplied with water again in twenty-four hours if only the city fathers put their minds to it. And although I am quite certain he was in this case exaggerating, his indignation is typical of that of thousands of others.

Almost everything is being blamed on the authorities: the lack of food, water and light, the mishandling of salvaged art treasures, failure to warn the population about the extent of the danger. This last point, together with the causes of the flood itself, is now the subject of judicial inquiry but I think it is fair to quote the opinion of an American permanent resident who seemed confident that had a citywide warning been given, the resulting chaos and panic would have far outstripped the dislocation that in fact occurred.

It is also, however, clear that had the banks burst a few hours earlier when thousands were asleep at ground or below-ground level, or a few hours later when they were in the streets, the casualties would have been higher. As things are, the place is in the most frightful mess, with thick brown oil from the city's heating installations leaving ugly marks on stonework that in many places will be ineffaceable, and with the river's filthiest deposits, including of course the carcasses of animals, permeating innumerable living-rooms, shops and offices. It is commonplace to see the entire furniture of a house being carted away for final demolition and on stalls all over the city you can pick up for a few lire goods that three weeks ago were spanking new but now look as if they have been cast up from a shipwreck.

In all this misery and deprivation, the Florentines have remained astonishingly good-mannered – which they always were, anyway – and, even in intervals of complaint, cheerful. One clothes shop, selling off its ruined Scottish tweed, has a nicely worded sign up saying DRY BRITISH.

I think the truth is that many are still suffering from shock. What this disaster will do to next year's tourist trade and to the city's long-term economy is anybody's guess, but I would like to make clear that within a matter of months, Florence will be fully habitable for visitors and that the overwhelming majority of its immense store of art treasures remains entirely intact.

DEATH OF MARTIN LUTHER KING

Charles Wheeler

WASHINGTON, APRIL 1968

The assassination of Martin Luther King meant that Americans, who were already at war in Vietnam, had to face up to the prospect of violent unrest at home as well.

At the moment of Dr Martin Luther King's death, I was sitting in an aircraft waiting with a hundred other correspondents to take off for Honolulu. My American neighbour and I were talking about the ups and downs of Lyndon Johnson, agreeing that the week's developments on Vietnam had put Mr Johnson back into the presidential race. L. B. J., we said to each other, is now exactly where he likes to be: facing an attentive audience on the brink of loud sustained applause. He is moving in harness with public opinion, trying to find a way out of the war. And then somebody shot a national Negro leader. And with his death, the prospect of talks to end the war seemed to fade into the background, to be replaced by the prospect of civil war at home. We piled out of the plane. Johnson cancelled his programme. He had spent most of the night on the telephone calling mayors of towns now torn by rioting, begging them to use the least possible violence in restoring order lest their local outbreaks should spread across America.

All Friday, the President struggled to convince the Negro

community that it was not white America that had killed Dr King, but a single killer. He summoned the Negro establishment to the White House, told them his own plans and asked for ideas. He was told it was too late for words and appeals for restraint. He was asked for concrete action, programmes guaranteeing jobs and homes and equal opportunity for black Americans. The President did what he could to show that white America cares. He proclaimed a national day of mourning. He lowered the nation's flags to half-mast, he cancelled his conference in Hawaii, he asked the Congress to assemble in joint session to hear his recommendations for action. All this he did on television, broadcast nationwide.

But, at that moment, the people he needed to reach were not watching television. Some of them, only five blocks from the White House, were looting television sets at that moment. Others were setting fire to shops, others again were pelting police and firemen with bricks, and the same was happening in far-off Chicago, Detroit and who knows where else.

For those who were listening to the President's appeals for calm and promises of action, it must have seemed late. When the cities were in flames last summer, Mr Johnson proclaimed a national day of prayer and set up a commission of inquiry. When a month or so ago that commission produced a damning indictment of white prejudice and white inaction, he all but ignored it. In all his speeches, even in the State of the Union Address, he put the emphasis on the need to maintain law and order, on the fight against crime in the streets, the accepted euphemism for Negro violence, just like any politician in the country seeking re-election.

Yesterday, there was no mention of law and order. No warning to the violent. It was a speech that recalled his addresses to the people of 1965, when white America was all for civil rights, and Congress was responding with an avalanche of progressive legislation. He even used the phrase once more, 'We shall overcome.'

There can be no doubt that in his response to Dr Martin Luther King's murder, the President has set himself against majority white opinion. Most Americans, though they may deplore his murder, had come to regard Dr King as a rabble rouser, as a Negro leader who was willing to hedge on non-violence in order to keep his position in the community. Many have said so in the past twenty-four hours and some have added that Dr King got what he deserved. President Johnson then is swimming against the tide. He is doing so on a major issue for the first time in his presidential career. He would have been applauded for making an example of the rioters and restoring order in a short, sharp show of irresistible force.

As I record this report it is just after midnight, about 6 a.m. in England. The President is in the White House basement Situation Room, usually the nerve centre in foreign crises, like Cuba and the Arab–Israeli war. Outside, infantry are stationed in the White House gardens, there are tanks in Hampshire Avenue and a machine-gun nest on Capitol Hill. Washington is now quietening down. But the fires are still burning. And if this has been a disastrous year for predictions this must be the worst morning for predictions yet. All one can do at this moment is look back a few hours to the middle of the week when America, with a real prospect at last of peace talks, was more united in purpose than at any time in the past three years. And now it is Saturday and it is not so any more. And President Johnson, down in his operations room, must be wondering how much else has died with Martin Luther King.

HOME FIRES BURNING

Martin Bell

WILMINGTON, APRIL 1968

After the murder of Martin Luther King, rioting broke out in several American cities.

Imagine the Parachute Brigade bivouacked on Clapham Common, its troops patrolling through Brixton and Balham and whole streets devastated by looting and arson. That, in British terms, would be an equivalent of what I saw in Chicago. And Chicago is only one city among many that have suffered some kind of insurrection. In Wilmington, Delaware, I found snipers in action and smoke pouring out of the downtown slums. In Trenton, New Jersey, after a similar conflagration, Negro youths were on the streets awaiting a confrontation with the state police. In all these places there was a night curfew and a restriction on the sale of liquor and petrol. In all of them, the army was on the streets. And in all of them, I was reminded of nowhere else so much as of Saigon – the same sense of emergency, the same omnipresence of American troops, except that in my experience, which pre-dates the Tet Offensive, Saigon was more relaxed.

The parallel with Vietnam is one that Americans themselves are uncomfortably aware of. The Negroes certainly acknowledge it. One youth surveying the scene in a burning part of Wilmington remarked that the street corner looked like Vietnam. And another,

94

referring to the sheer size of the army contingents deployed, commented that, 'Out there they must think we're the Vietcong.' It so happens, too, that most of the federal troops called into Chicago were Vietnam veterans. They had served their year in the war, and now they were back in their own country guarding against civil disorder and arson. This was not the sense in which they had expected to find the home fires burning.

The sense of siege prevails not only in the Negro ghettos but right in the commercial centres of many cities. It is a common sight to see guardsmen on duty outside city halls, in front of the main banks and public buildings, patrolling main streets among the throngs of shoppers. Their very presence in the cities where they appear is a token of the failure thus far of local schemes to improve the conditions that the Negroes live in. There is a recognition now among the leadership of many communities that too little was done too late. The burning and the looting is a price that has been paid for a long indifference.

And the Negroes themselves? 'Talk to a hundred of them,' a city mayor told me, 'and you'll find a hundred different grievances.' But unemployment is a big one. So is bad housing, though neither cause has been advanced by the recent rioting which happened, after all, mostly in areas where Negroes themselves live. The latest estimate is of forty-five million dollars' worth of damage and two and a half thousand people made homeless. In their case, even what they had before is better than what they have got now.

What has been done these last two weeks though, and done at a high price, is that some change has been wrought in the public attitude to slum problems. Citizens viewing the divisions in their cities find that apathy is no longer tolerable. Their recognition of this expresses itself in many ways. Some constructive, some merely rhetorical. There was a full-page advertisement placed by a patriotic organization in the local Trenton newspaper calling on the people of that city to 'strike down each violent act of destruction as if it were a foul beast and to rebuild that which we have helped to destroy: our faith, our hopes, our dreams, our city'. But in fact the actual task of rebuilding and of staving off further trouble will fall, as usual, to the civic leaders who have been putting in long hours on this already. Much has been made, and rightly, of the part played by New York Mayor John Lindsay in 'cooling it' in Harlem.

But other mayors, too, have acted with courage in other cities. The Mayor of Trenton, Carmen Armenti, insisted on going up to the troubled section of town to reason with the Negroes on the sidewalk. He was told he might get 'roughed up'. 'Nobody roughs me up,' he said – and they did not. But many Negroes, while willing at times to listen to the advice of their more moderate leaders, and indeed of their mayors, were also, while the burning was going on, quite indifferent to the destruction they were causing. Instead, I sensed they were in some way proud of having drawn attention to their plight, of having actually achieved something. 'This isn't a riot,' one man told me, 'this is a revolution.' He was overstating the case, of course. What has happened here since the death of Martin Luther King has fallen far short in scale and seriousness of what happened last year in the cities of Newark and Detroit. And even now, those in official positions are inclined to optimism, to the feeling that the very shock of recent events may itself cool things a bit.

But people not in official positions I have found to be rather less sanguine, pointing out that some kind of trouble had been expected this year in America's cities, but nothing like so bad as this, so soon.

MEMORIES OF PERÓN

Noel Clark

BUENOS AIRES, JUNE 1968

Former President Perón had been in exile for thirteen years, but much of Argentina's workforce looked back fondly on the days of his dictatorship.

I recently found myself sandwiched between the driver of a heavy goods lorry and his mate, plunging and jolting along a potholed road in the suburbs of Buenos Aires. 'Look at the state of this road,' said the driver, 'not been touched for years. Perón would have fixed these holes.' 'Ah,' said his mate, 'Perón.' I could not be sure whether his tone implied nostalgia or disillusionment. But the fact is that the persona of Perón, an ageing exile in Madrid, is still bathed in a reverential glow for many Argentines, a glow that tends to become rosier as the memory recedes. A middle-aged schoolteacher in Córdoba told me 'If he came back now, there's not a hall in the country that could hold the crowd.' A senior official said, 'Election? You know who'd win if we held them? So, of course, we're not going to.' Thirteen years after his dismissal, Perón's name still hovers on the fringe of any conversation. And yet, I wonder if one is not in danger of getting the picture wrong?

One of the great slogans of the Perón era was, 'My life for Perón.' But when the forces decided to get rid of him, very few people indeed were prepared to go that far. Yet one of Perón's most notable creations was the mighty confederation of Argentine Labour – the CGT – which in a very short time won concessions

97

from management so dramatic in the context of time and place that they are still resented in some quarters even today.

The dictatorial excesses of Perón's later years in power are forgotten by many humble folk who hanker after the days when workers enjoyed at least a very convincing illusion of their own supremacy. Even Argentines who detest the memory of what for them was an unscrupulous dictatorship, concede that what Perón offered the workers, both spiritually and materially, may have saved Argentina from one day going Communist. Be that as it may, the present military-backed government made it clear from the outset two years ago that it would tolerate no dictatorship from field or factory, or for that matter from the railway workers – the toughest union of the lot. Most troublesome unions were put under government management in effect, 'intervened' as the saying goes. And the others were warned to watch their step.

When workers show signs of getting restive over austerity measures, the wage freeze and the like, they are sharply dealt with. Several hundred employees who barricaded themselves inside a Buenos Aires paint factory a few weeks ago were literally smoked out by the police. More recently still at Córdoba, centre of the motor car industry which has been suffering a recession, four thousand workers held a protest rally against proposed lay-offs. But their attempt to march through the city was broken up by riot squads.

There are said to be about one and a half million unemployed or under-employed workers in Argentina. But, oddly enough, it is not that, nor indeed the government's toughness, which seems to have been uppermost in the minds of Argentine labour leaders. Priests, even one or two bishops, have been far more active and successful in drawing public attention to the sufferings of workers in depressed areas. The established leaders of labour, for their part, have been primarily concerned, to judge by their actions, with trying to revive the former prestige and power of the emasculated CGT. But their efforts seem only to have resulted in a further disintegration of the movement. No further action by the government has been needed. What was once Argentina's most effectively organized body after the forces has simply been rent asunder from within, by a combination of conflicting opinions and ambitions.

This auto-fragmentation, so to speak, of the Argentine labour movement suggests that, while one is constantly being reminded of the Perónist mystique, and while Perónist may be a convenient way of labelling a still substantial body of Argentine opinion, Perónism is no longer a force capable of cementing serious opposition to the government.

So far, President Ongania and his ministers have simply let the unions stew in their own juice, neither recognizing nor suppressing the federations which have emerged in recent weeks.

Earlier this year from Madrid, Perón formally dissolved the so-called, but already non-existent, front of Perónist unions within the CGT, as a prelude to reorganization. The gesture was perhaps recognition of the fact that times have changed.

SORBONNE SIT-IN

Kenneth Matthews

PARIS, JUNE 1968

Rioting students, at first supported by striking workers, occupied the Sorbonne and almost succeeded in bringing down the French government.

The tourists who go to the Sorbonne to stare at the students in unorthodox residence there have certainly picked on the most extraordinary sight of modern Paris. White and black, whole and bandaged, boys like girls and girls like boys, and some so covered in tangled hair that they might be reversing the process of evolution – they seem to have only their youth in common. And when they pour out of their lair for a raid into the night streets, they are indistinguishable from hooligans, leaving a trail of burnt cars, uprooted trees and broken windows behind them.

But they are intellectuals, or should be – reasoning creatures, the élite of the society of the future. Is it possible that they carry a message for the age, which has been obscured by the smoke of their fire-raising and by police tear-gas bombs? A Paris publisher is bringing out a book of fifteen hundred slogans collected from the scrawlings on the walls of the Sorbonne, though it would be an ingenious brain which could distil a coherent philosophy from such a wild mixture of the screams of competing revolutionaries.

And yet, standing in one of their serious discussion groups, listening to these young people talking – and heavens how they talk – I have been struck by the way in which certain words crop up again and again, as if they provided the key to the whole situation. Vogue words or living ideas? It is hard to judge. There is the word – I will give it first in French: *decloisonnement*. It is not in the dictionary. It can be translated as departitioning, and it means breaking down the partitions in society. Pressed to illustrate it by an example, they will tell you that in factories and offices the workers in one grade never speak to those in another. They want to open up new channels of communication between people. They have tried quite hard to make common cause with the strikers recently, but after a brief flirtation they have been snubbed. The Communists too have snubbed them, jealous of anyone who steals their revolutionary thunder. So the way of departitioning has proved rather stormy and unrewarding so far.

Another favourite word is *contestation*. I have been told about six times that it will not translate into English. The nearest try seems to be questioning. The students distinguish between inward and outward questioning. The inward sort was not hard to understand and made me think of Socrates' 'The unexamined life is not worth living.' But when I asked for an example of the outward sort, a very earnest young woman in trousers and thick glasses told me, 'Well, we go into a theatre, interrupt a play, and invite the actors and audience to question what they're doing.' I could see that such interventions might not always be received in the spirit in which they were offered. However, the politicians have taken notice of the word. A Gaullist spokesman told us, 'Government can't be in a state of perpetual questioning.'

The students, the more serious of them at any rate, accept this sort of criticism, and talk a lot about the need for creating. There is a vulgar English sense of this word in which one might say that the students have been creating more than somewhat already. But they mean by creating, making an imaginative effort to get the social order out of its rut and helping the brave new world emerge.

More of them would probably be willing to express regret for the recent riotings, but for the unhappy proof it has provided that violence gets things done. They have seen senior professors, university administrators, leading educationalists lining up in the newspapers and on the platforms to explain how they have long been conscious of the need for university reform, and in some cases how their proposals for reform have been side-tracked and neglected. And one student is actually a candidate in the coming elections on the government side. He says, 'It's more difficult to be a reformer than a revolutionary.'

Well, an older French revolution called for 'Liberty, Equality, Fraternity'. I cannot quite see a new one taking up the cry of 'Departitioning, Questioning, Creating'. But at least these watch-words provide a welcome alternative to the smashing, burning, and fighting, of which we have seen so much in Paris in the last few weeks.

PRAGUE WINTER

Robert Elphick

CZECHOSLOVAKIA, AUGUST 1968

The short-lived 'Prague Spring', when Czechoslovakian Prime Minister Dubček steered the country close to democracy, was shattered when Russian troops swept into the country and the Czechoslovakian leaders were taken away to Moscow.

As the days go by, the harsh realities of what the Russians intend for Czechoslovakia become more and more apparent. The leaders have returned from Moscow, it is true: they have survived those incredible negotiations, if one can call them that, at the point of Russian bayonets. And they are home again. But it is becoming more and more obvious that they are, none the less, hardly better than prisoners of the Russians, although they may speak in the name of the people from Prague Castle.

Effective rule in Czechoslovakia is coming nowadays by dictation from Moscow. And the tactics of the legally elected representatives of the people, like President Svoboda, Mr Dubček, Mr Černik and Mr Smrkovsky, are to save what can be saved of the freedom since January and bide their time for better days. But for now there seems no alternative but to accept the Kremlin's orders, backed up as they are by an army of some six hundred and fifty thousand men with modern weapons, all carefully planned and selected to outgun anything the Czechoslovak allies had.

Not that the Czechoslovaks would have had any chance at all if they had been ordered to fight. The occupation was in fact a coup, carried out in the first instance by the local manager of the Soviet airline, Aeroflot, who turned up at Prague airport just after dusk on that black Tuesday, 20 August, with forty-five plain-clothes men and a Russian serving officer. They seized the control tower and the main buildings. And after that it was a relatively simple matter to guide in the huge transports, which brought in the paratroopers who were the first into Prague, while the heavier stuff was lumbering in from the frontier.

The sheer courage of the Czechoslovakian people as a whole and the integrity of the leaders faced with such overwhelming force can only be admired, particularly if, like me, you happened to have been watching it all at close quarters. The disciplined defiance of the population as a whole; the activities of the secret radio broadcaster; the journalists who went underground and turned out the free newspapers, which just made the Russians occupying their ordinary premises look ridiculous, were and are beyond praise. They enabled the voice of an entire people to be heard in what the Kremlin had hoped would have been a private piece of bullying; and, in the end, they won back the leaders they wanted and prevented the Russians from simply imposing a puppet regime.

But the question must now be put: how much power does the Dubček–Svoboda government actually have? It is already pretty obvious that the Russians are not giving it any room for manoeuvre at all, despite the statement in the Moscow Agreement about non-interference. They are ruthlessly putting on the press-ure to get it to implement the Russian demands; stop that dangerous freedom of speech; conform to Moscow's ways; rein-state the Iron Curtain.

The brief Prague spring and summer have already turned to deep winter. Many of the more talented Czechoslovaks that I have known are getting out of the country while the going is still good, aided and abetted by the government itself, which evidently wants to keep a nucleus of reliable people out of harm's way until better times come round.

As of now, the Russians seem determined to root out anything that they think smacks of counter-revolution. They have already as good as wrecked the premises of the Writers' Union, when their patrols went in to look, apparently, for subversive literature. They have also destroyed the million-book card index of the National Library, and nobody can quite explain that. They are still trying to stifle discussion by ordering Mr Dubček to bring the censors back, and they are importing, according to reliable accounts, some one thousand KGB men to sit in at all the ministries to make sure that everything is run Moscow's way.

The lights are going out in Czechoslovakia, but the picture is not entirely dark. If there is hope for the future, it is in the spirit of the leaders and the unity of the people against the invaders. Getting them out is now the mainspring of everyone's thoughts, even of some of the people who had thought to benefit from Russian support, but who have been appalled at the form it has taken.

Strangely enough one of Mr Dubček's strengths – perhaps the only one – is that he is, after all, a Communist, with a party at hand well-versed in conspiratorial action. The party underground is already working well in the full knowledge that it has the support, not only of everyone at home, but of pretty well every Communist Party in Western Europe. The message from the top is to call for patience, dignity, a boycott of the invader. Truth shall prevail, but until that day comes, the best the leaders can offer is to say, 'We are with you; be with us.'

The most poignant scene in Prague these days is played out daily round the big equestrian monument of the Saint King of Bohemia – our Good King Wenceslas. Since the beginning of the invasion it has been the focus for protests, hung with black flags and the Czechoslovak national tricolour. But now it has been scrubbed clean of all the posters and slogans telling the Russians to go home, and it has become something like a national shrine – a shrine, moreover, which is not kept up by the government but by the efforts of the ordinary people.

Fresh flowers appear daily at the foot of the statue, and the national flag and the black flag of mourning get carried in informal relays by young people, old people, long-haired beatniks in jeans and spruce young soldiers. They have been keeping it up for days now, sorrowing for the people who were killed in the early days of the invasion, and also for Czechoslovakia's lost independence. By contrast, the most macabre of my experiences has been perhaps to watch a full-scale Soviet concert party entertaining the troops with concertinas, balalaika music and those exuberant Russian dances. It was something like a celebration at a wake.

It is now a fortnight, though, since the armadas of tanks poured across the country to strangle Czechoslovakia's attempt to mix Communism with democracy and it is quite clear that the Russians grossly miscalculated the temper of the people here in believing that they had only to act decisively to destroy Mr Dubček's position. They obviously placed high hopes on the veteran President, General Svoboda, as possibly providing a respectable head of a puppet regime. But the old President was having none of that, and it is reliably reported he threatened not only to resign but to commit suicide, unless Mr Dubček and the other leaders were freed and restored to their positions.

Not that this — a gain though it is against the possibility of widespread bloodshed — is making much difference to the general Soviet tactics of putting Czechoslovakia back into a rigid strait-jacket. No more dreams of independence within the Communist movement; no more thoughts of holidays abroad or contacts with Western Europe, of freedom or democracy at home, or even better pay, except by leave of the masters of the Kremlin.

What has been published of the dictated Moscow settlement is already onerous enough, and nobody believes that there are not any secret clauses. It is clear, for instance, that there is no fixed date for withdrawal. It is believed they have also insisted on stopping all tourism, and closing the frontier with Western

Germany altogether. They have also warned the Cabinet that any signs of unrest will be taken as proof of the government's incapacity to rule, and that any attempts to resist the invading forces will be ruthlessly suppressed.

Although the Russians are now withdrawing troops from some of the more conspicuous places in Prague and elsewhere, nothing can conceal the fact that their agents are taking over, as rapidly as possible, all the key posts in public life. The calculation is evidently that, having failed to push Mr Dubček and his colleagues out of office, they will make them do their work for them, in the expectation that as they take the unpopular measures they are told to do, they will lose all credibility with the public. The Russians have already forced the government to bring the censors back. They have also forced changes in the Ministry of the Interior, literally over the dead body of one of the deputy ministers, who is reported to have committed suicide rather than hand his files over to the KGB.

The best that Mr Dubček and his colleagues can do now is perhaps to mitigate the consequences of Russian domination, and wait for better times. Initially, at least, they will be helped by the massive feeling of national solidarity that the arrival of the foreign troops has engendered, and also by the natural patience of a people to whom foreign invasion is only too familiar.

HUNT THE EXISTENTIALIST

Daniel Counihan

PARIS, SEPTEMBER 1968

Our correspondent searched the cafés of Paris for signs of the city's famed intellectuals and existentialists.

A character in one of Len Deighton's tough novels says: 'Paris lives in the past. Manet is at the opera and Degas at the ballet. Escoffier cooks while Eiffel builds. Lyrics by Dumas. Music by Offenbach. Oo là là, our Paris is gay, Monsieur, and our private rooms discreet, our coaches call at three, Monsieur, and Schlieffen has no plans.' A friend replies: 'They're not all like that.'

And 'they're not all like that' was what I wanted to feel about Paris when I first used to come here for any length of time just after the war. With the Germans gone, Paris, one was told, was bursting out all over in a creative, intellectual artistic spring that would enliven all the jaded world, and indeed one knew that Monsieur Sartre was holding court somewhere or other on the Left Bank, that Mademoiselle Simone de Beauvoir was around, and Monsieur Camus. I certainly never met any of these people, as I sat and drank in pavement cafés feeling more grown-up than ever because I was no longer in the army, but it was nice to know that they were there.

Just the other day though, in this very different Paris, I asked some of my French acquaintances, 'Well, where does it all happen now? Who are the intellectual leading lights? Where are they to be found?' Some people said vaguely, 'Well, there's Sartre, you know, and Simone de Beauvoir, of course, and there's Camus – but didn't he die?' Someone else said forthrightly, 'Oh, there's nothing like that now.' And yet another, more thoughtfully, said 'Well, you know, there wasn't any fuel just after the war, impossible to keep warm in your own place; so people who wanted to write and discuss went to the cafés which had proper heat and light. There is no need for anything like that now.'

Just the same, it did seem worthwhile to go and see for myself. The places are still there, the Café de Flore, first shrine of the existentialist cult, sprawls its little chairs and tables still on one side of the boulevard St-Germain and they are always full. But you could throw a handful of olives without much real chance of hitting an existentialist. A businessman and his secretary from Dallas, Texas, would be more likely victims, or a couple from Earl's Court.

And so, on to Procope – a nearby restaurant which has a plaque on the wall, claiming incorrectly (as enthusiasts about London will know) to be Europe's oldest restaurant. The plaque also recalls that Voltaire and Diderot fed there as well as d'Alembert, Danton, Desmoulins, Robespierre, Alfred de Musset and George Sand. 'But not all at once I hope,' as a colleague of mine remarked. Anyway, inside there was nothing but excellent food and I suppose an 'atmosphere', which was quite good enough to be going on with.

So next, it was to the ancient rue Jacob and the Bar Vert where a good guidebook told me the poorer existentialists used to meet. There used to be notices on the wall: *I dream day and night of the animals at Bikini. Man, an animal who sings the 'Marseillaise'. Ask for an arsenic crème-de-menthe to appease your thirst for eternity.*

The Bar Vert nowadays is somewhat larger than a good-sized linen cupboard, hellish dark and smells of Camembert. The notices on the wall said: *Service not included, fifteen per cent.* There were a lot of these. Some French Africans grumbled in one corner, a young couple held hands and were silent in another; the waiter was old and moody. I supposed he might have been an existentialist. So, where next?

I was told, 'A lot of writers really do go to the Coupole Montparnasse. You can get served quickly there and buy just one dish if you want.' I think I may well have seen a lot of famous writers at the Coupole, but like the rest of the enormous crowd there, they were eating steadily as if at pasture. So how was I to know? It was quite late by then.

What, no intellectual ferment in all Paris? Well, there might be. I cannot pretend that this was an exhaustive enquiry. But anyway, 'Twenty years after,' as Dumas said, 'there's Sartre, you know, Simone de Beauvoir of course, and there's Camus – but didn't he die? Oh, and there's General de Gaulle.'

BACK TO THE BATTLEFIELDS

Daniel Counihan

PARIS, NOVEMBER 1968

Fifty years after the end of the First World War, our correspondent visited the fields, the towns and the villages where the worst of it was fought.

It is not the cemeteries of Belgium and northern France that most recall the Great War. In their quiet, tucked-away, almost Home Counties cosiness, they speak less of war than of the men who died. But the Great War, too, lies under the ground very close to the surface. That war, as it must be for many whose childhood came after it, has always been for me a shattered night landscape in the mind, a string of names from books and overheard conversations – Ypres, Béthune, Bapaume, Cambrai, Arras, Albert. Plug Street Wood and Hill Sixty, Vimy Ridge and the Menin Road – names that were something separate from those one saw on maps of Belgium and northern France, not simply because one always heard them Anglicized but because they were places in a dream. Yet when I visited them it was astonishingly easy on the ground to conjure up the reality. In the fields of Flanders mud round Ypres I saw even a few late poppies that in that laden atmosphere and at this time of year recalled far too facilely, I fear, sad winter flowers, the starchy red cloth and wire of school ceremonies on Armistice Day when it always seemed to rain.

The real poppies were a few hundred yards from the famous Hill Sixty to which a faded blue and white sign on the roadway pointed. I suppose this sign is a relic of the days when the battlefields were the centre of a pretty lively tourist trade. This, I think, is now somewhat in decline. An almost invisible inscription on a plank door under the ramparts of Ypres recalls that General Plumer's old headquarters was within, and prices of admission to this scene of disastrous decisions are stated. But the padlock and chain on the door are deeply rusted, and cobwebs lie thick across the cracked boards.

The superb Cloth Hall and its square, and the one-time death trap of the Menin Road, are reborn phoenix-like from utter destruction, and already look respectably old. A few shops sell souvenirs and postcards which have an unmistakable stamp of the 1920s. They seem irrelevant as the Menin Gate further on does not. One could be with it and mocking about its 'last days of the Empire' architecture, but impertinence is silenced by the shock of that mass of names of those who have no known grave. No doubt I should have been aware, but I was not, that this is the condition of most of our Great War dead, many of them vanished into the mud, pitifully few miles from the Gate, on the way to the German lines. 'Passchendaele?' I asked at the hotel. 'Turn left,' said the waiter, 'just after the Menin Gate, then it's left again at Zonnebeke.' He warned me, 'Don't turn right to Moorslede,' and that may have raised a hollow laugh from a few ghosts of 1917 who did make that mistake fatally in their day. But they had been on foot. It took me only fifteen leisurely minutes to get to Passchendaele by car. In the valley on either side the plough furrows were holding water or letting it rot away in a soupy slime in the lower hollows. Percheron horses plodded fetlock deep where two British armies, wading up to their thighs, progressed four and a half miles in four months of butchery, and suffered half a million casualties.

Passchendaele itself, reduced to nothingness in the fighting, is long rebuilt, already ageing and drably at peace, bearing no scar.

But the turf in the fields round about, as in many a field throughout the old Ypres Salient, heaves and puckers restlessly, not yet quite able to hide the wounds of fifty years ago. Sometimes, with an imaginative eye, you can guess at a few yards of trench helped out by the positioning of an old concrete strongpoint which has spent most of its existence as a farm building. Shells and grenades, I was told, still come to the surface and every year someone gets hurt. Warning notices are quite frequent. One needs less imagination to detect signs of battle in the chalky Somme Valley. It was there that I met a man who might have stepped from a book of First World War French Army drawings, almost absurdly a blue-jowled *poilu*. He was the guardian of a one-franc-entrance peepshow of old Great War photographs. He liked the British, he said, he had fought beside them. He waved vaguely towards Vimy Ridge down the road, but a dimness in his eyes showed this to be too old a memory. They brightened angrily when he spoke of the Second World War. The Germans came, he said, and stole some of his photographs.

Beneath Vimy Ridge the First World War lives vividly in the equipment-strewn miles of tunnels, the walls covered with soldiers' names (some near the floor) scored by the wounded, and among those a tiny cross carved by a dying Canadian. By Beaumont-Hamel both British and German trenches, and the littered wilderness between, are as they remained when an attack by men from Newfoundland swept the war beyond them. And stumbling about there in a drizzle under a veiled moon with a hint of thunder and lightning along the horizon, I suppose I approached nearest to my childhood notion of what the Great War had been like.

But I shall remember best in all the battlefields a meeting of wars at Warneton. Outside the church, which has been destroyed by many wars and rebuilt, the memorial to the First World War is pockmarked by the bullets of the Second. A First World War British gun stands where it fought its last action, its trail braced against an oak sapling which, now a tree, has grown round it. Some little boys played nearby. They ignored the gun, that was history. They had a tank ingeniously made from wooden boxes and a broomstick gun on pram wheels. One put his head out of the turret. 'Bang,' he shouted. 'You're dead. Bang. Bang. You're all dead.'

SKELETONS IN THE BUSH

Peter Stewart

LAGOS, MARCH 1969

The Federal Nigerian Air Force was accused of bombing civilians in breakaway Biafra. But life, and death, were continuing as normal in the Nigerian capital.

N'nandi Azikwe Street in Lagos is a blur of traffic and a blare of sound, a cross between Old Bond Street and the Faubourg St-Honoré and a suburban High Street. Here the cloth merchants have their showrooms and here come the fashionable women to examine the materials and be examined, in their gold earrings and glittering dresses.

Recently, from my perennial position in the traffic jam there, I saw a middle-aged man run across the street and drop dead on the further pavement. A blanket was thrown over his head and shoulders and trading went on, the high heels of the shoppers contrasting in their delicacy with the worn, heavy boots sticking from under the shroud. Death on N'nandi Azikwe Street is very different in many ways from similar tragedy in Bond Street, W1.

Outside Onitsha, the wrecked cathedral city on the River Niger, human skeletons, picked dry by vultures, gleam through the bush, white against the green reflection from thousands of broken beer bottles trampled into the mud. Dead men here are as useless as empty bottles.

In a war without casualty lists and few letters home, it is as hard to keep track of the individual soldier's fate as it is to return the empties for resupply. Death in Nigeria, and in so many sub-Saharan African countries where the life expectancy can be as low as thirty to thirty-five years, death is so near in families where the new-born mingle with the elderly – it is reverenced in retrospect, with wakes and memorials, rather than at the time of death.

Where there is no public account of casualties on the Federal side, and no clamour for one from the shoppers on Azikwe Street, concern in the world outside for rebel dead looks, to the Nigerian, first misplaced, then hypocritical. The new vehemence of protests from the State Department and in Parliamentary debate, therefore, may prove to have been counterproductive. Checked by stubborn resistance and newly delivered rebel weapons on the ground, the Nigerians have understandably stepped up the air war in which they have total superiority and the capacity to hit hard and cheaply.

Civilian casualties in the raids are regarded now as inevitable as were German dead in Royal Air Force attacks on Dresden in the Second World War. With communications so inadequate that one Federal divisional commander at least has personally super-vised the unloading of his short-wave transmitter at Lagos docks, it is admittedly impossible to control from headquarters each mission flown by an assortment of pilots – who have more enthusiasm than experience. Faced with the practical difficulties, and with a propaganda war for world sympathy largely lost already, Federal military leaders can only reissue their orders that no civilian targets are to be attacked and let the flights continue as before.

There is talk that the Egyptian pilots, frequently used, are to be sent packing to appease world concern. But since the Federal side has never admitted having them anyway, their going would have to be as inconspicuous as their arrival, and could not be publicized as an act of good faith. As the head of the air force told the international military observers in Nigeria recently, from the

Federal point of view, the blame for civilian casualties in the rebel area rests with the secessionists. They should site their head-quarters, ammunition and supply dumps and training establish-ments, which are all considered to be legitimate war targets, outside the towns and villages. Or, as he put it more succinctly later, 'Ojukwu has put his military headquarters in civilian cities like Umuahia. If, in the search for him, any civilian is touched, then, hard luck. This is war.'

HOW NOT TO STEAL A MISSILE

Ian McDougall

DÜSSELDORF, SEPTEMBER 1970

The more hilarious side of espionage and the international arms race was illustrated at a trial in Germany, where the presiding judge had difficulty in getting spectators to control their mirth.

Those on trial were three men in early middle age; an architect, a locksmith and a former German Air Force staff sergeant, who had piloted American-built Starfighters, the main West German combat plane. They were charged with attempted high treason, theft and breach of confidence. Behind these accusations, on which the court has not yet passed judgement, lies a story that might not only have supplied the script for one of the old Ealing Studio comedies, but also throws a disturbing light on NATO security. The allegation is that these three men stole a Sidewinder rocket missile from a NATO airbase in southern Germany, and shipped it to Moscow, together with secret aircraft navigation instruments. They are also said to have planned to steal a Starfighter.

According to the evidence produced in court, the accused were recruited by Soviet agents in Cologne, and were paid altogether the equivalent of some £13,000 for their services. It should perhaps be pointed out that this took place three years ago, at a time when the Russians were presumably more interested in

Sidewinders and Starfighters than they would be today. From then onwards the episode slides rapidly into farce. The three men began their exploit by hiring two professionals from the under-world to break into the NATO air base. These two promptly disappeared, and later blabbed out their part of the story in their cups. Then the locksmith concealed himself in the boot of the staff-sergeant's car, and having been driven thus into the airbase, broke open various doors and removed the secret navigational equipment. This was taken by the third man, the architect, to Moscow by air in his personal luggage. He says that in Moscow he was asked to get hold of a Hawk, a Nike or a Hercules rocket, if possible all three. At first he refused, but under pressure agreed to steal something 'a little smaller', to wit a Sidewinder. So, back to the airbase in southern Germany, where his two comrades this time got in by the simple expedient of climbing the outer fence.

Two hours later they duly returned, staggering under the weight of a genuine Sidewinder, which is nine feet long and weighs one-and-a-half hundredweight. It was too long to fit into their car, so they broke the rear window and let the pointed end of the rocket stick out behind. They then travelled several hundred miles across country to Krefeld in north-west Germany. Nobody on their route took the slightest notice of the Sidewinder, a fact which the defence attributed to their precaution of attaching a red flag to the protruding end of the rocket so as to comply conscientiously with traffic regulations. Throughout the long journey, as it later emerged, the Sidewinder had been fully primed, ready for instant detonation. It was later taken to pieces in a garage and packed in a cabin trunk and in a wooden case specially commissioned from a carpenter. At the airport, the architect and the locksmith were courteously advised by an official of the national airline, Lufthansa, that it would be cheaper to send their excess luggage to Moscow by air freight. Before agreeing to this the two travellers asked if this meant they would have to open the cases. 'No,' replied the helpful official, and I quote from the trial evidence, 'No, we are interested only in what comes into the country, not in what goes out. Any customs duty will have to be paid in Moscow.'

It appears that even the Soviet intelligence services at the other end were flabbergasted by these proceedings, being astonished, as one of the accused put it, not only that the Sidewinder had actually arrived, but that it had arrived in quite this fashion. Still, the Russians paid up as promised. As the trial continued, and as it became clear that the gravity due to the process of law was being somewhat impaired by the spectators' hilarity, the presiding judge was moved to observe that there must be something seriously amiss with the supervision of West German defence establishments. It seemed a fair comment.

COMING HOME

Charles Wheeler

In the Philippines, preparations were being made to greet the American prisoners of war being released in Vietnam.

Lieutenant-Commander Everet Alverez was shot down and captured by the North Vietnamese on 5 August 1964. He has been a prisoner of war for eight and a half years. The commander is one of five hundred and sixty-two American servicemen whose names are on the lists provided by the North Vietnamese and the Vietcong, and are due to be released in the next fifty days or so. Under the Paris agreements a first batch should be freed by Monday. They will be collected from Hanoi and in the case of the prisoners of the Vietcong, from South Vietnam, in an American hospital aircraft. Nobody knows who will be in the first party or what state the men will be in, so the planes are equipped for emergencies. The crews include doctors and flight nurses. There is an intensive care unit in each plane and men can either sit up or travel on stretchers. The flight from Hanoi to Clark Air Force Base in the Philippines will take three or four hours.

The plans for their arrival at Clark Base, the first stop on the long journey home, are elaborate and sensible. There will be no bands, no ceremonial at all. Because this first appearance of the prisoners is a major national event, it will be covered on television by satellite, but the cameras are being kept at a distance and reporters will not be allowed to talk to the prisoners or even get close to them. And for once the Press is not quarrelling with the authorities about arrangements. When the planes have landed, the first men to disembark will be the stretcher cases. Deliberately they will be unloaded out of sight of the cameras. The idea is to spare relations at home unnecessary distress. Then the walking prisoners will come down the aircraft steps, and these we shall see. They will board special buses fitted out as ambulances, and these will take them straight to the base hospital two and a half miles away. There they will wait, two to four men to a room, until the doctors arrive. A team of sixty doctors and dentists is standing by and the medical examinations will be thorough. The doctor will decide who is fit to fly home forty-eight or seventy-two hours later – the flight to the west coast of America takes fifteen hours – and who, if anyone, will have to be kept in the hospital here in the Philippines. In that event a man's family will be flown out here to join him.

As soon as the medical examination is over, each ex-prisoner will meet his personal escort. This is a serviceman of equivalent rank and in a few cases a personal friend, whose job it is to ease his return to normal life. For example, he has been carefully briefed about his charge's personal circumstances. He will hand over letters and photographs of wife and children, and if there is bad news to be broken, the escort is the one who will have to break it. He then takes his prisoner off to a private room, puts through a call to his family in the United States, and leaves him alone. This done, the escort produces a uniform complete with the right medal ribbons and badges of rank – many of the men have been promoted while behind bars – and a tailor appears to make adjustments. Fitting the ex-prisoners with proper clothes is regarded here as an important morale raiser and one can see why. Many of them have spent years in the same depressing prison overalls. The escort flies home with his charge and he stays with him until he is reunited with his family.

Each man will also get two hundred and fifty dollars for his immediate needs, a statement showing him how much back pay he is entitled to – in some cases the amounts are considerable – and a copy of a special edition of the Army's tabloid newspaper *The Stars and Stripes*. Now this is something of a collector's piece. It is a fifty-six-page round-up in words and pictures of the principal news stories from 1965 to the end of 1972. The front page lead, chosen in a poll of the paper's staff, is the first landing on the moon in 1969. It is all there in striking detail: the big city riots in America from 1965 to 1968; the assassinations of Robert Kennedy and Martin Luther King; the civil wars in Nigeria and Bangladesh; the re-marriage of Jacqueline Kennedy; the deaths of Churchill, Nasser, Schweitzer, Khrushchev, de Gaulle and Harry Truman. And there is a blow by blow account of the war in Vietnam and of the making of the peace.

At some point in the homecoming routine, the ex-prisoners will have to eat and drink. Any man who announces on boarding the hospital plane at Hanoi that he has spent the past seven years dreaming about his first whisky and soda and wants one now will have to wait at least until the doctors have finished their blood tests. As for the food he gets, it all depends on his condition. The dieticians have made up nine sets of menus, anticipating every imaginable condition of the human stomach, and the most exciting dish is described as 'bland Burgundy stew with curled carrots and noodles'.

There is also to be a prolonged debriefing session here at Clark Air Force Base. Hundreds of American servicemen are still missing and not accounted for, and the men who do return may have valuable information. This has to be done early before a man's memory becomes confused by a mass of fresh impressions.

One thing the ex-prisoners will not be subjected to is an automatic session with a psychiatrist. There was a battle about this behind the scenes and the general practitioners won the right to decide whether a man needs psychiatric help or not. The view that prevailed was a simple one – that the best treatment is to make the men comfortable: make them feel cherished, and get them back to their families as quickly as possible.

ESCAPE FROM THE EAST

Bill Treharne Jones

Commercial escape organizations went into business to help East Germans flee to the West.

Two weeks ago a group of East Germans, four adults and five children, managed to escape by a tunnel underneath the Berlin Wall. This was only the second successful tunnel escape in nine years. Few people even try to build tunnels nowadays. In the early 1960s many people used to start burrowing from the cellars of houses close to the Wall. But the East German authorities have knocked down these houses to make way for their death strip, and few would-be refugees contemplate burrowing the much longer distances from the houses set further back.

But this has not stopped people escaping, indeed about six thousand manage to get out every year. Some risk their lives climbing over the Wall, but most of them escape via other Communist countries, often with forged passports. Since last summer a new method has become possible, indeed it is so easy that many West Germans and West Berliners have been smuggling out friends and relatives. But most of the escapes are arranged by commercial escape organizations of a rather shady character, who are making a lot of money out of the business. For a price which can be anything up to £12,000 sterling per head they are bringing out at least a hundred people a month.

Ironically they are taking advantage of one of the more generous provisions of the four-power Berlin Agreement, which has done so much to make life more bearable for Berliners. This provision lays down that East German guards may not search cars which travel on the three East German highways which link West Berlin with West Germany. This makes escape easy. One refugee I spoke to recently described in vivid terms how he got out. He had an evening rendezvous in a wood near the motorway. There he found a large car parked in some bushes so he could not read the registration number. Two men were waiting for him. They asked him, 'Do you know how to get to the next town?' He said, 'No,' as he was travelling with his bicycle. That was the password. He and two companions climbed into the boot of the car. A special light was on in the boot so they would not be in the dark. The car drove off. The refugee told me he was absolutely terrified when they reached the frontier, as he felt the car slowly weaving its way round the concrete obstacles which force cars to drive in a zigzag.

'My denim suit,' he told me, 'was soaked with sweat.' The car stopped briefly for the East German controls, then it drove on. 'The next thing I know,' he said, 'the boot was opened and a man we had not seen before said, "Welcome to West Berlin."' The three refugees got out to find themselves in a multi-storey car park.

Not everyone is so lucky. Recently, a prominent East German gynaecologist was nabbed as he was just about to be driven across the frontier. But enough people are getting out to cause anxiety. The East German authorities have warned that they will in their own good time act to prevent what they call 'misuses of the transit route'. The West German government fears this means interference in some way with traffic on the route to Berlin. To avoid this, the West German government has said it will prosecute escape organizations which break existing laws. Theoretically this is not so difficult as the twenty or so escape organizations are known to use illegal, if not downright criminal, methods. For instance, they have been known to extort unusually high sums from their clients and blackmail them if they refuse to pay.

It may seem strange that people want to escape from East Germany, after all the country has made undeniable economic progress and enjoys the highest standard of living in the Communist Bloc. But the fact remains that the average West German worker enjoys a standard of living some 35 per cent higher than his East German counterpart. And this gap is not getting any smaller.

Professional people earn even more in the West. A young West German doctor can earn three times as much as his colleague receives in East Germany. This discrepancy explains why professional people figure so prominently among the refugees. For instance more than fifty doctors have escaped from East Berlin alone since the beginning of this year. But it is not just money. Many of the professional people coming out complain of the political pressures on them, pressures to join the party and the discrimination against their children who may have difficulty getting university places because they are not of working-class background.

East Germans often tell one that they do not want to leave East Germany but they would like to be able to visit the West – 'Just a few times,' they say, 'we would always come back.' The sad truth is that many would not come back. The hundreds of refugees every month prove this. That is why the Wall is necessary for the East German Communist regime today as it was twelve years ago when it was built. Economically East Germany has a labour shortage, it cannot afford to lose people, least of all those who are highly qualified.

SOLDIERS OF ISRAEL

Martin Bell

TEL AVIV, OCTOBER 1973

The officers of the Israeli Army led by example as the tide of war turned in their favour to the north and south of their country.

'It's not like 1967,' said one Israeli, 'this time the Syrians are fighting.' He was speaking during a combined artillery barrage and airstrike with which the Syrians were trying in vain to dislodge the Israelis from their soil. Four MiGs attacked an Israeli artillery battery, and two of them fell in flames. Later, still more MiGs streaked low over the battlefield. 'Christ,' said the Israeli – and it seemed a strange expletive for him to be using – 'Christ, how many MiGs have they got?'

The Israelis were surprised by the initial Arab attack only in a limited tactical sense. They expected war. They always do. The State of Israel – born in war – has consistently fought its neighbours to survive. But the Yom Kippur War was not at all the kind of war that they expected: bloodier, more protracted, and initially more defensive in nature.

But one thing that has not been affected is the troops' morale. Of course, no army in combat, however hard-pressed, will ever admit to its morale being anything less than sky-high. But it is among the advantages of reporting from Israel that one does not have to take it only on the say-so of the army spokesmen. One can go out and check for oneself.

In a bunker close to the Syrian front line, I talked to a mortar unit as the incoming shells dropped outside. Most of them had been mobilized on the day of Yom Kippur, or the eve of Yom Kippur. All of them were reservists, some of them veterans of the Six Day War. But even for these, this present conflict was the longest one they had fought in, and the only one in which they had met more than a token resistance.

The one thing that they could not conceive of was the possibility of an Israeli defeat, either on this front or on the southern front. Israel had not lost a war yet, indeed, could not lose one and survive, and it would not lose one now. Such cast-iron faith in their own invincibility may have helped induce Israel's early reverses in the war.

The talk in the bunker was not only of war. It was also of home life, new cars, the world outside. But every hour, the voices went quiet and the radio was turned up for the latest news bulletin. These front-line troops were avid for news of what was happening even on their own front line. All they knew was the small world of their bunker, and their mortar position.

The small things that are important to soldiers in combat were well provided for: mail deliveries twice daily; as many meals of K-rations a day as they could eat; a total absence of unnecessary spit and polish – indeed of any spit and polish at all. While the Arab armies are regular armies, Israel's army is a citizens' army, with only a small force of regulars and conscripts to absorb the first attack while the reservists mobilize.

The soldiers, by the standards of Western armies, are unkempt, dishevelled, but not undisciplined. This is the second of Israel's wars that I have reported, and I have never yet seen a soldier throw a salute to anyone. The way you can pick out the officers is: they are the ones above ground during the shelling attacks. And when they go forward, they do not say, 'Forward,' they say, 'Follow me.'

ON THE RAILS

Mark Tully

NEW DELHI, MAY 1974

India's vast and rambling railway system has always been a source of fascination to Indians and to visitors. But the railways, which were on strike when this dispatch was written, also play a key part in the nation's economy.

There is a marvellous sense of timelessness about Indian railways. A businessman once had to meet an important customer of his, travelling on the Madras Howrah Mail, at Waltair where the train was due to stop for thirty-five minutes. Even mail trains tend to stop for a long time at stations in India. The businessman showed up at Waltair Station five minutes before it was due to arrive. As he walked on to the platform he saw what was unmistakably the Madras Mail sliding out of the station. He rushed into the stationmaster's office and asked him what he meant by letting the Mail go out forty minutes early. The stationmaster calmly replied, 'Oh, that, sir, that's yesterday's train.' This sense of timelessness is reinforced every time you get out at a station and see the notice under the train running board which reads, 'Late running trains are liable to make up time.'

The extraordinary thing about travelling by train in India is that you actually welcome the timelessness. A long railway journey is like being in another world, and most train journeys in India are long. It still takes two nights and a day to get from

Calcutta to Bombay. It is like taking time off from the real world. I suppose the answer is that Indian railways still have romance. There is still plenty of steam and the trains on the broad gauge are vast, while those on the metre gauge are delightfully squat. They have marvellous names like *32 Up The Frontier Mail, 16 Down Grand Trunk Express, 1 Up Avadh Tirhut Mail*, and *Frontier Mail 308 Down the Black Diamond Express*. The station names have something about them too, Barabanki, Budge Budge, Clutterbuckgunj, Mokameh Ghat, Sawaimadhopur Junction and Mughal Sarai, to select just a few.

The food served on the trains is not an attraction but the food sold at railway stations is. Chai wallahs sell tea in lightly baked earthenware pots which unlike their plastic counterparts in the West disintegrate when hurled on to the line. The snacks served on leaves vary as the train moves across the country. The sounds at the stations also change although not the decibel level. Indian railway station vendors have a way of hawking their wares which sounds like the croaking of a raucous frog, but an experienced traveller can always tell the difference between the croak of the tea wallah and the samosa wallah.

Every day some seven million people travel by train but most of them in very cramped third-class carriages. But it is not even the third-class passengers who count most as revenue earners for Indian railways, particularly as large numbers of them do not bother to buy tickets. Goods are far and away the most important traffic. India literally cannot function without its railways. For instance, all its coal is in the east but its industry is spread all over the country. Its surplus wheat is in the north but it is eaten in the west, and so on. But the management of the railways faces tremendous difficulty in moving all these goods around the country because railways have become so much part of India's life that everyone resists change on them. Take the case of bulk loading. Grain and fertilizers are still packed in gunny bags before being loaded into goods wagons because the jute industry has a vested interest in seeing that gunny bags remain in use and the government does not want to lay off all the men involved in bagging up the grain and fertilizers.

But perhaps the greatest single problem the railways face is a human one. In India as in so many other places a railwayman was once a proud man, but is no longer. It is not just a question of pay. In fact the heart of the matter is a breakdown in morale and discipline caused all too often by political interference. As one railway officer put it to me, 'It no longer matters whether you are good at your job or not. All that matters is what *sifarish* or favour you can do for a politician.' So railway officers make wrong decisions to please the politicians, the wrong decisions affect the staff who lose all respect for the officers and discipline collapses. I remember asking a veteran Anglo-Indian driver at Abu Road Station in Rajasthan why the mail train was still being pulled by a steam engine when there were so many diesels available. 'Damned silly officers,' he grunted. But left to get on with the job Indian railway officers are anything but silly. In fact, their services as expert advisers are in demand all around the world. But even the best railwayman in the world cannot do his job if he is not allowed to do what he knows has to be done.

THE HEARST KIDNAPPING

Chris Drake

SAN FRANCISCO, MAY 1974

Patricia Hearst, the daughter of a newspaper magnate, was kidnapped in California by the Symbionese Liberation Army. Two months later she declared that she intended staying with the terrorist group.

Whether one is talking with the rich in the bar of an hotel here, where the cost of the cheapest room for a night is £40, or with the bedraggled looking individual who is begging in the streets for any loose change you can spare, it becomes abundantly clear they are both concerned about the Hearst case, albeit for different reasons. For it is a bizarre drama which has had its effect on San Francisco society at every level, and each new incident, coming as it does more daring and dramatic than the last, gives one the feeling of participating in a best-selling play, but one for which the script of the final act has yet to be written.

To the wealthy it represents the despicable actions of a fanatical group who should be denounced as common criminals, arrested and sent to gaol for life, since execution is ruled out by law. They will tell you that over a Martini in the bar, their voices hushed to avoid being overheard by the group at the next table, just in case they are terrorists in disguise, and going on to explain that they fear for their own lives, their wealth good enough reason for becoming a kidnap victim. So they vary the times of departure and arrival at the office, the routes to and from home and the venues for lunch and that after business hours cocktail. They are scared. Some of them have bought guns, increased security measures in their houses and now go around only in groups.

At the other end of the social scale are the poor, those who are destined to receive the millions of dollars' worth of free food, handed out by the Hearst empire as part of the deal for the girl's release. They are not scared, they are worried. For if the girl is not released unharmed they will lose the opportunity to take advantage of another four million dollars' worth of that food. They were criticized for accepting the earlier supplies but the majority did not care. Indeed they were grateful to the Symbionese Liberation Army for publicizing their plight. But while at first they regarded the members as Robin Hoods, who robbed the rich to feed the poor, now I find an air of disenchantment creeping in: those mythical heroes turning into a bunch of thugs, who care not for the so-called oppressed and needy but just for themselves. And unless the girl is freed, they say, the future looks grim. That publicity afforded to their problems will now be overshadowed by the criminal aspects, the bank robbery, kidnapping and attempted murder.

A twenty-minute drive from the city centre takes one to the suburb of Hillsborough and the Hearst home. When I visited them there this week I was invited by the girl's father, Randolph Hearst, to assist him in improving security around his own house by lifting a heavy rusty gate with a broken hinge, which had remained open for years, into a closed position. As we worked he talked about his daughter, his firm belief that she is an entirely innocent victim, and his increasing pessimism for her safe release.

He hopes social changes will come to improve the plight of the poor, his regrets being that demands for such actions should have had to come at the expense of his daughter. And no longer does he hide his anger and bitterness towards the Symbionese Liberation Army. 'After all, they stole my girl,' he says, 'they took her and brainwashed her, and turned her from being an innocent child into a puppet, a puppet for which they now pull the strings to further their own fanatical ideas.'

Like his wife and other three daughters, Randolph Hearst is learning to live with the situation. They have become accustomed to having the FBI camped inside the home and reporters camped outside. But it is Emmie, the loveable plump German-born cook, who seems to play the most important role in keeping up morale. Always a smile on her face, she fusses around preparing the meals, cleaning the windows and cutting flowers to place in vases, her difficult aim being to create the impression that all is normal. Obviously it is not, though; indeed, whatever the future holds it certainly can never be the same again for the Hearst family.

PARADISE THREATENED

Adrian Porter

Buenos Aires, August 1974

Brazil's economic boom was threatening to bring 'progress' to a quiet island off the coast.

There is this island off the coast of Brazil where I have just had three weeks of idle loafing and where I head for at every possible opportunity because it has managed, though with increasing difficulty these days, to remain a close proximation of everyone's idea of a primitive tropical paradise with some easily available but unobtrusive mod cons. About half an hour's boat ride from the coast, it rises high out of emerald green water and its slopes are covered with thick tropical vegetation. Dotted around the island, which is about four miles long and half a mile wide, are six small beaches all with fine sand and fringed with palm trees. On the main beach is a small hotel – run in unostentatiously first-class style – to provide the modern comforts such as a bar and restaurant.

It is very much the ideal place for getting away from it all. Not many other places I know offer you a stretch of beach with – as was my experience last week – only two other people on it; with a couple of native canoes to go fishing in or just paddling about if you felt like it; or a couple of small sailing boats to use if a wind came up to cool you off in temperatures of eighty to ninety degrees under cloudless blue skies; or a quick run round on water skis behind the hotel's speedboat before lunch under the palm trees.

And if you felt even that was too much like a touch of civilization you could walk on the jungle trail that goes round the island to the next beach a quarter of an hour's walk away accompanied perhaps from time to time by huge blue butterflies as big as birds fluttering in friendly fashion beside you. On the next beach you might find one of the inhabitants of the few fishing huts there mending his nets but you would most likely have the beach to yourself.

You could then prepare a simple island meal for yourself. First, prise off a dozen oysters from the rocks and use them to stuff an avocado pear taken from one of the trees on the island. Sprinkle them with lemon taken from another tree on the island. Next, buy a few giant prawns from the man mending his nets (he is bound to have some) and grill them over an open fire on the beach. Swill them down with the milk of a coconut which has probably dropped from one of the palms in the meantime.

You could add a touch of dreaded civilization here by adding a tot of gin or rum to make a tropical cocktail. To finish with – some succulent wild bananas from yet another tree or, for the sweet-toothed, a stick of sugar cane to chew on. After lunch you could fish for dinner by throwing a line into the water baited with bits of the prawns left over from lunch and get some exercise fighting off the scores of the local equivalent of small Dover soles who seem desperately anxious to offer themselves up.

Along with the good side of tropical island life, of course, you have to take the bad. And this includes some of the local fauna and insects which can, at times, be alarming both in size – the local cockroaches have to be seen to be believed – and in habits. When I am on the island I normally stay in the cottage of some friends of mine and on my past two visits I have been disturbed at times by the noises kicked up at dusk and dawn by a small family of bats who have lodged in the roof and who keep regular bat hours. My tolerant regard of the creatures changed to abhorrent suspicion when I was informed that they were, in fact, vampire bats. It appears their local source of nutrition is a poor mule that carries panniers of sand for the construction of a new house not far away and who sleeps out at night.

And there is also a bird that has the disconcerting habit of going 'Pssst!' in the night as you walk past whatever tree he has perched on. Upsetting, if not downright frightening, until you know what it is all about. However, there are signs that my primitive island paradise is beginning to be caught up in what still is known in these parts as 'progress'. In fact, part of Brazil's famous economic boom can literally be heard on the island when, if the wind is in the right direction, a muffled roar of an explosion creeps across the sea. You notice these things because, joy of joys, transistor radios and similar noises are banned from the beaches on the island.

Anyway, these explosions come from a quarry on the mainland supplying material for various new constructions in the area. The mainland's boom, with its prosperity for more people, has brought, too, more leisure time and more boats along the coast. At weekends they arrive in what seem like hordes, though there are probably only twenty or thirty of them, to clutter up the beach and the hotel, and the lucky few who live in weekday isolation sigh with relief as Sunday evening takes them away again.

But the permanent reminder of all this progress and prosperity and profit-motive are the excavations on parts of the island to accommodate people who seek isolation and the simple life. So far, there are not too many of them. And their homes are typical of Brazilian undemonstrative good taste. And I suppose one cannot really complain if the progress and accompanying pollution still allow you to observe the sea bed twenty-four feet under water – even though it was twenty-five feet a year ago.

NIXON GOES

Kevin Ruane

WASHINGTON, AUGUST 1974

When President Nixon finally resigned as a result of the Watergate scandal, there was a palpable feeling of relief throughout the United States.

Writing of another crisis more than a hundred years ago, an American historian said that a large proportion of the political tensions of those days could be attributed to what he called 'the hazards of health of the capital city'. He referred in particular to the heavy atmosphere – the humidity which presses down on Washington, like an oppressive blanket, during its sultry summer months. Modern air-conditioning has made things easier these days of course, but during last week's crisis, the pressure of the atmosphere was still very tangible to the newcomer and seemed to provide a very natural background to these historic events which unfolded themselves painfully in the space of five days. Towards the end of the week when President Nixon resigned, the skies definitely grew darker, and on the evening after he had left the White House and Washington, and Gerald Ford had assumed the presidency, there was thunder and lightning and torrents of rain washed down the window panes. To anyone with an eye for the dramatic, there was more than a suggestion there of portents in the sky. This was unreal, perhaps. But so, too, was much that had gone before. Mr Nixon was so isolated in his final week that he might just as well have been lying in some

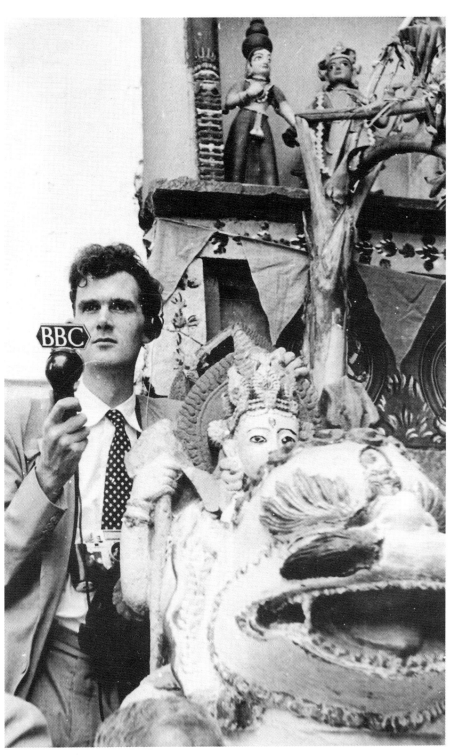

Gerald Priestland, India, 1956.

Christopher Serpell, Washington, 1954.

Ronald Robson, Broadcasting House, 1959.

Lionel Fleming, Broadcasting House, 1955.

Douglas Willis, Washington, 1956.

Erik de Mauny, Moscow, 1963.

Above: Angus
McDermid,
Congo, 1964.

Right: Charles
Wheeler, Washington,
1966.

Martin Bell, Sarajevo, 1994.

Robert Elphick (left), Prague, 1976.

Mark Tully, Bangladesh, 1992.

Brian Barron, South-East Asia, 1969.

Mike Wooldridge (centre) with cameraman Mo Amin (left) and
Michael Buerk (right), Ethiopia, 1984.

Bob Jobbins, Bush House, 1985.

Above: Elizabeth Blunt, Chad, 1990.

Left: Tim Llewellyn, Baghdad, 1991.

Mark Laity, Saudi Arabia, 1991.

Kevin Connolly, Sarajevo, 1992.

Carole Walker, Tbilisi, 1992.

Above: Stephen Jessel,
Paris, 1993.

Right: Fergal Keane,
southern Africa, 1994.

Malcolm Brabant, Bosnia, 1993.

inaccessible political deathpit. Correspondents who thronged the White House briefing room, asking if the President was going to resign, were told that there was no change.

Mr Nixon's family were then said to be gathered around him. He was seeing only his closest associates and friends. Members of his staff apparently nursing him through the crisis let it be known that Mr Nixon was serene and tranquil. One of them suggested that he was no longer listening to what they said to him; that he was getting out of touch with reality. Later, it was said that he was showing great courage, and three Republican leaders who went down from Congress to see the President on the Wednesday said afterwards that they had talked as old friends, but had not mentioned resignation. Almost as if that was too indelicate in so terminal a case.

But if Richard Nixon's resignation as President was the end of a political life, it could not be described as a happy death. He made no act of contrition. As he left the White House, emotional and defiant, he left a clear impression that he had no intention of doing penance, and before he had got back to his home state of California as a private citizen, his successor, Gerald Ford, had asked Americans to pray for him, but Mr Nixon got out of his plane and made a speech, promising continued work for world peace — unconscious of the apparent wilderness in which he stood.

The relief felt at Mr Nixon's departure was palpable, and when the new President declared at his swearing-in that the long nightmare was over, it sounded something like an act of absolution. People wanted to believe that it was true, though most will concede that it is not all over. But for the past weekend, at least, Americans appear to have been relaxing, wallowing somewhat in thoughts of honesty, decency and loyalty — the virtue said to be typified by their new president.

Whatever he is, Mr Ford is certainly welcome. One of the many sightseers who filed through the White House at the weekend, for instance, is quoted as saying that the place even smells better today. That may not be an entirely objective observation, but it says something possibly about a state of mind which wants to hear no more about Watergate. Unfortunately, though, there will be more. No one is in a hurry to decide what happens to Mr Nixon now, but many people want to know whether he will be prosecuted over the Watergate affair. Congress, it seems, no longer has the stomach to pursue him further. The Watergate Special Prosecutor, who could do something, is now taking a break, but next month several of Mr Nixon's former aides come up for trial and then, perhaps, the former President's name at least will come back to haunt Washington again.

DISASTER COUNTRY

Brian Barron

DACCA, AUGUST 1974

In the mid-seventies, it seemed as if Bangladesh faced one catastrophe after another. After war and disease, a cyclone disaster meant that the beleaguered people had to endure widespread flooding.

When a cyclone warning threatened to give a new twist to Bangladesh's latest agony, there was a headline in a Dacca daily reminiscent of that famous Fleet Street top, SMALL EARTHQUAKE IN CHILE: NOT MANY DEAD. Bangladesh's freshly printed equivalent read, FEW HUNDRED FISHERMEN SWEPT AWAY: NOT MANY MISSING. And so, one naturally asks, is the suffering in this waterlogged corner of the world so great and continual that it no longer registers? It is less than ten years since a Bengali historian wrote that 'National disasters like cyclones, tidal waves and floods do not touch the heart as they used to. Even the feelings for the tribe, for the community, for the nation are being replaced by an urge for personal prosperity. Survival of the fittest has become the ideal.'

In the spirit of Evelyn Waugh's 'Boot of the *Beast*', Bangladesh does serve as one of the headline writer's most reliable stand-bys. Death and destruction always seem on a biblical scale. If it is not flooding, it seems to be smallpox, or cholera or famine, and it is only thirty-one years since two million Bengalis starved to death while their rulers, the British, were fighting off the Japanese.

These days the Bengalis do not help themselves by being

notoriously shaky with figures. At a news conference last week a minister contradicted his own statistics in the space of forty minutes and, with an apologetic smile, rendered inoperative another morsel of official information which had sped round the world the day before; he amended a figure of ten million flood refugees to one million.

Dimly discernible through today's fog of uncertainty and exaggeration are the seventy-plus million Bengalis themselves, mostly living on the land. It is a confusion of waterways and paddy fields and floating banks of water lilies bearing whole communities and their livestock. Most of this grossly overcrowded area stretching from the Himalayan foothills to the Bay of Bengal is less than thirty feet above sea level. Due mainly to the introduction of antibiotics and a consequent drop in the death rate, the number of Bengalis has doubled since the Second World War. As more people are born and pressure on space grows even more intolerable, communities arise in the lowest-lying land which is always prone to flood. These are the people who die first.

The Muslim farmers of Bangladesh are deeply superstitious, God-fearing folk, who regard this disaster as the will of Allah. One man standing waist-deep in water outside his flood-damaged house told me that in his case it was divine retribution for a personal transgression. Life is governed by elemental forces, by the rice crops, by the need to produce lots of children as an insurance against old age and an inflationary future – not to speak of the child mortality rate of twenty-five per cent.

Of course, the Bengalis are inured to floods. Thousands of square miles are inundated year in year out, though not, it seems, on this scale. In many places the floods destroyed the crop just before it was due to be harvested. And the water is draining away so slowly that planting for the next crop is imperilled. Many people, it could be tens of thousands but no one knows, are facing hard times. Whether they starve, survive or grow thinner, depends, in part, on how much grain they have been able to hoard in previous months. Over the centuries they have become a wiry, resilient breed. These days, beset by poisonous water snakes, their mosques under water, their cattle drowned, often lacking light and heat, the Bengalis need to muster every ounce of fortitude. Flying low over their tiny, marooned communities in recent days, watching the water washing away the remaining soil under the already submerged houses, one still got the feeling that most people will see it through. Still, stoicism will only go so far, it is not going to help find bread – that is where the Bangladesh government bears a heavy responsibility. Despite the empty coffers and sheaf of outstanding IOUs, food supplies must be found quickly.

SOVIET TRAVELS
AND TRAVAILS

Philip Short

Providing coverage from the far-flung corners of the Soviet Union meant developing an intimate knowledge of crowded airports and second-rate hotels.

Usually if you can go somewhere by train in the Soviet Union you are also allowed to fly there, and most people do, especially over long distances. But travelling by train does have its advantages too, as I found when I went from Baku, in Azerbaijan, to Makhachkala, the Daghestanian capital, a couple of hundred miles north up the Caspian Sea coast. For one thing, it is punctual. The ticket clerk tells you that train number six always leaves ten minutes late and that is exactly what it does. And it is also one of the best ways of meeting Russians for, in the south at least, a train journey is not so much a means of reaching your destination as a social occasion; a great exercise in communal living. In the sleeping compartments, men and women are lumped indiscriminately together; unshaven figures in string vests wander up and down the corridors; music programmes from Radio Moscow blare out over the loudspeaker system and you find yourself being invited in to share someone's vodka, or to meet a village schoolmaster who says he wants to be able to tell his friends that he has had a drink with an Englishman.

Each carriage has its own *dezhurnaya*, robust ladies who bring round endless glasses of Russian tea, and who are equally capable of bouncing a drunk, or of arbitrating in a dispute over who has which bunk. And at the stations along the way, peasant children sell apples and tomatoes from tin buckets.

The problems really start when you arrive wherever it is you are going to, for then you have to take on the system of Soviet hotels. The lift, for instance, with its small handwritten signs – *No service after 11 p.m.* – and when you complain that the once-daily train does not arrive until midnight back comes the reply, 'Are we responsible for railway timetables?' Or your room, which turns out to be already occupied by someone else who has to move out. 'But I have booked it,' you say. And the answer to that: 'You didn't expect us to leave it empty, did you? What if you hadn't turned up?' And this, you are told, is not sharp practice, but just raising productivity for the Five Year Plan; and that is only the start. There is the bath you paid extra for to discover that there is only hot water on Fridays, and of course this is not Friday; or the television set for which you also pay extra, whether you want it or not, because the town plan for television rental is badly under-fulfilled.

And what about the noise like a cross between a jet engine and an air-raid siren that wakes you up in the morning – the cleaning lady's Hoover. Perhaps that all sounds just too far-fetched and vituperative; and if so I must disclaim responsibility. For it is all from a report on provincial hotels by two Soviet journalists, which appeared in the central government newspaper, *Izvestia*. My own experience, in fact, was rather better than that, but there was always some little quirk which made me realize that *Izvestia*'s description was not far-fetched at all. There were plenty of things which the paper did not mention. The practice, for instance, of charging foreigners ten times the Russian rates, so that a night's stay is £20 instead of £2; and if you query it, you are told with total conviction that it is the international norm and that exactly the same thing happens to Soviet tourists in Britain.

And there are other differences in the way foreigners are

treated too. At Yerevan, in Armenia, I watched a receptionist, who had gone out of her way to be helpful to me, turning away a Russian woman who was almost in tears because she had nowhere to stay, with a completely callous rudeness and indifference. Perhaps that was an isolated case, but certainly the system of foreigners being privileged operates all the time when you travel by air.

Flights in the Soviet Union may be astonishingly cheap; as little as £6 for the equivalent of London to Paris. But all too often they are subject to overwhelming delays, and airports in the provinces can look like transit stations for wartime evacuees – old peasants with great shapeless bundles of belongings; whole families encamped on suitcases; a woman breast-feeding a baby. They may have been there four hours or twenty hours or two days, quietly resigned. Sometimes you are lucky and there is no delay at all, but at Yerevan I waited eighteen hours to fly to Baku, and at Baku ten hours to fly back to Yerevan. You queue at the enquiries desk and at five minutes to twelve they are still telling you, 'Yes, your plane will leave at twelve o'clock,' and then it is postponed till four, and when four o'clock comes round it is the same story again. The reason, I was told each time, was the weather, but when there were enough foreign tourists waiting they arranged a special plane, which for some reason, the weather did not affect. Perhaps part of the explanation lies with the kind of incident I saw as I was waiting at Baku. Just as a group of passengers were at long last about to board their flight, a petrol lorry drove into the aircraft's tail. The passengers returned inside; lorry and plane were solemnly towed away and a little old lady with a broom appeared to sweep up the broken glass.

GHOST SOLDIERS

Brian Barron

Hong Kong, January 1975

While the North Vietnamese forces were associated with toughness and commitment to their cause, some of their counterparts in the South were better known for cowardice and corruption.

Landing in a whirling dust-cloud on a dried-up river-bed the other day our helicopter gunship picked up five refugees from a stranded convoy in as many seconds. The last to throw himself on board, among the women and babies, was an army major. At this deliverance he was so overcome that he presented his service issue revolver and holster to the helicopter pilot. It was a gesture wasted on the pilot, a combat-hardened lieutenant with a profound contempt for most officers, especially someone like the major who, on all available evidence, should have been four hundred feet below us helping to lead the convoy through a series of Communist ambushes which claimed hundreds of civilian lives.

Tragically for Saigon, the armed forces are stricken by a raging attack of fright and inferiority. The years of widespread corruption in the officer corps, of generals setting the example of making money first and war second, is having a deadly effect: a cancer within probably of more importance than the physical threat without posed by the North Vietnamese. The South Vietnamese army, the ARVN as it is called, is in a worse mess than ten years ago, when the US came to the rescue just as the Communists were threatening to do what they have now done with arrogant ease: cut the country in half. Many people outside Vietnam believe the government soldiers are at worst a cowardly rabble and at best no match for the North Vietnamese. But anyone who has spent time with the ARVN will testify to the individual soldier's courage, stoicism and, very often, engrained anti-Communism. However, the standard varies enormously, the vital element being the quality of officers and NCOs: in this, the South Vietnamese can never match their Northern rivals. In today's battles the Communist troops are less experienced than the ARVN. They are seventeen- and eighteen-year-olds fresh from the Ho Chi Minh trail. But their officers are total professionals, so are the sergeants and political cadres.

The venality of the ARVN system is that one learns to accept it unquestioningly. On a recent trip to the Mekong Dam we stayed in an army base – one of the old American ones, complete with redundant hooch girls, an abandoned dance-floor and a cobwebby bamboo bar. Our host for the night, a young lieutenant, seemed generally too bright to be on permanent roster for this sort of uniformed tourist-guide job. And for someone describing himself as an intelligence officer, he had a curious lack of knowledge about his division's operations, insisting the main theatre was 'about a hundred miles north of here', which would have put it in another country, when, in fact, the fighting was but fifteen miles away. It turned out the lieutenant's parents were wealthy Chinese goldsmiths in Saigon and they paid the general to keep their son in a safe, rear headquarters. Just outside the same town was a whole divisional headquarters, 'top-heavy', as one American put it, with captains, majors and colonels discreetly paying the wife of the commanding officer, the same one-star general, for their non-hazardous postings. This vast enterprise was kept ticking over by a young warrant officer, another of the general's special appointees, who by training was an accountant and, of course, Chinese.

Such individuals, in the colourful phrase of disgruntled American combat troops here a few years ago, are known as REMFs, an acronym loosely standing for Rear Echelon Mother ... somethings. Time after time one encounters units whose officers are afraid to take even the tiniest decision without approval from above. This reluctance to act on initiative partly stems from vestiges of Confucianism still lingering in Vietnam, allied to traditional subservience to seniors.

Although most ARVN soldiers are country boys they are aware of how the system works. The number of deserters now tops twenty thousand men a month. If the soldiers are shrewd and have a compliant company or battalion commander they can become 'flower soldiers'; that means their names remain on the roster, but they give all their pay to their immediate superior and, in exchange, they are allowed to go home for good and work on the farm. Then there are the 'ghost soldiers' who do not exist at all except on paper, but whose pay cheques help keep the officers in cognac. Such abuses are not the exception, they are near-universal, and the gravy train, the handouts, extend from the lowest level to important generals. Recently an American contact here was spending hours every day trying to cajole and bully a Vietnamese commander into demobilizing his ghost units so that a proper evaluation of his forces could be made.

I know an outstanding ARVN colonel whose troops had been under heavy pressure in Military Region Three, near Saigon. He is one of those rare commanders who stays in the field with his troops when the fighting is hard. The colonel was supposed to become a regimental commander after twenty-one years in the army, including military academies in the United States and France. Last week in the chaos of Nha Trang on the central coast, I hardly recognized the colonel, in blue sports shirt and slacks. Holiday gear. He resigned from the army in February, he could do that because of long service, and had grown a moustache and longish hair. 'So the Communists won't recognize me,' he joked half-heartedly. The colonel quit because political string-pulling led to another officer being promoted to the regimental vacancy and when the fighting flared the new commander pulled back his headquarters to an ultrasafe rear position. Now my friend the colonel is considering leaving Vietnam if there is a way.

All this boils down to the truism that an army is as good as its leaders. The soldiers have so often been left in the lurch that the terrible events of recent days do not come as that big a shock. Hours before Da Nang fell, I watched drunken, barefoot soldiers reeling past groups of military policemen who took no notice. About the same time, at Da Nang airbase, an army colonel pulled out a fragmentation grenade and tried to hijack a plane to the South – he was shot. This entire military disaster has been characterized by the speed with which the officers contrived to remove themselves and their families, while ordering the rank and file to make their way to the coast by road.

Perhaps the real failure in South Vietnam is the political one: Saigon's inability to impart to its citizens and soldiers a national ideal or purpose, other than bare survival. Today the doctrine of every man for himself, or every family for themselves, is paramount.

AMERICAN SCHOOL VIOLENCE

Angus McDermid

WASHINGTON, JUNE 1975

A Congressional sub-committee examining violence and vandalism in the nation's public schools produced horrifying statistics.

The figures read like a wartime casualty list. More children were killed in the schools, often in gun fights with other pupils, between 1970 and 1973 than soldiers died in combat in the first three years of the Vietnam War. And teachers, too, are frequently shot to death by angry children.

Crime in American schools begins at about the age of eight. Last year there were more than eight thousand rapes (young women teachers are often the targets), nearly twelve thousand armed robberies, a quarter of a million burglaries and two hundred thousand major assaults on teachers and pupils. Drugs, alcohol, extortion rackets, are all found in today's American classroom. And knives, clubs, pistols and sawn-off shotguns are more often taken to school these days, either for attack or self-defence, than an apple for the teacher.

It has to be said clearly that not all schools are in such a state. There are many where behaviour is exemplary and the products excellent. But if the wave of school crime grows – and the figures have more than doubled in many cases in five years – good schools will soon become hard to find. Headlines in local papers like DRUG BUST AT WOOTON HIGH – that is, a narcotics raid at a secondary school – are frequent. The official Congressional report reads like a lurid paperback; in New York a seventeen-year-old boy was clubbed on the head with a pistol butt and stabbed in the spine; sixteen shootings in Kansas City schools; in Chicago, a headmaster killed and a school official wounded, and a sixteen-year-old shot dead over a gambling debt of five cents.

In North Carolina, two children forced two others on pain of death to hand over one thousand dollars – their ages: nine. And in Los Angeles, where there are one hundred and fifty recognized school gangs, the biggest call themselves the Cripps because they are dedicated to crippling their victims. And there are girl Crippettes and the junior Cripps for eight- to eleven-year-olds.

American schools have not always been dismal, fearful caverns with armed police in the corridors. In 1964 only three per cent of the children had disciplinary problems. Ten years later, two-fifths of the country's teachers claim to have been assaulted. The experts can only suggest that it is a reflection of the condition of society as a whole, in which persons under twenty-five commit the majority of crimes and violent juvenile crime has increased two and a half times in thirteen years. 'The school,' says one report, 'has simply become a convenient battleground.' Other experts, however, say that crime is generated in schools themselves. Vast numbers of pupils – a high proportion of them black – are suspended or drop out and eventually come back seeking revenge against authority.

And, of course, there are the drugs. It is apparently beyond the wit of the authorities to stop them. If there is a crackdown, pupil riots often follow. A third of the country's eighteen million secondary school pupils habitually use drugs; in addition two-thirds get drunk at least once a month. Certainly, many of the children shot dead are mixed up in the drug trade; much of the pushing and trading takes place in the school buses that, because of the desegregation laws, cart the children from school to school. And what about vandalism, the thefts and the arson, which costs the government £200 million a year? Well, if the stolen goods are saleable then the money goes for drugs. But how do you prevent youthful arsonists from burning down their schools, the hated symbols of authority? In Los Angeles alone, £2.5 million are spent annually on security guards and armed police, fire detectors and closed-circuit televisions. In Boston, young thieves even stole three electronic burglar alarm systems.

Well, what is to be done about this terrifying educational jungle? Nothing much, it seems, about drugs. In New York, one pusher may sell £250 worth of drugs a day to school children. Many teachers seem inclined to ignore the problem; some do not bother or dare to keep the peddlers out of the schools. And school doctors often fail to examine children for signs of addiction. But gradually the authorities are acting. In North Carolina, a pupil can get sent to gaol for six months for provoking violence. In San Francisco there is automatic suspension for carrying a weapon. Yet teachers' hands are frequently tied. They are often sued by aggrieved pupils who can now demand a hearing with lawyers present if they think they have been unjustly punished. So how is an American teacher ever going to be able to teach? It is a question that will not be answered until there are solutions to the other big issues, like the decay of the cities, the state of the prisons, racial antagonism and all the other major social problems that are central to the condition of life in America today.

1976–1985

HANOI REBORN

Brian Barron

NORTH VIETNAM, FEBRUARY 1976

After the war, our correspondent became one of the first Western newsmen to visit North Vietnam in ten years.

If you arrive in Hanoi from the Western world, the atmosphere seems curiously muted and self-contained, suggesting a sense of weariness and resignation, evoking recollections of post-Blitz Britain, austerity and ration cards for food. For those foreigners who arrive from Peking with visible relief, as one of my colleagues did, Hanoi seems a gay, flirtatious place of brightness and laughter where young people are less secretive about their emotions. The rationing of cloth in North Vietnam, five yards per person per year, creates the illusion that most are still in the army, small figures in pith helmets and jungle jackets. For those who have done military service can wear their old uniforms.

Hanoi has everything that Saigon had squandered. It is a community with soul, a city of colonial elegance, leafy, murmuring to the swish of a million bicycles. Hanoi is poor but honest; clean and well-behaved, almost Confucian in its frugality; not without a few beggar women who carefully avoid importuning foreigners, but thankfully lacking the soiled amputees and pimp-exploited urchins who work the pavements of disordered Saigon.

Haiphong is altogether different. I went there expecting a large port still showing signs of war. Instead, it seems more like Penarth, in South Wales, on a grey day, very small with fewer than a dozen ships tied up at the only quay. The port is a quarter-master's nightmare, overflowing with thousands of tons of goods from the Communist world, including crates which have been there for months if not years. So great is this vast stockpile that it has spilled over into surrounding streets. It is a damaged city that wears its scars like a very old man. The American bombing of Haiphong was so sustained that it has yet to be wiped from the collective memory. Fatigue, even resentment, is written on many faces. Still, a start is being made on the construction. The burned-out wreckage of the oil depot is being strengthened and rebuilt. Outside Haiphong, dykes guarding the Red River delta are being strengthened and roads widened. Most of this work is done laboriously, painfully, by hand, without steamrollers. Women workers pound pieces of tar-covered stones into the road surface with hammers. With this absence of machinery and the bombing of many factories, no wonder North Vietnam admits that some of its important industries are still below the 1965 level.

As we left Haiphong, a train passed pulling trucks loaded with tanks and heavy artillery. It seems to complete one valid image of North Vietnam, a relatively small country, which, after immense sacrifice, won total victory with an army that is now the most tested and perhaps the most effective in the world. But now a radical change of direction is needed. There is a crippling lack of experienced managers, technocrats and specialists. As a short-term measure the army has been milked for such people. But there are not enough, and one of the problems is that, although there are many trained South Vietnamese, they have yet to prove their political reliability. After all, less than a year ago Vietnam was at war.

Will Vietnam demobilize? It is a question asked anxiously but unrealistically around South-East Asia, especially by those who respect if not fear the Vietnamese and believe that their national genius responds best to stress and struggle, if not war. The speculative answer must be that Vietnam's army of six hundred thousand will remain at that level for at least a few years. To demobilize would be economic folly at a time when there are three million unemployed south of the seventeenth parallel, and occasional security problems arise. That is why the Communists keep at least fifteen divisions inside Vietnam. For months now Hanoi has been immersed in political and constitutional matters. The decision to sprint towards formed reunification within the next three or four months is straining Vietnam's administrative abilities. Thousands of Communist soldiers who returned to their homes on rotational leave are discouraged from bringing large quantities of consumer goods.

But if the North is imposing its will on the South, there is also influence the other way. In Hanoi, women's hairstyles are more frivolous; girls can be seen with lipstick; blouses are brighter; there are more cars and motorcycles – all rather superficial, but exciting in Hanoi. After the years of self-denial then victory, the expectations of the Northerners have been aroused. To a very limited extent, these are starting to be met.

BEIRUT RESIDENT

Chris Drake

Damascus, July 1976

Living amid Beirut's warring factions meant a life of constant danger and a minimum of creature comforts.

The reason one does not notice is simply that, having lived here since the trouble began back in April of last year, I – like other foreigners and the Lebanese themselves – have become accustomed to it. I have been, as it were, 'dragged down' with the country and so if each day another of the services we once took for granted disappeared, it did not make much difference because it all happened relatively slowly, and we made allowances as we went along. However, having now come out of the country and been able to compare life there with life elsewhere it is a bit of a shock, to say the least.

The worst part is the lack of electricity, which was cut several weeks ago when part of the system was shelled. It has happened before, but the cuts never lasted so long we could not cope. It is different now, though. Very different. And I suppose the best way of describing the problems lack of power presents is to suggest one imagines one's own city or town in a similar situation, and then work out all the things that will not function as a result. The obvious one is lighting. When darkness comes, that is it. Candles are scarce and torches not exactly convenient, so people tend to go to bed much earlier, and rise again once the sun has come up.

Sleeping is not easy anyway. The sound of night-long battles raging in the suburbs – the machine-gun fire and the exploding shells – usually keeps one awake, and constantly worried too, for there is no telling when the shells will begin landing in one's own area. So the best way is a stiff nightcap (strictly for medicinal purposes, of course), cotton wool in the ears and a mattress placed either in the corridor or, for added protection, the basement of the building.

Now, without lights, without television, without lifts, without washing machines and irons – even without telephones – one can still manage. But a power failure is much more than that, for it also prevents water being pumped to the taps; and this adds yet another dimension to the vast amount of suffering and depression which those in Lebanon are already enduring because of the war.

For people who have not experienced this sort of problem, once again it is a question of putting oneself in similar circumstances; for instance getting up in the morning, and being unable to take a bath or a shower, being cautious about how much one uses even just to wash. Then going out to search for a broken mains pipe and queueing in the intense summer heat, often for a couple of hours, to fill a bucket or a bottle. The luckier ones have wells below their buildings, but even that has to be got out and the precious liquid then carried upstairs. Drinking water, more important than ever because of the dangers of disease, is still available in some shops; but it is so expensive, it is almost cheaper to drink the local beer.

Hot water is very rare, because canisters of gas are so difficult to obtain – and cooking is a major problem for the same reason. But it is possible to get food, though not easy, and anyway there is little variety. Usually, it is fresh fruit and vegetables. But because there is no refrigeration, preventing it all going bad is no easy task. To find those shops and stalls which are open is a job to be done on foot, for petrol is another of those precious liquids and without electricity it has to be pumped by hand if one is lucky enough to find a garage which has some, and one can pay the asking price.

The cars are all in bad shape because of the poor quality of the fuel, and most bear the scars of battles – bullet holes, dents, smashed windscreens or often no windows at all. As far as the standard of driving goes, well, that has certainly deteriorated. As an example, when my taxi driver pulled away from the hotel in Damascus (where I had been getting a great thrill taking a hot shower and watching water actually come out of the taps), he suddenly stopped again. I could not understand why, until he pointed out that the traffic lights were red. Well, we have not paid any attention to those crossings. You see, there is no law and order. No police force. It is the rule of the gun there – and it has become so bad that if a car full of gunmen is driving across an intersection at high speed, they will just fire their machine-guns in the air to warn people out of the way, and I must admit it is very effective. Of course, it can also be very frightening, and I confess to having lost count of the times when the muscles in my stomach have tightened and the cold shivers of fear have run up my spine, as I have found myself facing the guns of young men who have been ready to kill me for no particular reason. Simply, life does not mean much to them – after all, no one is going to arrest them for murder. And what is one more dead body in a country where nearly thirty thousand have already died?

THE CORRESPONDENT'S TRADE

Ian McDougall

LONDON, AUGUST 1976

On returning to Britain after twenty-seven years abroad, during which he sent more than ten thousand news stories from over forty countries in four continents, our correspondent reflected on some of the changing aspects of his trade.

The reason why a broadcasting correspondent has an easier time now than he did in the forties is simple: it is that communications have improved. Communications are the only things that change in news. The news itself – despite what some may claim about there being more of it today, or less of it – remains remarkably the same from one decade to the next. And, in fact, the only really novel events that have happened in my time are space travel, political hijackings, mass tourism and the plastic explosion in household equipment – what one advertising man once described to me as 'the breakthrough in plastic toys for budgerigars'.

When I first started in the forties, as number two in the Paris office, we had to send nearly all our stories at fixed times over a microphone hook-up, a music circuit, as it is called in the trade, and only occasionally did we use the phone, because at that time for various tedious reasons the use of the phone for broadcasting voice was forbidden. Tom Cadett, the chief Paris correspondent at that time, and myself used to scamper up and down a flight of stairs to a converted attic bedroom in a hotel and seclude ourselves behind a thick curtain, as if in a confessional, screaming ourselves hoarse till contact was established with London and praying that we would emerge without dying from suffocation. It was, incidentally, the only broadcasting studio in the whole world equipped with a bidet – in that as in so much else the BBC led the field.

It was not until the early fifties that I recall being equipped with a portable recording machine. The first of these was unbelievably heavy and big enough to pack a fair-sized puppy in. The tape had to be wound back by hand, which is the perfect recipe for instant calamity. A two-year-old child would have been an easier travelling companion, and I once said so in a cable from Burma, which was the only message I sent from Burma that got any notice taken of at all. Then we were issued, as a kind of over-reaction, with a sweet little machine about the size of a school-child's pencil box and about as robust as a piece of Dresden china. This also broke incessantly, but at least it was so small that one could forget about it, which was more than could be said for its predecessor.

As time went by, the telephone was rehabilitated as a legitimate means of sending dispatches by voice, and the extension of the automatic system for international calls greatly reduced the need to maintain bad-tempered arguments with exchange operators in various languages. On the frontier between Malaya and Thailand, I once got through to London in a few seconds from a jungle telephone which was having its cord chewed by a sacred goat as I used it. And in the remotest part of the Carpathian Mountains of Romania, I was taken by a heavily armed escort to a railway signal box half a mile away in the middle of the night – we had been sleeping in a train while accompanying the then Soviet leader, Khrushchev – in order to receive a call from the BBC. I thought this was good staff work on the part of the Romanian Post Office. I thanked my escort, who, however, stolidly informed me that they had only been protecting me from the packs of mountain bears which infested the region. I understood for the first time why they had made me change from my light-coloured pyjamas into something dark – a disconcerting instruction at four in the morning in a Communist country!

Broadly speaking, you can get almost anybody to a telephone these days, which is perhaps why some editors and producers think that there should be nothing very difficult abut getting Ford, Carter, Giscard d'Estaing, Schmidt, Amin or whoever into a programme at very short notice. On one single day in Bonn I was asked to get Chancellor Brandt, then just newly installed in office, into three different BBC slots at more or less the same time. The trouble is that foreign politicians tend to give priority, just as do British ones, to their own audiences.

However, while improved phone systems – not to mention cable and telex and satellite – have made human contacts much faster, they have also reduced the frequency of the old-fashioned scoop, by which I mean a story which no one else has got and which – and this is the crucial point – is worth having. There is no merit at all in being first with a load of boring old rubbish. My idea of a reasonable and feasible scoop today would be for a reporter to land on Mars, or authenticate the Loch Ness monster or prove that Mao Tse Tung is already dead. But scoops cost money and editors tend to be closer and closer fisted. When, some time ago, Henry Morton Stanley of the *New York Herald* questioned his editor about expenses for an interesting assignment he had just been given he received this magnificent reply: 'Draw a thousand pounds now and when that is spent draw another thousand: and when you have finished that draw another thousand, and so on. But find Livingstone.' In fact, Stanley spent about nine thousand pounds on the job, which would of course be equivalent to a far greater sum today, though still cheap at the price.

But my point is that today the editor would not have put it like that. His message, probably in garbled telex, would have read,

'Find Livingstone, but remember cost-cutting has absolute priority.' Stanley's great scoop, incidentally, was fully believed in by
his editor, though at the time others had doubts. A scoop today is
suspected by all.

I am none the less proud that the profession of foreign
correspondents survives. Democracy needs it, even though some
people claim to be vague about what foreign correspondents do,
and whether indeed they do anything at all. There is a lunatic
fringe which thinks they drink champagne out of their mistresses'
shoes and live at the local Ritz. There is another fringe, not
entirely lunatic but almost so, which believes they are on
Christian-name terms with everyone in their territory from the
President downwards and are occasionally called in to advise on
foreign policy.

My own experience throughout twenty-seven years has been
that the job is extremely arduous, both mentally and physically;
that drudgery is of its essence, as in most other jobs, and that the
advantages of not having to keep nine to five hours are offset by
the disadvantages of being on call at every hour of the day and
night, a requirement which correspondents share with, almost
uniquely, medical practitioners.

When all is said and done, however, it also seems to me a
profession which teaches you to cope with literally any situation
without flapping and without yielding to the pressures of
interested parties. Over a very long time, and on a day-to-day
basis, this is harder than it sounds. It defines, too, the frontiers of
your powers of endurance and rubs in the valuable lesson that the
way things appear on the spot are nearly always different from the
way they are visualized by the reader or listener in an armchair.
Now this has nothing to do with inaccurate reporting. It has to
do with the human imagination, which seems unable to cope
with anything smaller than twice life-size. I do not remember
being seriously frightened on a story I was actually covering, but I
was often terrified when I read other people's reports of it
afterwards.

FESTIVAL IN OMDURMAN

Bob Jobbins

KHARTOUM, MARCH 1977

Close to Khartoum lies Omdurman, the site of one of Sudan's great religious festivals.

As you cross the bridge from Khartoum to Omdurman, look back to the south and from the bridge you can see the point where the two great rivers merge to form the Nile. To your left, the water is dark blue, to your right, bright silver. And there is a distinct line where the waters of the Blue and White Nile meet. Ahead, the eighty-foot silver dome of one of Sudan's great shrines dominates the town. This is the tomb of the Mahdi, the self-appointed religious leader who, at the end of the last century, launched a holy war and drove the British and Egyptian colonialists out of Sudan. The Mahdi died only five months after the death of General Gordon who was cut down by the Dervish army on the steps of the Governor's Palace. And it was thirteen years before Lord Kitchener stood in front of the tomb, victorious in one of the bloodiest battles in African colonial history.

As I approached the tomb, the whole of the dusty plain, which forms the centre of Omdurman, was surrounded by a high fence and above it floated the red, green and black banners of Islam with their gold crescents and stars. It looked like the camp of a vast army. As dusk fell the flags were lit by the harsh lights from hundreds of temporary carpeted mosques which formed a huge horseshoe facing the tomb. Inside were perhaps thirty or forty thousand jostling people, who had come to celebrate the birthday of the prophet Mohammed.

Some Muslims argue that this is not, in the true sense, a religious festival. But, for the Sudanese, it is the climax of a ten-day celebration which is part pilgrimage and part fair. It was difficult to see into the crowd, but overhead dust mingled with the smoke of innumerable small fires lit by kebab sellers and tea vendors. When I arrived, the crowd was being held back to leave a wide avenue from the main entrance to the tomb itself. And the martial impression was heightened by the throbbing of drums in the background and by the mounted policemen on prancing horses who rode up and down to keep the way clear.

Finally, Sudan's deeply religious President, Jaafar al-Numeiri, dressed in a long white djellaba and spotless turban, drove out after praying at the tomb, and the crowd surged forward and mingled. Tall tribesmen, some with dust-caked, tightly curled hair, from the eastern borders of Sudan, also in white robes, stood with young men in jeans and T-shirts. Women with brilliant coloured veils over their smart Western dresses strolled past the open-air mosques where the faithful prayed and listened to sermons from the leaders of rival sects, or stood and watched as swaying drummers circled, endlessly chanting, 'Allah, Allah.' The complex pattern of the drums was broken by the harsh clash of cymbals and the chant was echoed by the crowd, urged on by the leader of the sect dressed from head to toe in a heavy robe made entirely of brightly coloured rags. He conducted the chant with a staff and whirled and swayed with the music, pausing only to salute friends in the crowd.

In the centre of the vast open space, where the crowd was a little thinner, other groups of drummers with large tambourines, which they threw in the air as they struck them with the flats of their hands to give extra resonance, provided the music for small groups of youths who whirled and leapt to the rhythm using stout walking sticks, as if they were spears, in traditional Dervish dances. And between these groups, families strolled – the small children in their best clothes clutching dolls made from dark rose-coloured candy, the traditional gift on the prophet's birthday.

Indeed, one corner of the festival ground was taken up with booths selling nothing but garish gifts. Some of the candy figurines were in the shape of elephants, lions, soldiers on horseback or even, on one stall, what appeared to be missiles. It is this aspect of the birthday celebration which has led some devout Muslims to question the way the festival has developed. It has become, they say, too commercialized. The religious aspect has been over-whelmed by the family party, the feeling of having a night out. The event is clearly a religious one. The number of people kneeling on prayer mats in large tents, or squatting listening to a local leader preaching through a loudspeaker system, testified to that. And, in spite of the frenzy of some of the drumming, the atmosphere was strangely peaceful. In the centre of the crowd, the sound seemed to be lost in the vastness of the enclosure, and as the incredible mixture of Arab, African and Nilotic people strolled past, the main impression was one of relaxation.

During the whole evening, apart from my companion, I did not see another European. We seemed to be the only intruders in what is, after all, a national as well as a religious event. And yet we were greeted with smiles; there was little curiosity and absolutely no hostility. We were just left to wander around as we pleased.

As we left, looking back, the flag still fluttering against the ring of light, the drums and the chanting merged. The next morning was a national holiday and Khartoum was virtually deserted. The white streets were empty, the shops shut. The guards outside what was once Gordon's palace, now the President's official residence and renamed The People's Palace, were the only people in the street as I walked down to the bank of the Blue Nile to look across to the silver dome in Omdurman nearly five miles away.

DEATH IN CUSTODY

John Simpson

JOHANNESBURG, NOVEMBER 1977

The death in detention of Steve Biko focused world attention on the conduct of the South African police.

Two months before Steve Biko died, the South African Broadcasting Corporation carried out a series of interviews with security policemen about the treatment of suspects. Not something the SABC usually refers to much. A Major Trevor Baker told them that his personal method of interrogation was to offer a person brought to him for questioning a chair, to tell him the reason for his detention and to show an interest in him and attend to his well-being. The police did not, he said, make anyone's life unbearable.

Well, one thing is certainly true. Although a number of ordinary policemen have been found guilty of maltreating prisoners, not a single member of the Security Police has been among them, despite the high number of deaths among people they have detained. The findings in many of these cases have been 'death by suicide'. There was for instance the case of Mopotla Mohapi, who died in August last year in his cell at the Kei Road Gaol near East London. He was found by a Constable Smith, hanging with his back to the cell bars, with a noose made of a pair of denim jeans round his neck. A note was later found in his jacket pocket saying *This is just to say goodbye to you, you can carry on interrogating my dead body*. The handwriting of the note, to an ordinary observer,

170

bears no relation whatever to a known sample of Mr Mohapi's writing. Police handwriting experts said it was undoubtedly written by him. An expert brought in by the Mohapi family was just as certain that it had not been. Constable Smith, who found the body, did not belong to the Security Police. At the inquest, he said he had been deeply distressed by Mr Mohapi's death and had thought a lot about it. The way Mr Mohapi had hanged himself seemed strange to him and suicide was inconsistent with the Mr Mohapi he had known.

Captain Schoeman of the Security Police, who had been interrogating Mr Mohapi before he died, agreed that the death was inexplicable. In his evidence, he said he had 'borne no grudge' as the result of a formal complaint Mr Mohapi had brought against him after he had been arrested and interrogated once before by Captain Schoeman. The magistrate found that death had been caused by hanging, but he did not bring in a verdict of suicide.

Joseph Mdluli, aged fifty, died in the custody of the Security Police in Durban in March of last year. A post-mortem showed that he had cuts and bruises on many parts of his body, especially his head and stomach. Three ribs had been fractured and he had a number of small haemorrhages in the brain. His lungs were congested with blood and his Adam's apple showed a fracture. Four policemen, two black and two white, were charged with culpable homicide as a result. The police evidence was that Mr Mdluli had tried to escape during interrogation and that there had been a struggle but Mr Mdluli had not been injured. Afterwards, according to the police evidence, he had suddenly stood up then staggered and fallen, hitting his chest or neck on the back of a chair.

The Durban state pathologist, though, told the court that Mr Mdluli's injuries were too extensive to have been caused by a single fall over a chair and another senior pathologist suggested that death could have been caused by a karate blow to the neck. All four policemen were acquitted, since the judge explained he was not satisfied that they were directly involved. The medical evidence cast grave doubts, he said, on the evidence of the police.

The case was referred to in an associated trial at Pietermaritzburg four months ago, when another judge said that the injuries which had caused Mr Mdluli's death were probably inflicted by the Security Police, but he could not make a positive finding on that.

The cases of Mopatla Mohapi and Joseph Mdluli bring out two major points. Firstly, that the record of impartiality by judges and pathologists in South Africa remains a good one and all the cases have been fully reported in the Press. Secondly, that even if no security policemen have been found guilty in court of ill-treating prisoners, it does not necessarily mean that some have not been doing so. It should not be assumed, though, that everyone in South Africa is particularly upset by the deaths of detainees. The other day, a government MP, Mr Frekkie Le Roux, told an election meeting in Pretoria that he himself would have killed Steve Biko, the latest prisoner to die in detention. In South Africa, said Mr Le Roux, when a man disturbs law and order the way Steve Biko did, he should be killed.

IRAQ'S STRONGMAN

Tim Llewellyn

BAGHDAD, AUGUST 1978

The new President of Iraq, Saddam Hussein, eliminated much opposition when he had twenty-one of his senior officials executed for plotting against the State.

'A flag among flags.' 'A knight among knights.' 'A sword among swords.' Iraqi officials tend to become somewhat flowery when they talk about Saddam Hussein these days; perhaps it sounds better in Arabic. But there is no doubt who, for the foreseeable future anyway, is number one indisputable leader of this complicated and violent nation of Iraq. His face, sometimes glaring, sometimes beaming, gazes at you from every wall, every hoarding and, it seems, almost continuously from the television set. Old speeches are repeated, old rallies re-run, filling the gaps between the fresh ones.

He was still lecturing away from the little box as I staggered out of Baghdad Airport last night, after a seventeen-hour wait for a plane. Wealthy Iraq has not yet learnt how to translate its vast oil money into either stability or efficiency. And maybe the inherent, the endemic political and administrative complexities of Iraq do demand the presence of a tough, remorseless, even ruthless leader like Saddam Hussein who, for whatever reasons, has cleansed the Iraqi body-politic of twenty-one traitors – one of whom was his close friend and confidant, Adnan Hussein, a personable, bright man of thirty-two.

For an Arab, Saddam Hussein is big; more than six foot, broadly built and barrel-chested, but always decorously swathed in the draperies of Pierre Cardin. A ring glints on a ham-fist. The tie is colourful, but discreet. It is the sort of gear that Lee J. Cobb might have worn in *On the Waterfront*.

From the balcony of his palace last Wednesday night, as delirious crowds massed round him in echoing approval of that morning's executions, Saddam Hussein was an impressive, even awe-inspiring figure. The words were harsh, slow but articulate, emanating from below the thick black moustache that has become a badge for most Ba'ath Party hopefuls. Shawareb Tamania, the Arabs call it, Moustache Number Eight – a reference to the Arabic figure eight, which is a curling, inverted 'v' shape. When he paused for a word, or for a gap in the chants of adulation, the handsome but brutal face assumed a kind of slow, burning glare – the look that can kill, and quite frequently does.

Yet, for all the objections of the international, including Arab, world to the Iraqi way of political house-cleaning, and last week's was different in context but not in style, I received a definite impression from Iraqis around me that it was more than fear alone that had given him his renewed stature. Their responses, as it were, were genuine, the muttered Arabic equivalents of 'That's right, you tell 'em.' as he excoriated his nameless enemies, defended his actions and Iraq's steadfastness.

Here was the man in charge, the man who can shoot as well as pen the thoughts of the Iraqi Ba'ath Party in many pamphlets. The ruthlessness is that of a man who came up fighting, literally, the hard way in a harsh country; killing as well as out-manoeuvring rivals who tried to do the same as he did – and they will probably try again.

It is really not much beyond gang warfare with political labels. It is all a little much for the parlour liberal. It is even reckoned to be rather distasteful in the not normally sensitive or peaceful environs of other radical Arab groups. 'But this,' say the Iraqis, 'is Iraq. We need and deserve this kind of leadership.' And though they constantly stress that all flows from the Revolution, the Ba'ath Party, that the President is merely *primus inter pares*, the cult of the personality that is so necessary to impose order in the Arab world is more prevalent in Iraq now than ever.

A new Nasser, Arabia's Fidel Castro? The Iraqis only object mildly to the comparisons. Saddam Hussein is, after all, much more advanced than Nasser, they say, a different entity completely. Eleven years at the top, most of it shared with ex-President Bakr, have ended with Saddam Hussein's assumption of power in extraordinarily violent and confused circumstances. He has, though, assumed it, scything opposition from around him like a prophet with a sharp sword, and that is what Iraqis like and respect. But how long will this respect last? Iraqis are also tireless plotters, and no one doubts that there will be more tests of this man's leadership and ability to survive.

JONESTOWN MASSACRE

Paul Reynolds

GEORGETOWN, NOVEMBER 1978

More than nine hundred members of an American religious cult led by the Revd Jim Jones were found dead deep in the jungle in Guyana. Earlier, the body of a visiting US Congressman, Leo Ryan, was discovered nearby.

He lay back on the bed in the heat of the afternoon, his head propped up on a pillow. A short, stocky man in his forties, lean and bronzed. His name was Gerry Parkes, and in his soft, slow drawl he told me the story of how he had led his family into virtual slavery, and how he had tried to lead it out again.

Gerry Parkes, his wife Patricia and their five children, the eldest a married man, the youngest a twelve-year-old girl, were fundamentalist Christians who lived in California. Many years ago Gerry and Patricia used to go and listen to sermons given by a young preacher called the Revd Jimmy Jones in Ohio. Jones was a dynamic young man, Parkes said, and he himself, a methodical, reserved man, was attracted by the Jones personality. 'Everything Jones touched seemed to turn to gold,' Parkes said. 'He looked after drug addicts, criminals, the poor and the black.'

The Parkeses moved to California and kept up their close links with Jones, who by now had set up a commune in San Francisco he was calling 'the People's Temple'. Parkes broke off and stared ahead silently for a few moments. His twelve-year-old daughter was asleep on the bed next to his.

'Didn't you know there was terrible repression in the People's Temple?' I asked him.

'We rationalized that,' he said, 'we thought the punishment was necessary to keep some of those people out of prison.'

It took the Parkes family two years to make up their mind to go to Guyana. Gerry Parkes broke off again before resuming: 'It was the most terrible mistake I ever made,' he said. He explained that Jones had told them Guyana was ideal for a new type of community. The land was rich. The temperature never rose above eighty. The settlement would perhaps grow into a new city one day. Jones showed them films of the site and eventually the Parkes family sold up their house, gave the money to the Temple and set off for South America.

The family was greeted at the camp gate by an armed guard. 'I knew I'd made a mistake as soon as we arrived,' Gerry Parkes went on. From then on they lived the lives of slaves. The day began at six with a meagre breakfast. Everyone had to be at work by seven, some toiled all day in the fields, and at six in the evening there would be another meal, usually rice and gravy, sometimes vegetables as well. At around seven thirty the people would have to gather around the camp pavilion where Jones harangued them and built up the atmosphere of paranoia which was to culminate in the mass self-destruction. 'He told us our enemies would destroy us,' Parkes said. 'We had to be ready to commit revolutionary suicide. When the enemy attacked, we would foil him by destroying ourselves.'

The Parkes family arrived in Jonestown in April this year. They were not allowed to leave, so they began to work out an escape plan almost immediately. They did not dare to tell anyone else. There was no one they could trust – many of the settlers believed in Jones, others enforced his will with guns. Some even regarded the camp as a revolutionary base to help spread and ferment rebellion throughout South America.

By then the visit of Congressman Ryan was imminent, and when he arrived Gerry Parkes decided this was the moment to leave. Jones tried to persuade him to stay. He offered to give back their passports, get good medical help for his mother, give them better food if only they would stay. But Parkes had had enough. He gathered the family together and along with Congressman Ryan they set out for the nearby airstrip and freedom. A few others joined them. Jones and his followers saw them as traitors, though. 'People we had got to know stared at us with hatred,' said Parkes. 'We knew we were in danger.' And they soon found out just what that danger was. As they sat in the small aircraft one of the supposed deserters with them pulled out a gun and started shooting. Other gunmen appeared from the camp, and among the five dead was Gerry's wife, Patricia. The death of Patricia Parkes was the price the family paid for their escape. Nor was it the only price. As Gerry was finishing his story his eldest son, Dale, came into the room. He listened to the end then quietly went over to a wooden trunk in the corner, the trunk in which all their belongings had been shipped to Jonestown some months before. He pulled out a photograph. It was that of a smiling two-year-old boy, half black, half white. 'That was my adopted son,' Dale said, 'we had to leave him behind.' Dale put the photo back in the trunk. 'The police have told me he is dead,' he said. 'It was the children they killed first.' Dale Parkes went to lie down on another bed. A doctor from the American Embassy came in to see how they were. The girl woke up, her face was drawn and tired. From below there drifted up the noise of a steel band. I left the room and closed the door.

IDI AMIN'S LEGACY

Tim Llewellyn

Ten days after Uganda's liberation from the tyranny of Idi Amin, traces of the grotesque brutalities of the previous eight years still lingered.

The plain L-shaped, pink and white four-storey building is reached up a leafy path in a quiet, wealthy, residential area. Idi Amin lived next door along a drive. It looks like a post office or gas board in an English country town; inside are all those desks, corridors, filing cabinets, shelves and sterile furniture one associates with the tedium of bureaucracy. Its ordinariness sharpens the horror of this block – headquarters of Idi Amin's State Research Bureau. How Orwell would have relished that stark, anonymous name, redolent as it is of scientists and organization. Of course, the slaughter and torture whose stains still mark the walls and floors were planned routinely, relentlessly. These files, with their lies, their informers' suspicions, their litany of groundless, seedy, unnecessary paranoid detail are almost as nauseating as the rich smell of death that still pervades these offices. People, firms, are accused, quite without proof or even evidence. And this fragile web of suspicion, fear and misinformation caught thousands who eventually met shoddy, brutal deaths, some of them dispatched in a callous farewell gesture just a few days before the forces of Tanzania and the new Ugandan National Liberation Front made their cautious way into town.

But it is not only the bloodstains, the decomposing corpses, the stench of murder among the soft glades and bougainvillaea, the guns, shells and clips of ammunition piled at reception, just where they made afternoon tea or coffee, or opened the mail, there are other disturbing contrasts as well. The macabre pilgrimage through this chamber of horrors reveals the questionable taste of those comedians – alas, some of them British – who made a fun figure of Idi Amin. I found a letter from a young Irishman asking Idi for his favourite joke, a Greek technician offered his services, a young Swedish boy requested his autograph. And would that humorist who aped Amin in *Punch* magazine not swallow his words now if he could have talked, as I did, with an old man in his Sunday best, recalling the beatings, the shootings, the degradation he witnessed, and somehow survived, in those dank, black dungeons? A young woman, a relative of his, as they revisited this awful scene, as she trod through the carnage, and the strewn files, lifted her calf-length, neat cotton frock even higher, as if afraid of being sullied by the proximity of such squalor – but it was something everyone had to see.

Around the central and dominant International Hotel, where bored and often drunken Tanzanian soldiers view from trees and bushes the prize they now possess, the gardens are still lush with flowers, greenery, palms, exotic and vivid African growths tidied with English precision, sweeping down past the old colonial-style Speke Hotel until they tip suddenly into the looted, broken shambles of the business district.

It is an image of Kampala's problems: easy-going, humorous, fine-looking, friendly Ugandans, citizens of East Africa's richest and most beautiful nation, but oppressed by a hard core of criminals, racked by tribalism, misled by corrupt and incompetent rulers. And is it over? One Ugandan I found, a post office worker, had worked on through all the tedious dangers, staying resolutely at his telecommunications post. He was concerned more that he could not wash or change, did not have a chessboard, than at the prospect of being shot or savaged or starving. As we looked out of the window at the girls cheering the Tanzanian troops, their liberators, he said, 'It is a great welcome, yes. People are naturally happy; but there was a much bigger welcome for Idi Amin in '71 when he kicked out Obote.'

POL POT'S PEOPLE

Adrian Porter

BANGKOK, MAY 1979

Our correspondent was on the Thai side of the border when a group of Pol Pot's workers briefly appeared while on a march from one part of Kampuchea to another.

The guerrilla army and its column took two days to pass through Thailand and the junction of a dirt road and a muddy farm track about half a mile from the frontier was the point where they turned left to go back into Kampuchea. Right there were a couple of shacks that were Thai general stores, and one of them sold a kind of ice-cream block made out of powdered milk, frozen water and sugar. It tasted awful but, under the hot sun, it offered something cool, and watching journalists and Thai villagers bought some of the blocks and gave them to the children in the column. It was obvious that they had never tasted ice-cream in their lives before and their eyes lit up and they began to smile as they ate it and let it dribble down their chins. But even before they got halfway through eating, a guerrilla, aged maybe seventeen or eighteen, pushed the muzzle of his gun at them and ordered them to move on. Dejectedly they obeyed.

It summed up in one scene the essence of Kampuchean life – its brutality, its inhuman attitude to anyone who might step out of line (even children), its unfeeling discipline, its exercise of power by an élitist set, most of them uneducated teenagers, and the total subservience of those who do not have this power.

Everything I had heard about Pol Pot's Khmer Rouge was confirmed as I watched the column pass me, or talked to a few peasants who dared to speak or was pushed around myself by the guerrillas who were not even in their own country at the time. The Khmer Rouge were hard, unsmiling, dead-eyed and used to being obeyed without question. They gave the impression of brain-washed automatons who obey orders as blindly and as cold-bloodedly as they give orders or kill those who disobey. They were laden down with guns and ammunition but those in the rearguard of the column whose job it was to herd what can only be described as the slave labourers carried the real staff of authority in Pol Pot's country – the short wooden-handled hoe. This was the tool used, according to every account, to kill any Kampuchean who opposed or was thought to oppose them. I saw a group of peasants lying in the shade of a tree almost unable to move from heat and exhaustion. A Khmer Rouge guard shouted at them to get up and get moving but they were a bit slow about it. Slowly he unslung the hoe from around his shoulder and before he had lifted it in his hand the peasants were up walking again.

But even among the guards and guerrillas there was an upper élite, just as there was, for comparison, among the hand-picked divisions of Hitler's SS. They led the column and were well clothed, well fed and had the best weapons. They had wrist-watches, ball-point pens, battery torches and even transistor radios. And if they were very important they rode bicycles, or mopeds or red mountain ponies. But most of them marched or walked and they were as fit as marathon runners.

Behind the main force and their families came the civilian supporters. Then came the thousands and thousands of ordinary peasants who had formed the workforce of Pol Pot's new society, labouring from dawn to dusk in the rice fields under the guns and hoes of the Khmer Rouge. They were the nearest thing to serfs I have ever seen. They shambled along, bare footed, with their heads down, or they lay in the bullock carts looking neither left nor right. Walking or riding with them were their guards, often boys of eleven or twelve, keeping them moving and preventing anyone from trying to make a break for it. Occasionally there would be a stretch of the column without guards. Twice I managed to find a man who spoke a few words of French, and who would tell me where he came from and how long he had been on the march, but that was all. In any case, by the time the contact had been made, a guerrilla would be approaching and the conversation would stop.

The only communication I had with the guerrillas was to be told in no uncertain way in sign language, grunts and gestures that I should keep out of their way. However, I managed to walk with them almost to the dry watercourse that marked the border where they were crossing back into Kampuchea, but when I dallied, watching, a group of guerrillas ostentatiously unslung their guns, so I walked hurriedly back the way I came. But at least I could walk away. Not many of those in the column could do that.

END OF A DYNASTY

Harold Briley

BUENOS AIRES, JULY 1979

A civil war led to the downfall of President Somoza, the last in a dynasty of dictators who ruled Nicaragua with little regard for their people.

He brought his own unique stamp to the role of dictator. He was full of Latin boastfulness – a general in his own right, trained at America's military academy, West Point, who liked to don his jungle-green uniform and fly his helicopter to the fighting, but not too close. He was intelligent – a brilliant businessman; approachable, with a great deal of charm. He liked company. Sometimes got drunk, berating us journalists with insulting language. He was estranged from his wife, and kept a mistress. Deep down, he had a hard streak of cruelty, and a total lack of compassion for his fellow men.

He was a small dictator writ large, hardly known for years outside his own country, but inside it, dominating all political, economic and military life, as his father and brother had done before him. A dynasty spanning more than forty years, savagely impinging itself on this small nation of two and a half million people. With his talents, he could have done so much for them. He did nothing, and worse than nothing. He brought them blood, sweat and tears, not in the cause of liberty or self-improvement, but for his own lust for power and his own greed.

The Somoza family grew rich – fabulously rich – as the mass of people stayed poor, desperately poor. The statistics cried out

for action. Forty per cent unemployed. Half the children dying
before the age of four, and half the survivors suffering malnutri-
tion. Half the population with a wage less than $150 a year. The
Somoza fortune was all of $500 million, owning much of
Nicaragua's arable land, most of its major businesses and a mansion
in Miami, where he has gone into exile. Many of his people live
in shanty-towns, with plywood walls and tin roofs, amid squalor,
disease and millions of flies. Yet they are charming, delightful
people, never begging for help. They bear their hardships with a
simple dignity, which never deserted them in the awful ordeal of
war. War of a kind, the Red Cross said, which had never before
so closely involved the civilian population. It was a war fought
around and through their shanty-towns, hit by bombs, rockets,
mortars and machine-gun bullets. No one knows for sure how
many died or were wounded. Nearly a quarter of a million of
them were displaced, pathetically wandering the countryside with
their white flags and their few belongings in plastic bags, or
crowding into Red Cross relief centres.

All the time, the dictator in his bunker spoke of 'his people,
of honour, freedom and the defence of democracy against
Communism'. That is what brought him support for so long from
the United States – the nation that created the dynasty, putting
his father in power and giving him the National Guard, devised,
trained and armed by them. But there came a time, and a
President, Jimmy Carter, to cry halt. Economic and military aid
was cut off, signalling a change of American policy. That dictators
should no longer get unqualified support simply as a bulwark
against Communism. That human rights must enter the equation
on both sides. Many people said that Somoza's actions created
more Communists than they deterred. Now, as happened with
the Shah of Iran, President Carter faces criticism that he has
abandoned an ally for something worse. Not a personal dictatorship and tyranny, but a doctrinaire, systematic one – the Cuban-
backed Communist menace, spreading through this strategically
vital region of Central America. Well, that is the big question

mark now over Nicaragua. What comes next? Whatever it is, ex-President Somoza has departed, unloved, unlamented, unmourned. I doubt if many Nicaraguans will say, 'Come back, all is forgiven.'

DESERT DISASTER

Clive Small

WASHINGTON, APRIL 1980

An American military mission to rescue the fifty three hostages being held by the Iranians in the US Embassy in Tehran ended in disaster. Eight Americans died when a helicopter of the assault force collided with a tanker aircraft in the Iranian desert and the mission was aborted.

I had been up late at night putting over a dispatch to London about the growing concern in Washington that Mr Carter might be moving too quickly towards some form of military action against Iran. Ironically, the action everyone was talking about was a non-violent naval blockade some time in the future. At midnight I went to bed. Not much more than an hour later the phone rang next to my bed. A voice on the other end said, 'The White House here, Rex Grenham speaking. Is that Clive?'

I sat upright quickly. Rex Grenham is deputy to Jodie Powell, the President's spokesman.

'I've got a statement,' said Mr Grenham. 'I'll read it and at the end I won't take any questions. Are you ready?'

I scrabbled for my pen and notebook. 'Go ahead,' I said shaking the sleep out of my head.

'The President has ordered the cancellation of an operation in Iran.' And so on.

As that astonishing story unfolded I felt a fleeting second or two of doubt. One of the strange features of Washington in the early hours is a number of what are officially described as 'nuisance calls'. Several times my wife and I have been woken by the phone ringing and an official-sounding voice trying to put over a hoax of some kind. Was this another? But no. By the time I had taken down the first few sentences of the statement I knew this was only too tragically genuine. Rex Grenham was giving me the first few details of an historic disaster. He spoke calmly at little more than dictation speed. 'Rex,' I said, 'have you given this to the news agencies?'

'Jodie's doing that at the moment,' he said.

'Thanks,' I said, and he hung up.

I rattled the phone cradle frantically to clear the line and got my call through to the foreign news traffic manager on the late shift in London. I hurried through a quick sentence telling of the mission that had failed in the desert in Iran. Within minutes I was reporting the White House statement live into the *Today* programme. After putting over a news dispatch and being interviewed by the *24 Hours* programme on the BBC External Services, I dressed hurriedly, swung my car out of the garage and headed in to the BBC office in the centre of Washington. I drove fast through the scattered banks of mist in the empty streets. It was just after three in the morning. Suddenly my mind flashed back to a hotel room in Nairobi. It was about three in the morning then and it was Sunday, 4 July 1976. The phone next to my bed rang and it was a voice telling me of the raid on Entebbe. The traffic light changed and I put my foot down and the car shot off again. Now I was thinking about something else. Why had the White House phoned the BBC so quickly with the first news of the raid on Iran? Ever since the hostage crisis began President Carter's officials have become more aware of the BBC's ability to get news in and out of Iran through its Persian language service. In this case was the White House trying to get a message through to people in Tehran by way of the BBC? If so, what people? Was it the militants in the embassy, letting them know through news broadcasts that the American raid had failed in case they heard rumours of an assault under way and panicked and shot hostages?

Or could it be something else? A raid like that would have to have had supporting groups inside Iran. Perhaps the White House was hoping that BBC broadcasts would tell those groups that the raid was off and they should keep their heads down. Well, perhaps all that it proves is the way a journalist's imagination can speculate privately at three in the morning. Still, the BBC was given the news surprisingly quickly. As I drove past those darkened houses it looked as if no one in Washington was aware of what had happened a few hours before on that stretch of Iranian desert. The British Embassy, like the other foreign representatives here, had not been told. But now, as I listened to the car radio, the talk shows and the phone-in programmes were well aware of the failure of the rescue mission. And nearly all of the listeners who were calling in were worried. What would happen to the hostages now? And would the disaster in the desert mean that the crisis would spread and threaten peace? The announcer interrupted. 'The President will speak to the nation at seven this morning,' he said. I parked the car and crossed the deserted street to the office. It was still dark. And it felt darker.

THE WRECKING
OF ITALY

David Willey

BOLOGNA, AUGUST 1980

A wave of terrorist killing in Italy, culminating in the bomb explosion at Bologna railway station in which more than seventy people died, threatened to plunge the country into chaos.

It has been a week of funerals charged with symbolic meaning. Many Italians are wondering if they have not been witnessing the sabotage of their republic by criminals who will stop at nothing in the pursuit of money and power. I shall not easily forget the state funeral of the victims of the Bologna railway station massacre; it took place in an incomparable setting, one of the finest squares in Italy, the Piazza Maggiore in Bologna, surrounded by superb Renaissance palaces. The summer heat was suffocating. For hours the mourners, many of them from other parts of Italy, kept on arriving in the piazza and the tension mounted. Then the red banners were unfurled and you realized that this was more a political than a religious occasion.

In the cathedral on one side of the square the coffins of only eight out of almost eighty victims of the terrorist bomb were spread out in front of the main altar. Most families had opted for a private burial. It was an eloquent way of protesting to the authorities of their failure to protect ordinary citizens going about their legitimate business; setting off on holiday, meeting a friend or a relation at the railway station, driving a taxi. The politicians began to arrive; there were whistles and catcalls, even for the Communist Party leader, Enrico Berlinguer. The only man to get any applause was the eighty-three-year-old President Pertini. He walked stiffly up the aisle of the vast Gothic edifice and paused for a moment with his hand on the tiny white coffin of the youngest victim of the disaster, a three-year-old girl. Outside the pigeons wheeled overhead in droves and a police helicopter chattered menacingly from time to time. The funeral mass was relayed outside, but when the politicians emerged again into the sunlight, there were renewed catcalls. The entire political establishment of Italy was there on the platform and they had to listen to the funeral oration of the Communist Mayor of Bologna, who catalogued the lapses and inefficiencies of those who govern this country, and because it was a funeral oration, they had no right of reply. The politicians literally scuttled away, as the crowd erupted into well-orchestrated calls of, 'Now is the time for the Communists to take over.'

It was a fine piece of theatrical management by the Communist city authorities, who showed they were capable of organizing a disciplined political meeting that many cities might envy. The politicians barely had time to fly back to Rome when disaster suddenly struck again, this time eight hundred miles to the south in the centre of the city of Palermo in Sicily. The man in charge of a battle against organized crime in Italy, the Mafia, the Chief Public Prosecutor of Palermo, stopped for a moment at a newspaper kiosk to look at a book. Suddenly a volley of shots rang out and he was lying crumpled on the ground; the Mafia had executed a man who they considered was getting uncomfortably well informed about their organization of the transatlantic drugs trade. So he was eliminated, as his predecessor had been, as were two senior police officers last year who prepared the prosecution of a group of more than fifty businessmen, lawyers, bankers – 'pezzi grossi' as they call them here, big shots accused of complicity in Mafia crime. With the help of the American Drug Enforcement

Agency, the prosecutor had prepared a powerful counterattack, not only against the drug traffickers, but against those who are believed to be recycling the enormous profits earned from heroin. On Friday, another funeral; a widow and relations desperate with grief; more grim-faced ministers who flew down from Rome; another sermon by another cardinal-archbishop. It was a replay of a scenario that we are seeing all too frequently in Italy.

What the government finds particularly disturbing is that neither the terrorists, be they black or red, nor the Mafia, respect normal frontiers any more; they hop away abroad into hiding and even immunity with the greatest of ease. The chief of police in the home town in Tuscany of the main suspect wanted in connection with the Bologna bombing said yes, he knew exactly where this known neo-Fascist was living, but he could not touch him for technical and legal reasons. Perceptive Italians noted that behind the messages of condolence flowing in from abroad lay perhaps the realization by Mrs Thatcher, by President Giscard d'Estaing and by Chancellor Schmidt that only international cooperation can solve what can only be described as trans-national terrorism. The connections are not always clear, but as one newspaper has put it, 'The leaders of Europe are worried about seeing the worst happen right on their own doorstep. What is the most immediate threat is not the American crisis, or the Soviets in Afghanistan, but the wrecking of Italy.'

BAGHDAD UNDER ATTACK

Michael Vestey

IRAQ, SEPTEMBER 1980

As Iran and Iraq waged war, our correspondent was among a group of Western newsmen invited to the Iraqi capital.

For a regime that is very secretive, the Iraqi government seems surprisingly anxious to allow Western journalists into the country to report on the war with Iran. With only a few minor hitches, I collected my visa in London, and prepared to fly to Baghdad. Then the Iraqis closed their airport here and that meant I had to go to Amman in Jordan. At Amman airport there was the man from the Iraqi Embassy waiting for me and my colleagues; and off we went to the embassy where we were told a bus would take us across the desert to Baghdad. They handed out apples and tins of Pepsi Cola to keep us happy while we waited for the coach to arrive; but then the problems cropped up. The Iraqis, I think, began to wonder what they were doing, because jetloads of journalists were arriving at Amman from throughout the world, and in the case of American television crews bringing with them huge cases of equipment and personnel required to carry and operate it. One American network came in with thirty-five large boxes to hold its ENG television cameras – probably the most cumbersome media invention of all time though, once in position, quicker to use. As the evening wore on and the daunting pile of

194

boxes began to occupy the front garden of the embassy, the Iraqis began to look disconcerted. However, the first bus arrived and off we went into the warm Jordanian night.

The journey took eighteen hours, including the inevitable hold-ups at an Iraqi customs post. But even there a man from the ministry was waiting to help smooth things over, and we managed to avoid a systematic search of every case and box of camera equipment. In Baghdad we were checked into a new state tourist hotel which had a tiny switchboard and one operator. Immediately, a hundred journalists tried to phone their offices across the world. The switchboard collapsed and the operator seemed to be in a state of shock. At that moment Iranian jets roared over the hotel to begin an air raid. The Iraqis clearly had not expected that so many journalists would descend upon them. But fortunately, we were moved to another hotel which had more than one telephone line; four direct-dial phones and a switchboard with several lines. But again the hotel could not cope and that switchboard gave up and it took twelve hours to repair it. And more coachloads of correspondents and camera crews were still arriving from Amman. What became obvious was that the Iraqis were determined to keep control of most of the news being sent out of Iraq. The state-owned television service refused to send foreign television reports by satellite. Unless television networks managed to transport their film and video reports overland, Western broadcasting companies had to rely on Iraq's television coverage, and that was obviously biased; and our only source of information about the war comes from military communiqués and government ministries.

However, we do manage to catch glimpses of the Iranian Air Force in action here in Baghdad. The morning after I arrived I was woken by a persistent sound that at first I was unable to identify. It was like someone wearing hobnail boots clattering down a concrete staircase. It was, in fact, anti-aircraft fire echoing around the city and coming from batteries placed on buildings a hundred yards away. From my hotel balcony I saw two American-built Iranian Phantom jets flying at a tremendous speed straight for me. The markings and colouring were quite clear. These jets had dropped their bombs on a military base on the edge of the city and were making for home. It was one of many air raids on Baghdad in the past week. They are rather odd affairs; the jets move in, drop one or two bombs, and then depart, almost as if they are not completely serious about what they are doing. Many Iraqis cannot understand why more bombs have not been dropped and why the Iranians have not attacked many civilian targets. Perhaps the jets have been concentrating on military and oil installations and on their way home have disposed of their remaining cargo on Baghdad. Who knows?

The Iraqis, however, are remarkably disciplined in their reaction to air raids. If there is enough warning, air-raid sirens begin their mournful wailing like the calls from the mosque summoning the faithful to prayer, and the streets empty astonishingly quickly. I was caught in an air raid and within seconds was ordered off the streets into the nearest doorway where we peered up at the clear blue sky for a glimpse of our attackers. Thousands of young people, members of the Civil Defence Corps, a civil militia, ensure that the streets are empty when the raid begins. In a sprawling and chaotic city of several million people, this is no mean feat; and at night the city is blacked out – we have to write our reports, this one included, by candlelight. How long we will be able to report on the war is a matter for conjecture. The Iraqis have stopped issuing visas so freely; and a sign from the Ministry of Culture and Information has appeared in the hotel lobby inviting us to leave. After expressing the faint hope that we might want to go away, it ends with the words '*Happy to receive you on other occasions*'.

ORPHANAGE NUMBER TWO

Jack Thompson

PHNOM PENH, OCTOBER 1980

Thousands of children lost their mothers and fathers during the Pol Pot regime and were living in orphanages in the Kampuchean capital.

Phnom Penh today is the guard on duty at the Ministry of Foreign Affairs making verbal passes at the girls who ride by on their shiny new bicycles. It is a shy Vietnamese woman working as a technician with a group repairing Phnom Penh's telephone lines; tree-lined boulevards, bequeathed by the French who once ruled Kampuchea as they ruled Vietnam and Laos; public buildings and villas which would not be out of place in some town in Provence, except that they now bear the scars of neglect and vandalism, a legacy of nearly four years of vicious misrule by the government of Pol Pot. But for me, the most durable memory of Phnom Penh will be the children of Orphanage Number Two, where four hundred and twenty-five boys and girls from six to sixteen have, in the words of the orphanage's director, found '*la joie de vivre*' again. Mr Sam Ang is a jolly, avuncular Khmer in his fifties who is not afraid to show his emotions. He was in a Pol Pot prison for six months. 'They beat me and chained my feet,' he told me. 'My two sons and my daughter were all killed by Pol Pot's agents even though the regime had invited them back from Europe to play their full part in the revolution. What deceit, what treachery,' Mr

Sam Ang exclaimed. 'Believe me, I saw Pol Pot's men kill babies. It is not easy to forget,' he said, fighting back the tears, 'and these children, they remember. They are happy today. The sun is shining and they can play football, tend the garden or help the new arrivals. Five or six turn up at the orphanage every day; sometimes they are so disturbed they start to smash the nearest thing in sight. At night you can hear them crying; they wake up from horrible nightmares. No, they will not forget their mothers or fathers or how they lost them.

'We are here to help the children,' said Mr Sam Ang, 'not exploit them.' I think he thought I was going to get the wrong impression from some of the activities – gardening, sewing, pig-rearing and cooking. 'But they're the ones who organize everything. They're divided into groups with an elected leader and each leader is a member of the school council with an elected president. It's a children's republic,' said Mr Sam Ang with a chuckle. 'We are only the counsellors.'

But Orphanage Number Two is no utopia. When it rains the whole place is flooded to a depth of a foot. Playgrounds, gardens and the repaired volleyball court are awash. Like all buildings in Phnom Penh, the dormitory blocks and the classrooms, the kitchens, the canteen and the administration block are in a sad state of disrepair. 'We need everything,' said Mr Sam Ang, 'exercise books, pens, pencils, tools and light bulbs. UNICEF [the United Nations Children's Fund] has provided a great deal and Oxfam has donated a minibus so that the children can have occasional outings.' But like all Kampuchea, Orphanage Number Two is short of essentials.

Mr Sam Ang makes up for a lot. He plainly loves every child as his own, but at his elbow there was a rather hard-faced man whose name I never learned. Communist dogma came rather too trippingly from his tongue. 'The children will be taught according to the principles of Marxism-Leninism,' he affirmed. The reception room in the administration building was dominated by a picture of Ho Chi Minh – the founder of the Vietnamese

Communist state. There was a photograph of President Heng Samrin, head of government in the People's Republic of Kampuchea, but it was much smaller, somewhat faded and a little to one side, further down the wall. Then there were some banners, presented by visitors from the Soviet Union, East Germany, Cuba and the Popular Front for the Liberation of Palestine. They were no different in their way from the pictures of the king and queen I have seen in every public building in neighbouring Thailand. Young minds, it seems, are for moulding, even those that have passed through four or more years of living hell.

But, as I left the orphanage, all was laughter and smiles again. The tiny ones had just sung me the Kampuchean version of 'Here We Go Round the Mulberry Bush'. When I played it back to them on my tape-recorder, their faces were a study in astonishment. Mr Sam Ang said he wished they had got a machine like that at the school. But he knows and I know that it will be a long time before sophisticated teaching aids reach Orphanage Number Two. Priorities in Kampuchea are of a rather different sort.

CAMPAIGNING WITH LECH

Tim Sebastian

WARSAW, OCTOBER 1980

After a Polish court gave legal recognition to the independent trade union Solidarity, its leader, Lech Wałęsa, later to become the country's President, went campaigning in Poland's industrial south to gain support for the union.

Lech Wałęsa, sometime worker, sometime striker, now a leader of millions, began his campaigning tour by looking after essentials. He arrived in Warsaw for talks with a government commission and then went out to buy a new pair of shoes. It was as much a symbolic gesture as anything else; he was setting out on the first campaign tour of its kind ever seen in Eastern Europe. The steps he was taking had never been made in a Communist country and would be unthinkable even now outside Poland.

Wałęsa took with him a gruff manner which alternates between difficult and less difficult. He is good with crowds but personal contacts are not so successful. One worker who got up to ask a question and began with his name and place of work was quickly flattened. 'Too long-winded,' bawled out Wałęsa, 'give me the facts, I only want the facts.' Cornered by journalists, Wałęsa was asked how the talks with the government had gone. 'They're over,' he replied, 'I haven't even had time to comb my hair.' This somewhat autocratic style is inevitable in a man who has had to claw and cajole, to elbow and kick his way to the forefront of a 'mini-revolution'. Wałęsa had to organize a workers' movement which had gone on for thirty years thinking only of the Communist state as its guiding force. Free legal trade unions have been dreamt of, even planned, but they had never ever come close to reality.

Whatever it achieved in the long term, Wałęsa's campaign was impressive at the time. He was, after all, down in the industrial south talking to the men who matter, a hard and uncompromising workforce with a reputation for obstinacy. These are the men who control the vital industries of coal and steel; without their goodwill Poland could grind to a halt in a matter of days. For Wałęsa they came out in their thousands, they crowded into a football stadium near the industrial complex of Nowa Huta, built as a symbol of the new Communist worker – something of an ironic memory in the present climate.

I caught up with Wałęsa at the climax of his tour in the southern city of Częstochowa. He had arrived at a factory club on the outskirts, where the red and white Polish flags were out flying a welcome in the sunshine. The only sign of authority was a lone police car at a discreet distance down the street. It was ironic that the Warsaw Pact foreign ministers had just left the country the day before. While Wałęsa was touring they had been arguing, perhaps also warning, that they do not like independent trade unions and they have attacked Wałęsa as anti-Socialist. They did not say so in public but they will have found Poland much changed since their last visit.

Lech Wałęsa never speaks with notes. He stands in front of the workers, timeless, his shoulders slightly drooping, and he speaks in long staccato bursts. He has become a lot more cheeky than he used to be, talking about tanks and Eastern Bloc intervention, telling people not to be afraid as they have been for the last thirty-five years. The new style is in, he says, the old days are over. It is an optimistic philosophy but the crowds enjoy it. In Częstochowa, the workers thought he was the best thing they had seen in a long time even though he did not think much of them. He criticized them for a poor turnout, for not organizing themselves better, for relying only on central trade union advice, without thinking up their own ideas. But they took it all from him, and in a time of crisis and uncertainty they look on Lech Wałeşa as a man they can trust.

That afternoon, though, he treated Częstochowa to a sight it had never seen before. He toured the town centre in a van sporting Solidarity posters, in front of it a police motorcycle escort, behind it a white Mercedes. On the streets people turned and looked in astonishment, some waved from the trams, a few of them smiled and shook their heads in disbelief. In a country where only the politicians in power campaign it was, to say the least, an extraordinary sight. Later that day, Wałeşa was back on the football pitch sprinting boyishly for the microphone for another display of unstoppable optimism. From the top of the stadium you could see the workers getting off buses hurrying along in lines through the industrial landscape, behind them the chimneys and the power stations and the grey provincial city of Częstochowa. It was not the prettiest place for a campaign tour but it certainly made an impact. Not a single worker went home that night saying he had heard it all before.

DINGO BABY

Red Harrison

The disappearance in the Australian bush of Lindy Chamberlain's baby daughter led to a series of inquests and a flood of innuendo.

The beginning of the story is simple enough. On the seventeenth of August last year, Mr Michael Chamberlain, a thirty-six-year-old pastor of the Seventh Day Adventist Church, was enjoying a holiday camping with his wife, Lindy, and their three children. That night, the youngest child, a girl only ten weeks old, vanished from her cot. Mrs Chamberlain, thirty-two and with the kind of looks reporters like to write about, cried out: 'My God! The dingo's got my baby!' The dingo is a wild and savage native dog of the outback, a kind of Australian wolf. Mrs Chamberlain told police she had seen a dingo running out of her tent with something in its mouth and then she had seen the empty cot.

Twenty-four hours later the names of Michael and Lindy Chamberlain were splashed in newspaper headlines and they have been there ever since in a bizarre story which reaches from the heart of London to the scorching deserts of central Australia, a story of death and mystery, of science and mythology, of truth, half-truth and rumour. It is a story which is making legal history in Australia and the end, the climax if you like, has yet to be written. The Chamberlain family was camping at a place called Ayers Rock, a giant geological absurdity which rises suddenly twelve hundred feet from an otherwise flat and featureless desert near the town of Alice Springs. If you look at a map of Australia and stick a pin right in the middle you will be pretty close to the town called Alice. Ayers Rock is a tourist resort and on the night the baby disappeared some two hundred tourists tried unsuccessfully to find her. To the Australian aborigines, Ayers Rock is a holy place, steeped in folklore and legends. In ancient times, some of its caves were used for childbirth and it is said that when twins were born the weaker of the babies would be left in the wilderness – for the dingoes. For days after the Chamberlain baby vanished, every dingo which showed its scavenging nose around the Rock was shot and its stomach contents examined. No one found a trace of the child. Indeed, her body has never been found.

There is still about the rock an element of the supernatural, and this, coupled with the Chamberlains' religious devotion, has inspired many unpleasant rumours: the baby was called Azaria, an unusual name which meant 'sacrifice in the wilderness'. At the first inquest last February, the coroner took the remarkable step of putting down this fiction. Azaria, he said, was a Hebrew name meaning 'the blessed one'. At that point, Mrs Chamberlain broke down in the court and cried. Some of the police enquiries into Azaria's disappearance went astray. The police camera used to photograph dingo footprints did not work. The duty policeman at Ayers Rock had no real forensic experience and when the child's bloodstained clothes were found a week later they were hardly examined. It has since been established that those clothes had been buried. But the questions of who buried them, who dug them up, who removed them from the baby and hid them in a rock crevice have never been answered. Instead, the coroner opened his court to live nationwide television to announce his finding that a dingo had taken the baby and that her parents had nothing to do with her death.

That finding did not satisfy some scientists and senior police officers. They sent the baby's clothes to London, to the laboratory of Professor James Cameron, a distinguished forensic consultant to Scotland Yard and the Home Office. His first investigations were enough for police to persuade the Supreme Court to order a new inquest. To reject the dingo theory. Enquiries since then have been nonstop, involving three universities, several government scientific departments, a zoo and police in three Australian states. The Chamberlains and their remaining children, now aged eight and five, have been questioned for hours. Their home has been searched, many of their clothes seized and their family car torn apart by scientists. Throughout all this, they have been subjected to the heated speculation and hearsay of a vivid communal imagination, a kind of never-ending trial by innuendo. But curiously, the word 'murder' has been mentioned officially only once. According to a detective, Mrs Chamberlain said police were trying to credit her with the brains to commit the perfect murder, an act she denied.

The second inquest opened in Alice Springs this month. Professor Cameron, flown out of London's bitter winter to the desert temperatures of more than a hundred degrees, was the key witness. He used slides, photographs and a videotape of a doll dressed in Azaria's clothes to show why he believed the baby's throat had been cut, possibly by a pair of scissors. The dying child, he said, had been held upright by a pair of young adult hands, hands that were soaked in blood. Mrs Chamberlain, on legal advice, has declined to allow police to take her hand-prints. Other scientists have given advice on bloodstains in the car and on a pair of scissors found in the car. Those stains, they say, have been positively identified as having come from a baby. The second inquest has been adjourned until next year. Whatever it decides happened to Azaria can be only the beginning of another chapter in the Chamberlain story. And Ayers Rock, that mysterious, mythical centre of the Australian continent, now has another legend which it will tell for evermore.

OUR MALVINAS

Paul Reynolds

As a naval task force sailed towards the South Atlantic, and even after the onset of hostilities, Argentines still believed that the conflict with Britain over the Falkland Islands could be solved by diplomatic means.

It was always fairly clear cut from here. We listened over the radio to the reports from London about the slow progress of the fleet south, and the slow progress of negotiations. And somehow one knew that eventually the talks must fail, and that Britain would make its move to regain the islands by military force. In those early days, the attitude of the Argentines was light-hearted, and a bit light-headed. They celebrated the recovery, as they always called it, of land they had always believed belonged to them, smiled at one, and said, 'Surely the British won't bother to try to get the islands back? After all, they are of no value to you any more.' One murmured vague replies, that of course, everyone hoped for a peaceful settlement, and for peace between our two countries, which after all had had such a close relationship over the years. Yet the reality was different.

I think for me the moment when reality set in was when I realized just how important the Falklands, or Malvinas, issue was in Argentina. It is very difficult for anyone who has not been here to understand the total agreement at all levels of society about Argentine rights in the matter. And so, rather quickly, it became obvious that the military government could not back down. And

I kept on reminding Argentines and Anglo-Argentines and anyone who would listen that they should not underestimate Mrs Thatcher. The personality of leaders is a factor in international crises and Argentina had clearly not learned the lessons of Mrs Thatcher's time in office. And so began the long and unreal process of negotiation. Mr Haig came down here twice, and departed with stern warnings about time running out. He, after all, was a general and he knew very well what Britain would do. But I remember even then a diplomat at the American Embassy saying that Britain would have to make a compromise eventually. Then military action multiplied. Britain regained South Georgia, imposed the blockade, sank the *Belgrano*, lost the *Sheffield*, yet still the talk was of a peaceful solution.

I remember going out into the British square with the English clock tower in the middle of it asking Argentines on their way home one evening what they thought. 'No, we don't want a war,' said two middle-aged businessmen, eyeing me rather warily. 'But no, we won't give up the islands, and no, there probably won't be a war, the politicians will sort it all out,' one said. By sorting it all out, he probably meant Britain giving up. Argentines everywhere expressed incomprehension that Britain should send the fleet. In a garden in a pleasant part of the city the roses were smelling sweetly as the middle-aged Anglo-Argentine couple told me they just could not understand the British attitude. 'Ridiculous' and 'absurd' were the common words used, though the Foreign Ministry usually added 'colonialist' or 'anachronistic'.

And now, inexorably, we have arrived at the moment when British troops have landed. Curiously the mood in Buenos Aires is not one of anger, partly because the propaganda machine has told the people Argentina will probably win, and partly because it is all still a long way from Buenos Aires. The mood is more one of sadness and resignation. It was quite remarkable, for example, how calmly everyone took the sinking of the *Belgrano*, with the loss of more than three hundred lives. One of the leading figures in the British community said he had been in close touch with the government stressing that Britons living in Argentina wanted a peaceful solution. But nothing happened, he said. And Argentines, he explained, had grown stoical over the years. They had grown so used to military rule and violence that they had learned to accept whatever happened to them. An American living in Buenos Aires had a similar, though more blunt explanation. 'They just don't care,' he said, 'they accepted the disappearance of fifteen thousand people here during the war against terrorism, so a few hundred more doesn't matter, they are just interested in self-preservation.'

And it is true that in Buenos Aires the restaurants are still busy in spite of the war and the economic crisis, and on the night the UN talks failed there was a lively fashion show in a leading hotel in town. Argentina, of course, will fight for the islands, but the private talk among the military, I have learned, is that Britain will probably get them back. Argentina will then try to mount its own blockade, and I have a feeling that the people may accept all this much as they have accepted so much over the years, and that it will be put down to big-power bullying.

STREET CHILDREN

Harold Briley

RIO DE JANEIRO, FEBRUARY 1983

While millions of dollars were being spent on Rio's annual carnival, Brazil's millions of poor, and their children, continued their struggle for survival.

As the samba bands beat out their frenetic rhythm and Brazil's bikini-clad beauties soak up the sunshine, I often watch a fifteen-year-old crippled boy drag himself along Rio de Janeiro's famous Ipanema Beach, his body pitifully deformed, his useless legs trailing in the sand behind him. At other times, I have seen him propelling himself along the main shopping centre on a skate-board, his only form of transport. He cannot afford a wheelchair. He is one of Brazil's fifty million unfortunates, what are known as 'marginalized' children. That is the social workers' word for children whose families are unable to feed, clothe or educate them, or who exist totally alone. Many live in abject poverty, in subhuman shanty-towns called *'favelas'*, the notorious slums of Brazil; frightening, festering areas of disease, destitution and uncontrolled crime. Their shacks, made of driftwood and other abandoned materials, give them a roof over their heads. Millions of the marginalized children do not even have that. They are known as *'Meninos da rua'*, 'street children', who bed down at night on the pavement or in doorways. Millions of Brazil's children are forced to take to the streets or the fields to work by the time they are five years old. One social worker told me,

'They go from babies to workers. They never know childhood or learn to play. They never have a chance to develop their minds.'

Child labour in Brazil is common, and for those who have reached the age of fourteen it is legal, with laws allegedly providing strict safeguards, guaranteeing a minimum wage, health care and other benefits and a safe place to work. In practice it does not happen, as you find when you look at individual cases. There is a three-year-old girl who goes into the streets of São Paulo's flower market each night at ten o'clock to sell flowers because her mother has no other way to get money for food. The little girl earns on average £2 a week. There are many worse jobs. São Paulo appears from its skyscrapers and bustling activity to be one of the world's most modern, richest cities. In the shadows of those skyscrapers children are working in worse conditions now than in Charles Dickens' London of the last century. Many of them are employed in glass-making factories, toiling long hours, six and a half days a week in one-hundred-degree heat, often in windowless buildings. The children are classed as apprentices and get only half pay. Because they start work so young, doctors say they more easily suffer lung disease, like silicosis from sucking in silicon as they blow glass vases and other objects into shape.

A few miles south of São Paulo lies a shabby brick-making town where whole families start work at three o'clock in the morning. Eight-year-olds help their parents mix the tough clay with water, fill the moulds and put them in the oven. They get paid, as a family, for every thousand bricks they make, so they keep their 6 a.m. coffee break very brief.

The hungry homeless street kids get caught up in crime and violence. Street workers in São Paulo were blamed in one year for twenty-five thousand criminal acts and for murdering two thousand people. They are estimated to possess as many as ten thousand firearms. When the youngsters get involved, they find it is dangerous to break away because they pose a threat to their former partners. Many of Brazil's homeless and unemployed are migrant workers forced to trek into the cities from an impoverished drought-stricken countryside. Others stay on the land, among them five- and six-year-olds who start work at dawn, picking coffee beans, collecting cotton and cutting sugar cane.

Many girls who should be at school find work as maids doing all the chores for middle- and upper-class families. Some are treated well, others almost like slaves, sleeping in tiny rooms without windows, allowed no visitors or telephone calls. But they are better off than the child prostitutes. In the northern Amazon city ironically called Belém, Portuguese for Bethlehem, there are as many as fifteen thousand child prostitutes. Some can be found in luxurious brothels, some wandering the streets and the bars, others established in shabby motels. They perform their services for the many skilled workers building roads, dams and other projects of Brazil's hectic industrialization, which has transformed large areas of the country in what a few years ago they called its 'economic miracle', which is now transformed into a debt-ridden nightmare.

Poorer families migrating from the rural regions have no obvious means of survival so small girls of twelve and upwards find that it is the only way they know of getting money. One priest who tries to save them said, 'They don't know they are prostitutes. Just as their brothers sell peanuts, they sell their bodies.' A social worker concerned with child welfare said, 'The Brazilian child is not working for self-realization but as sole supporter of broken or destitute families. The saddest part is that the family is the last to protest against the exploitation of their own children.' The child prostitute in the Amazon is a world away from the smart-suited bankers in their plush offices poring over the huge foreign debt built up by Brazil, Mexico and so many other nations, but it is all connected. It is a graphic illustration of the gap between North and South, the developed and the developing world, the rich and the poor.

FAMINE

Mike Wooldridge

ADDIS ABABA, OCTOBER 1984

Thousands and thousands of Ethiopians died of hunger in a tragedy that some said was avoidable.

On only one other occasion in my life have I seen anything quite like the tragedy I witnessed last weekend. This was when I saw bodies being pulled out of the rubble after the earthquake at Tabas in Iran six years ago. But even though the aftermath of the earthquake was horrific, and many people in the area were denouncing the Shah's regime for not having built quake-proof houses in Tabas, you felt that it was essentially an unavoidable disaster and that the high death toll was probably inevitable. No one, I think, could say the same about the ninety to a hundred deaths occuring every day at Korem in northern Ethiopia and the unknown number of people dying of starvation in the country-side, unrecorded by Ethiopian officials and the media.

A relief worker based in Addis Ababa, who last week paid his first visit to Korem since the death toll there rose so alarmingly in September, felt that an entirely avoidable disaster was taking place. He is right, but to have prevented it happening would probably have required more foresight and political will than either the Ethiopian or foreign governments have shown so far, and perhaps above all else an end to the wars being fought over some of the most drought-stricken terrain. There are signs now that both Ethiopia and the countries in the best position to give substantial help are taking significant steps to prevent the disaster reaching an even bigger scale, such as the Ethiopian Air Force ferrying grain with its Soviet-supplied Antonovs fuelled by the United States. But at the same time aid officials say so many people are now completely destitute, with no access to food supplies, that the situation is bound to get worse before it gets better.

It will be a miracle if Melkamu Getahun survives this famine. He is an eight-year-old boy I met in Korem. Unlike others who grabbed at your clothes to plead with you to give them some food or help them get medical attention, Melkamu's father simply came and stood in front of me with his son and gestured to me to look at him. He was extremely thin, with his ribs barely covered with skin. He wore just a flimsy cotton shirt for protection against the burning daytime sun and the chill nights. He looked as if all life had already been drained out of him. Through an interpreter, Melkamu's father told me he had harvested no crops for three years and the family had survived by gradually selling all their belongings to buy food. When they had virtually ran out of things to sell, they left their home and walked to the relief shelters at Korem, in the hope of finding a place in a shelter and some food. But the shelters and the rows of plastic tents were full and, he said, they had not been given any food. His wife and one of his sons had already died. The day before he had sold his vest to buy something for Melkamu and himself to eat. The surprising thing was that he related all this with evident sorrow but with little sign of anger, and I found this with many of the other men I talked to. It is the new arrivals who tend to agitate most for food, clothing and shelter, even demanding that the hard-pressed local officials send off messages to their superiors for more supplies that are probably not available; those who have been there longer tend to be more fatalistic. Relief workers say many of the men go to great lengths to feed their families before themselves, and the psychological strain of doing this is showing. Men in their twenties and thirties would normally be the last to die in a famine in Africa, but they are dying in this one.

The Ethiopian authorities face a genuine dilemma over the tens of thousands of people gathering in the roadside towns like Korem: the more food they send into such towns, the more people arrive, and the more chance there is of epidemics such as measles, which has killed many children in the past few months. The solution, everyone agrees, is to get food out to people in their villages. In some areas the mountainous terrain makes it very difficult to do that; in Tigre, where one and a half million people are said to be short of food, that would clearly mean reaching an agreement with the rebels that they would not interfere with food sent from government-controlled areas.

The tragedy now taking place in Ethiopia has a profound effect on anyone who sees it at first hand, however fleetingly. I asked a Church worker how he coped day in, day out with seeing so many people starve to death. All you can do, he said, is to distribute what food there is as widely as possible and help those who are dying to do so with a little dignity, even on the distinctly undignified deathbed of a piece of cardboard on the floor of an overcrowded relief shelter.

KENYAN ROADS

Mike Wooldridge

NAIROBI, JANUARY 1985

The reckless drivers of Kenya's matatus, *or communal taxis, were blamed for the country's huge number of road accidents and deaths.*

You are driving cautiously along one of the roads leading from the centre of Nairobi out to the sprawling suburbs, watching for deadly potholes, when suddenly in your mirror there is a Peugeot or Japanese pick-up right on your tail. The next moment it is overtaking you, probably swaying from side to side, the enclosed passenger compartment on the back jammed with people and sitting low on the rear axle, with suitcases, sacks of maize, bunches of bananas, even bicycles and chickens, perched precariously on the roof. Once it has passed you, likely as not the driver's young assistant – known as the turnboy – will open the back door and, standing on the tailboard, swing one leg to the left and stab a finger towards the verge. It is as well for the following driver to know what this gesture means, for suddenly the pick-up will lurch to a halt, not necessarily pulling in to the side of the road, and two of the passengers will squeeze their way out to be replaced perhaps by three or four people waiting at the roadside – for the *matatu* principle is that 'there is always room for one more passenger'. That is typical *matatu* driving, encouraged by the fact that many of the drivers have to hand over a fixed amount of money at the end of the day to the owner of the vehicle, and any earnings above that are for the driver and the turnboy to share. So the object is to make as many trips in a day as possible as quickly as possible, and with as many passengers as possible.

Matatus have in the past twenty-five years become a Kenyan institution, comparable to the famous mammy wagons of West Africa. Like the mammy wagons, many *matatus* now have hand-painted slogans on them ranging from the functional *Machakos Express* to the all too appropriate *See You in Heaven. Matatus* appeared first in the Nairobi area, often private cars, sometimes disused ambulances, carrying passengers quite illegally for three pennies or ten-cent pieces a time – *matatu* means three in the local Kikuyu language. The *matatu* operators played a cat-and-mouse game with the law until, in 1973, President Jomo Kenyatta formally exempted them from the need to have a public service vehicle licence. With buses unable to meet the ever-growing demand for public road transport, the *matatus* have flourished. There are now estimated to be thirty-five thousand of them, mostly operating in and around towns but some plying routes of two hundred miles or more. They carry more than two hundred thousand people every day in the Nairobi area. People move house in them, and they are frequently used as hearses to transport a body from Nairobi to the homeland for burial. But Kenyans have a love-hate relationship with the *matatus*. It is common to read in the local newspapers of horrifying accidents involving *matatus* which have defective steering or brakes, which are simply being driven too fast. I have one paper in front of me which reports that seventeen people died on the spot when two speeding *matatus* collided head-on in western Kenya, and several others died later in hospital. Letters to the papers complain about the recklessness of *matatu* drivers; about turnboys who demand extra fares or do not give any change, about gangs of thugs who rob *matatu* passengers at night. One woman who was robbed of all her money and the keys of her house received little sympathy from the secretary of the *matatu* owners' association. What could she have been doing out at that hour of the night? he asked.

Now the government has decided that all *matatus* must have a public service vehicle licence, which means they have to be tested for roadworthiness, and their drivers must be at least twenty-four and have four years' driving experience. The owners protested vigorously: they said the *matatu* industry would collapse and seventy thousand people would be thrown out of work. But there do not seem to be many fewer *matatus* on the road, and most are already sporting the sign PSV, with M for *matatu* in brackets. Public reaction has been favourable, though some people have said it is unfair to deprive younger drivers of a job. And one newspaper warned recently that when the present crackdown has eased and it is left to individual police officers to enforce the new law, the drivers know that a modest bribe can be enough to prevent prosecution. In contrast, a recent letter praised a *matatu* driver who leapt out of his vehicle to put out a fire in a car and then sped off without waiting to be thanked. And a well-known rally driver once paid tribute to the *matatu* men's potential as safari rally competitors.

Although *matatus* are involved in more than their share of fatal accidents, many others have to accept blame for the carnage on Kenya's roads. I have seen regular buses driven just as recklessly; it is common for slow vehicles to hog the fast lane of dual carriageways; and broken-down vehicles are often left where they can easily cause accidents. In the rural areas small children may have been taught everything about looking after cattle but little about crossing roads. It has been calculated that in Africa more people aged between five and forty-five die in road accidents than from any disease. Perhaps the only thing Kenya can take comfort from is that it is three times as bad in Nigeria.

AFTER HEYSEL

Paul Reynolds

BRUSSELS, JUNE 1985

The culmination of the 1985 football season, the European Cup Final between Liverpool and Juventus of Italy, ended in tragedy when a wall collapsed after a charge by British fans. More than forty people, mainly Italians and Belgians, lost their lives.

It has not been a good time to be British in Brussels: the British community here has learned something about the nature of society's collective responsibility for uncivilized behaviour. We have had an inkling of how decent Germans must have been feeling for the past forty years. It is not pleasant to be regarded as outcasts, because what this event has brought home is surely that football hooliganism can no longer simply be dismissed as the work of a few. Something is rotten in the state of Britain. That, sadly, is the view in Brussels.

As the first bodies left the military hospital on their way back to Italy, I was speaking to an Italian who was standing on the pavement watching the solemn convoy go by. He had lived in Brussels for twenty-three years. 'What a sad business,' he said, 'for Britain, a country which once civilized the world.' That same sentiment came to me as I walked through the Grand Place, the heart of the old city of Brussels, where just a few months ago the people of Brussels, and I mean the ordinary people, the people who were painted by the Flemish masters centuries ago, cheered and clapped as the veterans of the Welsh Guards marched into the square to celebrate the fortieth anniversary of the liberation of the city. Then it was warmth and welcome; now all the British are tainted with poison and English voices attract nervous looks in restaurants and on the street. One British resident rang to say she had spoken French to avoid being identified. The strength of feeling on the continent against the return of British football crowds is overwhelming. The owner of a restaurant in the centre of town said people had been revolted. She had not slept that night after learning that one of the Juventus supporters who had lunch in her own restaurant obtained a ticket to Section Z on the black market and had been killed.

It was in this kind of personal way that everyone in the city has been touched to some degree. For me the horror was brought home when I heard the account of an English friend who had been in Section Z with his eleven-year-old son. It had originally been my intention to be there with mine as well. The boys had been classmates at school in Brussels. His son had come over from England and was festooned with Liverpool colours. Immediately they arrived on the terraces they knew there was trouble. They began to feel the pressure of the crowd pushing against them as Section Z fell back in the face of the onslaught. Missiles rained through the air.

For five minutes, the friend said, he felt he might die and worse, that he would cause the death of the weeping child beside him. Somehow they scrambled out and went straight home. And that was supposed to be a football match. What has compounded the anguish of the Belgians has been a realization that their capital city, the centre of the Common Market and NATO, the great crossroads of the new Europe, had failed in its organization. The Belgian self-blame has sometimes even overcome their revulsion of the British. 'Gentlemen,' one newspaper announced, 'you have an account to render.' I thought this meant us but no, it was a message for the local authorities. The sight on television of three armed riot police retreating before young hooligans has simply added to the sense of local outrage, for when a country is invaded

– and that surely is not too strong a word in this context – then the forces which are supposed to defend the country are inevitably criticized.

And yet it would be wrong to divert attention in any way from the behaviour of the Liverpool crowd. After the match, after the riots and the deaths, a small group of Liverpool supporters were running past a parked police car. Quite casually and without a murmur they set about trying to turn it over. Having failed, quite casually and without a murmur they left and rushed on. There are some who have drawn a link between this violence and the British attitude to Europe generally. Over here they have never felt we have been at ease in Europe and now some of us are being kept out; even school teams are kept out of the country we liberated twice. That indeed shows how shame has fallen upon us.

1986–1995

AFGHAN FIGHTERS

Aernout van Lynden

KABUL, JUNE 1987

Soviet troops occupying Afghanistan were continually harried by groups of mujahidin Muslim fighters.

Going into Afghanistan with the mujahidin one can be certain of just one thing: that one is going to walk sometimes for stretches of fourteen to sixteen hours up and down steep mountain paths the likes of which I have never seen before. Apart from that, well, one is in the hands of Afghans so nothing is fixed or certain. The whole enterprise begins in Peshawar in neighbouring Pakistan. There in the lively and colourful bazaars one indulges in a form of secret fancy dress more commonly linked with out-of-date spy novels. Having collected an assortment of Afghan clothes, large baggy pyjama-type trousers, long shirt, skullcap, turban, waistcoat and the blanket the Afghans always carry with them, the next stage is to find a mujahidin group willing to take you with them. I successfully negotiated with an English-speaking commander of one of the Hezbi Islami factions. Three days later we were off.

Travelling to the border with a busload of mujahidin I felt more than normally conspicuous in, for me, new and therefore uncomfortable clothes. But we got past each police checkpoint without a hitch. For the next six days we walked, for how long or for how far was never certain. When Afghans say something is near, beware. It most probably entails a one and a half hour walk at a pace most Westerners would not even dream of, and we had far to go. But if the endless walking is, to say the least, a morale-breaking venture, the evenings make up for it. Then one sees the Afghans at their best. Ear to ear smiles transform their dark bearded features as they welcome you into their homes and, however poor, offer you a meal, pot after pot of green tea and a rug on which to rest the night.

It has always seemed one of the strange paradoxes of life to me that it is always the poor who are hospitable and not the rich, and this is certainly the case in Afghanistan. During the day, one is confronted by more unpleasant things. In the first three days we passed hundreds of Afghans fleeing their war-torn country for the safety of United Nations rations and a tent in Pakistan. They make a pathetic and tragic sight. After six days of walking, we finally reached the stronghold of one faction, whose young commander was just planning an ambush on the important stretch of road linking the capital Kabul to Jalalabad and further to the east, to Pakistan. His favoured site for the ambush was in the mountains which, although rising steeply, give plentiful cover for a quick getaway in case of any intervention by Soviet helicopter gunships. The Russians, having been hit there time and again, have simply strewn the area with anti-personnel mines. A more open and dangerous position is chosen. We walk there, now seventy men strong, in the late afternoon and evening. The last two hours on the road itself. A weird sensation, particularly if one keeps in mind the almost jovial air of the mujahidin. If it was not for the arms, more modern and plentiful than in the past, it would have been hard to imagine that this was anything other than some friendly midnight hike.

How deadly serious it all is becomes clear in some five minutes the next afternoon. Within that time anti-tank rockets home in with impressive accuracy on a small Soviet convoy of two armoured patrol cars and two lorries and the peaceful gorge is filled with a dense cloud of black smoke. The mujahidin are gone as quickly as they came and that includes the group of seven I am travelling with. Exalted by the success of the attack and the killing of some twelve to fourteen Russians, the Afghans rush off over the bare mountains as fast as their feet can carry them. They know that if they hang about the chances are the one Soviet weapon they are truly frightened of, and near impotent in fighting against, will descend upon them. But that afternoon the helicopter gunships stayed away and all that rests is their pleasure in the telling of their victory to their hosts later that evening.

KHOMEINI'S BURIAL

Alex Brodie

TEHRAN, JUNE 1989

Huge crowds paying their last respects to Ayatollah Khomeini, the architect of the Iranian revolution, took to the streets of the capital on the day he was buried.

The millions who swamped Tehran on Tuesday were almost to a man and woman dressed in black. From the air it appeared as if a black lake in the foothills of the mountains had disgorged into rivers which flowed south through the city of Tehran to a black sea fifteen miles away. The innumerable mourners poured out of the hundreds of acres of waste ground where the Ayatollah's body had lain in state, through the streets of the city to the Behesht-e-zahra graveyard where the Ayatollah was to be buried.

It was not a stately progress. There was no pomp and circumstance, and the austere old man who ruled Iran for a decade of turbulent, continuing revolution died and was buried as he had lived, in a manner which contrasted starkly with the flamboyance and profligacy of the ruler who came before him – the Shah. The body of Ayatollah Khomeini lay in state in the middle of dust and gravel, a half-built tower block and an electricity sub-station. The refrigerated glass of the Perspex case, in which the body lay, was raised above the waste ground, which will now become the capital's new prayer ground, on a pile of cargo containers and guarded not by a braided palace guard but by members of the green-fatigued bearded or unshaven Revolutionary Guard corps, created by Khomeini to be a ubiquitous presence throughout the life of the new Iran, to make permanent his revolution and to police the morals and behaviour of his flock.

The body was carried from the prayer ground on a simple wooden structure and manhandled into a refrigerated lorry which was then swamped by the frantic crowd. The Ayatollah's son, Ahmed, had to be carried out, passed from hand to hand across the heads of the throng. It would have taken days for the lorry to reach the cemetery had not a helicopter been brought down to spread the mourners and to airlift the body. But when the helicopter landed at the cemetery those waiting, in a frenzy, dragged the body out. It was enveloped in the crowd and fell to the ground; hastily retrieved, it was flown away. Later, this time encased in a metal box, the sort in which air cargo is carried, the body was brought back and the Revolutionary Guard escort just managed to take out the remains of Ayatollah Khomeini and partly bury him in a simple hole in the ground, before the frenzied mourners broke through and, howling in anguish, fell on the grave. A cargo container was winched in and placed over the grave to protect it.

Those who made up the sea of black which took over the capital were largely the poor of the slums and the villages; those who see the black-turbaned white-bearded Ayatollah as a holy man. To the embattled middle class, Khomeini's revolution is anathema, but even those who did not mourn the passing of the Ayatollah watched riveted on their television screen at home as the whole bizarre spectacle unfolded. 'Iranians love mourning,' said one, 'all our main religious holidays are mourning days.' But no matter how much he tried to make light of it, he knew that what he was seeing was evidence of the hold Ayatollah Khomeini had over the poor and ill-educated. No matter how much they want to, few of his enemies believe the Ayatollah's revolution will crumble. The funeral showed them that, as it was surely intended to.

TIENANMEN MASSACRE

James Miles

PEKING, JUNE 1989

An increasingly popular demonstration by students and others calling for democratic rights in China was broken up by troops with tanks. There was heavy loss of life.

At about two o'clock on Sunday morning I stood at an intersection about three miles west of Tienanmen Square. The night sky was lit by flames leaping from buses set up as barricades by residents in a futile attempt to keep out the army. Armoured vehicles had tossed aside the roadblocks and in the smoke and glare, truckload after truckload of soldiers passed in front of me. The air was filled with the sound of wailing sirens as ambulances raced up to the intersection to carry away the dead and wounded. Hundreds of people were milling around watching in horror and amazement, some of them young, educated people; men and women came up to me almost in tears and begged me to tell the world what was happening, and as we spoke the shooting began again about two hundred yards away, bursts of automatic gunfire. Terrified bystanders scattered and crouched by the roadside and the endless convoy of trucks kept moving towards Tienanmen Square. Others witnessed more horrific scenes. One of my colleagues watched as soldiers dashed in front of lines of advancing troops and sprayed unarmed civilians with bullets. Other witnesses spoke of tanks crushing students to death as they rolled into Tienanmen Square. Of angry crowds murdering and then burning the bodies of stray soldiers.

The death toll of that Saturday night and Sunday morning may never be known but it is almost certainly in the thousands, a massacre on a scale almost unprecedented since the Communists came to power forty years ago. The only comparable action has been in regions inhabited by ethnic minorities, such as Tibet. Not a single Peking resident I have met ever seriously expected the army to suppress its own race with such ruthlessness. None believed that Chinese leaders would resort to the methods of the Maoist era. Indeed before the army moved in many believed that people power had won, that the military and the leadership were paralysed in the face of peaceful mass defiance. Only about ten days before the soldiers came in, huge crowds of people were pouring on to the streets of Peking in a triumphant mood, sensing, it seemed, that the tide of hatred against the regime was unstoppable and that the forces of moderation would be victorious. Even after the army action a week ago, for a couple of desperate days, crowds continued to gather in the streets to taunt the troops and set fire to vehicles, but bullets continued to cut them down and now all resistance has been stamped out. Peking is under complete military control. Residents who for a few delirious weeks have enjoyed almost a free rein in the city are now subdued, shocked and frightened. The last remaining traces of their protest are being wiped out. Anti-government posters have been stripped from walls and burned-out vehicles towed away. The campuses are almost deserted, with most students having fled or left the city to spread news of the massacre. On one campus a wreath remains at the foot of a monument; on it are the words *The debt of blood will be repaid with blood*, but few expect that revenge is close at hand.

There are fears now that a new reign of terror is about to be launched with purges and widespread arrests. But if there is a ray of hope for the people of Peking, it is that the leadership can only now rule by force. In the traditional Chinese view, that means that it has lost the mandate of heaven and its days are numbered. When the army eventually eases its control, new unrest is almost certain to erupt with even greater force and in the meantime passive resistance will continue. Students and intellectuals will redouble their efforts to leave the country. Those who remain are unlikely to devote their talents to blazing new trails in the country's reforms, knowing now how dangerous it can be to step out of line. Workers in state-run industries, already disillusioned with the reforms because of low wages, rapid price increases and widespread corruption, are likely to become even more half-hearted in their labours. Similarly with government officials, many of whom took part in the demonstrations, and among the forty eight million members of the Communist Party there are bound to be many who, if not expelled, will abandon whatever faith they had in the system. Among foreigners resident here, business-men and diplomats, goodwill towards the regime has all but evaporated.

The sense built up over the past ten years that the Chinese leadership was becoming increasingly responsive to the demands of its own people and those of the international community has now been destroyed. The recent events have partially lifted the veil on the working of the leadership, revealing a system as much determined by the whims of individuals and factional struggles as it was before reforms began. The problem for the Chinese people is that there is no institution they can rely upon to check the abuse of power. If there is resistance in the army to methods of control in Peking, it appears at the moment to be weak. All of the seven military regions have expressed, on paper at least, their support for the army intervention. One institution that might have saved the day is the National People's Congress, China's equivalent of a parliament. The Congress has generally been little more than a rubber stamp but in the last two or three years it had become the scene of increasingly lively, and to the leadership embarrassing, debate. Students had hoped that the Congress standing committee due to meet later this month would challenge the legality of martial law. The chairman of the Congress, Mr Wan Lee, was once regarded by many students as a potential hero who could swing the balance in favour of moderates in the leadership but now Mr Wan has appeared on national television along with Deng Xiao Ping and other hardline leaders, congratulating the army for its heroic efforts last weekend. The news media might have been another ally in the search for moderation but newspapers and broadcasting networks have now been brought thoroughly under control. Over and over again television has shown carefully edited footage of the events of last weekend, designed to prove that the army showed the utmost restraint in the face of fierce onslaughts from counter-revolutionary rebels. In a spine-chilling distortion of the truth, army officers have been telling the nation that no one was killed at Tienanmen Square and that the people of Peking were grateful for the army action. Footage has been shown of people clapping as tanks rumbled past or offering food and drinks to soldiers. The propaganda campaign may well succeed in fooling, or at least confusing, some Chinese but, in Peking at least, the tragedy will never be forgotten.

CURTAIN DOWN

Ben Bradshaw

BERLIN, OCTOBER 1989

As East German President Erich Honecker prepared to welcome his Russian counterpart, Mikhail Gorbachev, to Berlin, trainloads of East Germans fled to the West as Hungary and Poland relaxed their border controls. The Iron Curtain was down.

It is quite difficult for an Englishman to understand the emotions that were unleashed on Hof's railway station in the early hours of Sunday morning. We do not have a minefield and fences running down the middle of our country. We do not have a wall cutting our former capital in half. I think anyone would have been moved by the scenes that changed a cold, dank, autumnal Sunday in a north Bavarian town into a world event. Train after train arrived to tumultuous applause; those on board, men and women, weeping copious tears of joy and relief. They had arrived at last. Some of them had waited years; had had repeated applications to leave turned down. Others had jumped on the bandwagon at the last minute. They had heard what was about to happen and they had taken their chance.

Going or staying is a dilemma that enters the minds of even the most steadfast East Germans. The difference is usually they do not have a choice. It was not just the arrivals at Hof who wore their emotions on their sleeves. The local people turned out in their hundreds to welcome them; stout men and women in their Sunday best, twice or three times the average age of those getting off the trains, wept as they clapped. 'These are our people, free at last,' they said.

And still the exodus goes on. The movement over the border between Hungary and Austria continues and what many people forget is that those leaving East Germany legally this year will number more than at any time since 1961 and the building of the Berlin Wall. And here of course is the crunch: the Berlin Wall did its job; so successfully that many commentators say East Germany only really began after its construction. It was after 1961 that the country managed to establish some form of stability. Its doctors and engineers were not running off to the West. It became the showpiece of the Eastern Bloc, tenth in the World Bank league of international economies. Its citizens enjoyed – as they still do enjoy – the highest standard of living in the Communist world. Then came the longed-for international recognition in the early seventies, when Western countries, apart from West Germany, established embassies in East Berlin. So, little East Germany with its population of just over sixteen million, proud of its Prussian and Saxon ancestry, flourished in relative terms.

But a concerted effort by its government to cultivate some kind of East German national consciousness failed. For most East Germans their condition remained an artificial one. They did not compare their lives with those of the Poles, Czechoslovaks or Russians, but with those of their German cousins in the West; cousins who drove a BMW and took three foreign holidays a year in countries of their choice.

Many of those leaving East Germany at the moment profess to be doing so for political reasons. There is no reason to doubt them. But for others the incentive is more basic. One forty-year-old arrival in Hof told me: 'I've been working my guts out for twenty years and what have I got to show for it – a Lada.' East Germany has survived by keeping its people in. It has been able to do so because it was a part of a solid political and military bloc in a divided world, and in which its allies played ball. But in rapidly changing central Europe they, Hungary and Poland at least, are no longer willing to do so. By tearing down its border fence with Austria and saying East Germans could come and go as they please, Hungary in effect tore down the Berlin Wall.

It must not be assumed that all East Germans want to go west. Many do not. Among them are the leaders of the numerous opposition groups to have sprung up in response to the country's current difficulties. By and large these people want to maintain Socialism in one form or another and the thought of being swallowed up by West Germany, with problems of unemployment, homelessness and drug abuse, fills them with horror. But they will tell you that every day longer that their government resists reforms, more people who essentially think as they do will give up and say, 'To hell with it, we would be better under rule from Bonn.' These are the people who could be East Germany's hope for the future, but there is no sign of the government entering a dialogue with them. Those arriving at Hof say it is too late anyway. They even report people lining the route of the trains in East Germany waving and clapping and holding placards saying: 'We're coming soon.'

So spare a thought for Mr Honecker, as he and his ageing Politburo colleagues try to raise a smile later this week. East Germany's seventy-seven-year-old leader suffered and was imprisoned under the Nazis. He devoted the rest of his life to building the first state of workers and peasants on German soil, only to be abandoned by their children and told by those who stayed they have had enough. What can the little man from the Saarland do? If he continues to resist reform, the mood of the people, dark enough as it is, will only get worse. But if he grasps the nettle and does what everyone, save his own ideological advisers, is telling him to do, what will become of East Germany? How could it open its borders and introduce free market structures but maintain its separateness from West Germany? As one senior East German politician recently put it: 'If we give up Socialism, we give up our reason to exist.'

As the world asks itself how many more birthdays East Germany can look forward to, I cannot help wondering what Mr Honecker really feels about the man from Moscow who will be sharing the podium with him in a few days' time. For all the bombast and rhetoric fired in the direction of the imperialist West during the current crisis, it is Mr Gorbachev, of course, who is really to blame for East Germany's predicament. It is his *glasnost* and *perestroika* that have brought the trouble. One wonders what he must be thinking, as the Soviet Union's most docile and reliable ally becomes suddenly a hotbed of opposition and unrest.

NIGHTMARE'S END

Mark Brayne

BUCHAREST, JANUARY 1990

The Ceausescu dictatorship in Romania crumbled quickly and violently.

For someone like me, brought up in the cosy liberal traditions of post-war British consensus, it is difficult to conceive of absolute right or absolute wrong. There are, after all, two sides to every argument, or are there? As the door closes on forty years of Communism in Eastern Europe, I am not so sure. For what the people of Romania have just experienced has been to my mind a confrontation between the power of good and that of absolute, indeed biblical, evil. What Nicolae Ceausescu and his wife Elena unleashed on their people has few precedents in history: the impoverishment of a nation and finally the slaughter by machine-gun of thousands of innocents, a killing far greater in scale even than that of Tienanmen Square in China last June.

Even for someone who does not believe in political violence, it is difficult not to share the view of so many Romanians that Ceausescu was evil and that with his security police still fighting the people to free him, there was, last Christmas Day, no alternative to his execution. The choice for Romania was absolute and at the start of the new decade the people of this extraordinary, brave nation have taken a stand as few before them for decency and justice and against an odious dictatorship. Europe, both East and West, may consider itself in Romania's debt.

As you recover from your peaceful British Christmas and

New Year with family and friends, that may all sound a trifle emotional, perhaps a little over the top. But to have been with the people of Romania these past ten days as they have stood, and died, as one, has been the most powerful experience in many lives here. A few particularly uplifting incidents stand out: dinner with new friends, for example, on Christmas night as it was announced that the Ceausescus had been executed. My host stood to toast the end of the nightmare. In the Romanian tradition we first tipped a little of our wine onto the floor to remember the dead. It was an intensely emotional moment. On New Year's Eve, as midnight approached, the radio and television of now-free Romania fell silent for one minute, remembering the martyrs of Timisoara, Bucharest, Sibiu and of so many other cities. At one of the many, many parties of celebration in Bucharest, men and women alike were convulsed with sobs as they hugged and kissed to welcome in the new decade.

Another new friend, a waiter here at my hotel, was insistent that I visit his family and meet the son and the daughter of whom he was so terribly proud. Never before had he dared invite a foreigner to his home. The Securitate, the secret police, would have interrogated him and stripped him of work. Once again, as we toasted Romania's new freedom, it was all we could do to hold back the tears.

I tell these stories because what Romania has experienced is something more fundamental even than the revolutions of the past month in Czechoslovakia, in East Germany and in Poland. Here, with the overthrow of Ceausescu and one of the most vicious dictatorships the world has ever known, Communism is, in a word, dead. There are no compromises to be made in Romania with an apparatus resisting the loss of its power and privilege. There is no party to be renamed; that has been completely destroyed. Romania can, in other words, set about building a genuine liberal democracy with concessions to no one. In the economy too, the prospects for Romania look possibly more promising than for any other nation in Eastern Europe.

Obsessed with independence, the dead dictator starved the people but he paid back all debts to the West. Unlike for Poland and Hungary and even for East Germany, there will be few reservations in the West about credit for Romania. And for all the horror of the Ceausescu years, this country has natural resources and scenery and fertile agricultural soil that could make it a land of great richness.

The people of Romania, flushed with the victory of their revolution, certainly seem determined to make that happen. For the speed with which the veneer of totalitarianism has been stripped away is difficult to believe, but it has revealed a mature, cantankerous no doubt, but self-aware society, ready to assume responsibility for its own destiny. There will be many problems, of course. The exercise of democracy and freedom, as so many Romanians have been telling us, cannot be learned overnight and there are strains already very plain between the ordinary people who have suffered so terribly and those mostly decent men and women who made their compromises with the old regime. But ultimately the emperor Ceausescu was seen to have no clothes and the instant the people in their desperation were willing, like the little boy in the fairy-tale, to stand up and say so and not flinch even when gunned down and crushed by the armoured might of the Securitate, the nightmare was over. In Romania, the people, with the help of their army, have been victorious. In China last spring, after the comparable euphoria of Tienanmen Square in May, the army sided with the oppressors. From Pyongyang and Peking to the capitals of Africa and Latin America, the message of Romania's revolution should make dictators around the world sleep a little less easy in their beds.

DOE'S DEATH

Elizabeth Blunt

MONROVIA, SEPTEMBER 1990

As Liberia's rebel factions continued fighting for dominance of the country, the country's President, Samuel Doe, was captured and killed.

For months Liberians had talked of little else; if Doe would go and when Doe would go. Everyone had a different scenario: he would finally lose his nerve and beg the Americans to helicopter him out; he would leave Monrovia for his home village and make a last stand among his own people; or perhaps he would stay until he went down in the flames of his bunker, the Executive Mansion. What no one ever thought to imagine was the way that President Doe did meet his end – being carried off from under the noses of an international peace-keeping force in a hail of bullets.

By the beginning of September, the situation in Liberia had reached one of its periodic states of uneasy equilibrium. Rebel leader Charles Taylor and his men had taken most of the countryside, but not the seat of government, where Doe was still clinging on, or the port area of Monrovia, which was held by a rival rebel faction. Five West African countries had tried to break the stalemate by sending in a joint force with a mandate to negotiate and maintain a ceasefire, and to use it to bring in an interim government which would hold the ring until elections could be held.

The peace-keeping force worked slowly, but two weeks after it landed it had made some modest progress. Those men of the

239

rebels in the port area – Prince Johnson's faction – had agreed a ceasefire and West African troops had gradually deployed in their area, despite harassment by Charles Taylor's forces. For what was left of the civilian population of Monrovia, there was now a little space in which they could move fairly safely.

But the city was a sad sight. Past the bullet-holed buildings and the wrecked cars, endless lines of thin, weary people trekked to and fro all day long, searching for food. The city was under siege; no ship had come in since July and no produce from the countryside could get into town. Liberians basically live on rice, and rice had finally run out. Now there was nothing except boiled wild greens and whatever could be stolen from the port. One day street vendors might have boiled sweets, another day it would be mayonnaise. The mayonnaise is sold by the tablespoonful; it is a common sight to see customers licking their spoons just to stay their hunger.

It was at this point that President Doe, who had not been seen out since July, took it into his head to visit the peace-keeping force in its port headquarters. He swept in with a large entourage – ministers, television cameramen and a heavily armed guard – and he went up to see the force commander, General Quainoo. But ten minutes later another line of jeeps burst into the port, this time carrying the rebel commander Prince Johnson and his young fighters, flaunting scarlet T-shirts and curly permed wigs, and armed with every conceivable kind of weapon. Members of the rebel group swear that they did not come to the port to kill the President. But when he arrived unexpectedly, on what they thought was their territory, the opportunity was too good to miss.

Soon there was a full-scale row going on between the two groups; voices were rising and guns were being cocked. Prince Johnson himself, flamboyant and irascible, was stamping about shouting and raving as officers from the peace-keeping force tried to calm him. Then he went to the window and shouted: 'Men! Open fire! Open fire!' And the gun battle began.

At least from inside the force headquarters it certainly sounded like a battle, a battle fought at close quarters with rifles, machine-guns, grenades and even anti-aircraft guns. For an hour and a half the only sound apart from the gunfire was the begging and pleading of officers from the peace-keeping force trying to stop the carnage. For, in reality, it was less a battle than a massacre, as the rebels mowed down the President's people, chased them into port buildings and machine-gunned them where they were hiding.

When they finally pulled out the President, they shot him in both legs, bundled him into a jeep and drove away. They left seventy-eight bodies behind, all from the president's entourage. They took President Doe to the rebel base camp. Whatever happened that night can only be imagined: by the following morning, the President's body was on public display, its fingers smashed, its ears and private parts missing. It was a bloody end for one of Africa's worst rulers.

In a sense that was the moment that everyone had been waiting for for months. And yet so far it has solved nothing. Now the two rival rebel groups are slugging it out for dominance, with the peace-keeping force getting more and more drawn into the fighting. The day before the shoot-out, a team of six aid workers arrived to assess how they could get food and medicine to people in Monrovia. The day they arrived, the port was being shelled. The next day, it was the scene of Doe's capture. The following two days, stray bullets were flying in the centre of town where the aid workers were staying. They left without having seen more than a couple of square miles of the city, and with the message that until the fighting stops, it is going to be very, very hard to send in any kind of help.

TUVAN THROAT-SINGERS

Tim Whewell

KYZYL, DECEMBER 1990

Tibet's spiritual leader, the Dalai Lama, travelled to Tuva, an isolated Russian region on the border with Mongolia, where people still live a nomadic way of life.

It is hard to decide how to approach the Dalai Lama, particularly at six o'clock in the morning in the waiting-room of a Siberian airport. He is fairly unmistakable as he sits in his flimsy red robes and incongruously sensible black shoes. So anything like 'I'm Tim Whewell; you must be the Dalai Lama' would clearly sound absurd. How forward can you be with a living god? But on the other hand, how long can you hover silently in front of someone who is already looking quizzically at you? In the end I went for the direct approach and was greeted not only with a disarming grin but also with a firm squeeze on the arms. His Holiness remembers faces and over the next few days, as he sat enthroned at interminable ceremonies, we exchanged several grins over the heads of the intervening monks and officials.

It was the Dalai Lama's first trip to Tuva, a wide tract of mountains and steppes on the northern fringes of Mongolia. For the Tuvans it was the first visit by a foreign statesman since Genghis Khan passed by in 1207. Stalin, Brezhnev and Gorbachev all avoided Tuva. Yeltsin has never been there either. And yet,

242

until the Second World War, the country was an independent state. In the tiny capital, Kyzyl, you can see the white-columned house that served as the Soviet legation and the former parliament where Tuva's Communist deputies voted, in 1944, to request admission into the USSR. But apart from the commemorative plaques on those buildings, virtually the only other traces of the country's lost independence are the triangular Tuvan stamps, preserved in schoolboys' albums all over the world.

The memory of those stamps, with the exotic name and pictures of camel and yak herders, inspired the Nobel prize-winning American Richard Feynman to embark on a ten-year struggle with Soviet bureaucracy in a bid to reach Tuva – then a region closed to foreigners. Feynman died of cancer just before an invitation finally arrived from the Soviet Academy of Sciences, but his friend, Ralph Leighton, did get to Kyzyl and wrote a moving and funny book, *Tuva or Bust*, about their joint quest to rediscover the mysterious, forgotten country. It is a measure of Tuva's isolation that, even now, few people there have heard of Feynman or Leighton. And of those who have, some get the story a bit mixed up. One told me that the American physicist had been unable to reach Tuva because he was not allowed out of his own country. Another said that Feynman's chief aim had been to stick a pole through the geographic centre of every continent, and he was frustrated because he had already done them all except for the centre of Asia, which is in Kyzyl.

Tuvans seem to regard their location at the centre of Asia as their chief claim to fame. One local businessman told me of his plans to set up an association uniting the centres of each continent, which could become an important international trade network. When I suggested that the centres of some continents, such as Africa and South America, were mainly jungle, he pulled out Tuva's other joker, its peculiar tradition of throat-singing. The art, developed by shepherds on lonely hillsides, involves a single singer producing two notes simultaneously; one can be a low, prolonged rattle and another a piercing whistle.

Tuvan officials hope that throat-singing concerts in the West can become a major source of hard currency for their country. Already several groups have made successful foreign tours and, when local people talked about Britain, the place they seemed to know most about was Llangollen, the Welsh town which, every year, hosts an international musical Eisteddfod. Not surprisingly, it is famous in Tuva, and when I visited people's homes they proudly brought out battered copies of the *Shropshire Star*, and its special Eisteddfod supplement – 'Not to be sold separately' – with pictures of throat-singers on the front. Showing a degree of self-confidence that would have been unthinkable in most Soviet citizens a few years ago, the Tuvan group that visited Llangollen this year deliberately missed their return flight to Moscow and went busking on the streets of Manchester. They caused a minor sensation in Chorlton-cum-Hardy shopping centre, and were soon being interviewed by Granada TV. It is all a long way from the high pastures around Kyzyl, where the singers' parents or grandparents move their round felt tents, or *yurts*, from season to season.

In fact, a surprising number of Tuvans still lead nomadic lives. One evening, just outside the capital, I was welcomed into a *yurt* by an old woman and her son, who immediately began apologizing that, since they had no torch or electric light, it was already too dark to kill a sheep for me. They did, however, offer traditional Tuvan tea, brewed with salt, and a strong spirit distilled, while I waited, from a boiling cauldron of sour milk.

Down on the main square of Kyzyl, the Dalai Lama had been sitting through hours of prayers and speeches. As a Buddhist monk, he avoids alcohol, even milk vodka. But his smile at the end of a gruelling day was as boyish and mischievous as ever.

LITHUANIAN ALAMO

Kevin Connolly

VILNIUS, JANUARY 1991

Fourteen people were killed when Soviet troops tried to seize control of the television tower in the Lithuanian capital.

His face, when I saw him first, was calm and serious. He was older than the other demonstrators, and had even taken the trouble to shave and put his best suit on before coming out to the television tower. He had not, he said, taken part in a demonstration before, and when the deafening whine of the tank engines drowned out our conversation, he shook hands with me, then linked arms with fifty other people in an attempt to stop the armoured column from reaching the building. It is difficult to remember exactly what happened for the next hour or so; the army convoy, a tank and a group of armoured personnel carriers, did stop for a moment; their searchlights, probing the clouds of tear gas, picked out his face – angry and resolute – and the crowds chanted their defiance. I lost him again as the tank moved towards the human wall around the building. For a few moments there was panic and chaos. The screams of the protesters were drowned out by the crackle of machine-gun fire from the tank, and from the paratroops, who poured from the armoured vehicles around it. Then, incredibly, the tank slowly began to move forward into the crowd.

A few days later, I was sitting at a news conference, listening to a general from Moscow calmly explaining how a picture showing a man being crushed to death had been an elaborate fake. In common with most of the other Western correspondents in Vilnius, I had been to his funeral the previous day.

In the week since someone in Moscow – or in Lithuania – took the decision to use force to demonstrate Soviet power here, what would once have seemed extraordinary has become sadly familiar. The shock of seeing troops and tanks deployed on the streets of a European capital has begun to fade. Political rhetoric about bourgeois nationalism, about the vanguard role of enlight-ened Communists and about the invalidity of the election last year which swept them from power might seem almost amusing in its datedness in Moscow or in London; here it seems chillingly cynical.

A pro-Moscow puppet body appealing to Mr Gorbachev to impose direct rule from Moscow has apparently been set up. But none of its members has been identified or seen in public; it is a time-honoured tactic to establish a puppet government, and then answer its appeal for help. To watch it being used by politicians who do not care whether or not the fiction is believed is very frightening. For Lithuanians, whose country was invaded and occupied by Stalin in just such circumstances fifty-one years ago, it is also tragically familiar. Then, they did not fight, and many people feel their case would have had more sympathy in the West if they had. This time many of them are determined that things will be different.

The day after the television tower was attacked, I went down to the parliament building, to find that it had become a fortress. 'Lithuania's Alamo,' said the guard who checked my papers. The work of reinforcing it has continued throughout the week. It is a symbol of defiance, and a symbol of Lithuania's desire for independence: the memory of what happened to the television tower is very vivid; but it was the preparation for the defence of parliament the following night, which will stay with me for ever, as a memory of what has happened here. In the corridors, darkened to make it more difficult for attacking troops, they handed out gas masks, and discussed how best to deploy the tiny handful of hunting rifles at their disposal.

Their mood was grim and determined – easy words to write now, but which seem inadequate for the task of describing their cold courage. That I decided to leave to my friend from the television tower who – unshaven now, but still in his suit – I found again inside the parliament that night. We were relieved to see each other but he, due to the experience ironically gained as a conscript in the Soviet Army, was helping to organize the defence, and was too busy to speak for long. In the darkness he wished me luck, and handed me a note asking me, if the building fell, to include it in a dispatch. So far, the attack has not come. The note says simply this: 'I am a schoolteacher, not a paratrooper. I know the battle we face is an unequal and perhaps a hopeless one, but we fight on so that in future, wherever freedom is discussed, the name of Lithuania will be mentioned with honour.'

YELLOW ALERT

Stephen Sackur

The Gulf War was underway: Allied aircraft were pounding Iraq as ground troops prepared to march into occupied Kuwait.

The news came just as I drifted off to sleep; it was three twenty in the morning. Two soldiers came into the tent and announced that the camp was on yellow alert. 'We're at war,' one said. 'This is not a joke.' Then, from the next tent, there was a terrified shout: 'Gas! Gas! Gas!' I struggled from my sleeping-bag in total darkness, feeling along the sides of the tent for my gas mask. I was thoroughly frightened. I knew I was not supposed to breathe, and risk inhaling poisonous gases, but I simply could not find my mask; had there been nerve or blister agents in the air, I would have died, without a doubt. It took me minutes rather than seconds to pull on the mask and find my chemical warfare suit. Fumbling with zips and fastenings in the dark merely tightened the knot of fear in my stomach.

Thus it was that the news of the onset of hostilities was greeted with a tangible feeling of relief across the camp: relief that weeks and months of uncertainty were over, that war was a reality for which everyone could prepare. On the face of it, many of the men I have lived with, and talked to at length over the past few days, seem to be less than ideally suited for the unrelenting ground battle that may well lie ahead. Many are very young, some no more than eighteen years old; far too young, one would have thought, to have acquired the psycho-logical toughness necessary for battle. Inevitably, there is much talk about home and family and a great deal of day-dreaming about the forbidden fruits of life in Saudi Arabia. Almost all of the men are deeply superstitious: tank crews stuff furry animals into the available nooks or crannies. Sappers write legends such as *Plymouth or Bust* on their wagons, and there is intermittent grumbling about what most of the British troops regard as the 'God-forsaken desert'.

At the heart of the British force, though, there is an impressive streak of determination and resilience. There is a tremendous internal pride within the ranks which operates at every level, from the company through the regiment and the two brigades to the division as a whole. If pushed, the men will talk about their views on the rights and wrongs of the war, but moral conviction is not the force that will motivate them when the ground combat begins. Indeed, a surprising number of them have told me that they see this as a war about oil and economic interests, not as a fight for the principle of sovereignty. There is a strong sense of duty and loyalty to each other and, now that they have been set a task – the liberation of Kuwait – they have every intention of seeing it completed.

Indeed, many of the men here say that the reality of war has brought with it a unity of purpose and a comradeship rarely found in the British Army bases in Germany. It is noticeable that some of the formalities in relations between officers and men have quietly been dropped: saluting, for example, is much less in evidence, and there is a great deal of banter and good humour about the privations of life in the sand. For a journalist unused to the military mind, whether it be that of an urbane and articulate officer, or a baby-faced private who is missing his mum, it is the overriding sense of duty that is most startling. Not only startling, but in many ways comforting as well; because, for the next few weeks, I am going to be reliant on the qualities of the men of the First Armoured Division – who knows, perhaps some of their self-discipline might even rub off on me. In one important matter of detail, I am already a reformed character: now, when I need my gas mask in the middle of the night, I know precisely where to look.

AIR SUPERIORITY

Mark Laity

DHAHRAN, JANUARY 1991

Three days into the Gulf War Baghdad and other parts of Iraq were coming under Allied air attack.

It should not have been a shock, and yet it was. The 3 a.m. phone call that said it had started: the Allies had, somehow, achieved complete surprise by doing the blindingly obvious. A powerful night air attack soon after the UN's deadline expired. In the end, military reality pushed aside the appeals for peace, the hopeless, last-minute initiatives, the lingering belief that somehow a little more time would produce a way out. And, freed from the constraints of a deadline, the Allies rushed to attack fearing that otherwise Iraq might strike the first blow.

It was the sensible solution, and yet Iraq seems to have been caught out: stunned by the ferocity of an attack that may be recorded as one of the most successful applications of air power in history.

There is a military saying that no plan survives first contact with the enemy and yet, so far, this one seems to have. Again the strategy is obvious. Use the Allied superiority and air power to blunt Iraq's own offensive potential by destroying their air force, their long-range missiles and their command system. With control of the air the Allies can, in comparative safety, turn to the task of systematically destroying other parts of Iraq's military machine. The plan's apparent success is, in part, due to the maturing of many weapon systems that have in the past promised more than they delivered. Highly accurate laser rangefinders, radar jammers and radar homing missiles have all combined with a sophisticated command and control network to produce an integrated and, more importantly, a reliable system.

The crews have also had five months to practise and to modify their aircraft while the commanders worked out the battle plan. As an avid reader of military history, I find the results so far little short of staggering, with casualties that in individual human terms are tragic, but in hard and clinical military terms are very light.

In effect the Allies have achieved air superiority. This does not mean Iraq's air force has been totally destroyed, or that its air defences are useless, but what it does mean is that the Allied air forces can operate with comparative freedom over Iraq, able to attack any targets they choose. The Iraqi response so far has been weak.

The Allies now have to maintain superiority, revisiting damaged air fields to ensure that shattered runways are not repaired and that Iraq's substantial numbers of surviving aircraft cannot easily take off. Meanwhile, the air forces can concentrate on destroying the rest of Iraq's considerable military potential, and that could take a long time. So far they appear to be within schedule, with an ever-expanding target list, as they switch attention from the weapons plants to tactical targets, such as ammunition dumps, army communications and tank concentrations.

Again there seems to be a puzzling lack of effective opposition, with one American defence official saying the Iraqis seem to have systems and equipment up to Western standards, but they are unable to operate them effectively. Automation, especially in the shape of the highly effective Tomahawk cruise missile, has served the Allies better; it has made precision attack far easier than in previous wars. And it is the Allies' ability to exploit their admittedly better technology that has given them the edge over the Iraqis, who are not short of advanced weaponry.

Britain's Tornado bomber air crews are a good example. Their aircraft is equipped with a JP233, which contains a combination of more than two hundred bomblets to variously crater runways, destroy aircraft and lay time-delay mines to hamper repair efforts. It has proved devastatingly effective and can be laid with great accuracy, but it still requires great skill and courage to fly a Tornado at low level through the curtains of fire thrown up by the airfield defences and then to go back and do it again and again.

The jubilation of the air crews at their initial success is already being replaced with an exhaustion that requires them to dig ever deeper into their reserves of experience and nerve. Another of the many imponderables about the war is also how the Iraqis themselves can bear up under the bombardment. An increasing number of air strikes are now directed at the Iraqi armies in the Kuwait area, trying to isolate them from Baghdad's control while destroying their supplies and equipment, softening them up in the military jargon for the ground offensive that the Allies expect will be needed.

Once again the coalition forces will try to overwhelm the Iraqis with firepower and once again it will be the skill and the courage of the tank and artillery crews that decide their effectiveness, and if it does come to a ground offensive, casualties could mount rapidly. As one Allied commander put it: 'They're hoping, but not expecting, that air power will do the job, without resorting to the grim and bloody business of an army offensive against an enemy well used to taking losses. The Allies may have made a remarkable start, but the task ahead still looks enormous.'

BAGHDAD SHELTER

Allan Little

IRAQ, FEBRUARY 1991

Allied bombing raids caused heavy damage inside Iraq even after the announcement from Baghdad that Iraqi troops were to be withdrawn from Kuwait. But, despite the ultra-modern technology being employed by the airmen, it was not only military targets which were destroyed.

We watch each evening from our fifth-floor window as the raids take place. It seems to many of us that we have been witnessing, little by little, the destruction of everything that makes a city a city. The electricity is gone, the telephones are gone, there is no fuel. Water is almost gone, government ministries have been destroyed and city centre river bridges reduced to rubble.

Many Iraqis, whatever their views on the origins of the conflict, now believe that the fabric of their society, everything that makes Iraq a modern nation state, is being unpicked. Sometimes the raids defeat Iraq's warning system and bombing precedes the air-raid siren. One night last week, shortly after dark, I was in the garden of the al-Rasheed Hotel where the handful of foreign journalists who are here are being accommodated. Suddenly, and without warning, the building across the street was struck by a missile. I felt it crack and felt its suction as it passed. Then the thud of impact as it entered. Finally the deep roar of an explosion that blew off the roof and gutted the inside of the building. It was the impressive Palace of Congresses, a vast showpiece conference centre built for the 1982 Non-Aligned

254

Conference and never used because of the Iran–Iraq war. Pieces of it landed on the forecourt below our window. It burned all night.

This morning, relatives of what Iran calls the Martyrs of Ammaria are still trying to count and identify those killed in the bombing of a civilian air-raid shelter in the western suburbs of the city. Yesterday we went to the city mortuary. Outside, trucks and cars carried shallow open coffins of rough bare wood. Small groups of black-veiled women kept a quiet, mournful vigil. In the mortuary courtyard was the first sign of the grotesque chaos that has overwhelmed the staff there: the body of a woman, burned and bloated, in a heap beside a rough dirt path. In the back of an open pick-up truck, a soldier was going through the pockets of a dead boy, searching for clues of his identity.

We entered the mortuary through a small ante-room. About half a dozen bodies lay there in a pile. One man was squatting nearby weeping. He was fingering a bracelet from which he had identified the body of his wife. He had found her still cradling their baby in her arms. Another man had wrapped the remains of his daughter in a blanket before placing her in a coffin. Staff were helping him carry it outside. We walked into the cool mortuary chamber. There were bodies everywhere, many of them tiny, placed, not in serried ranks and covered in blankets, but dumped hurriedly and chaotically, limbs contorted. Two marble dissection tables were caked in blood. There is water to wash neither the bodies, nor the floor, nor the furniture. Two women moved among the corpses, examining scraps of scorched clothing for clues. They were sifting the dead like sifting rubble, searching for their relatives.

At the shelter, those we addressed spoke with passion but always with courtesy and restraint. One man, upright and composed in a blue robe, showed me five small plastic identity cards: those of his wife and four children, the youngest four months, the eldest six years. They had all died in the shelter.

Those of us who watched the nightly raids from our fifth-floor window will never again watch with the same detached curiosity. For a few brief moments yesterday, Baghdad thought the war was over, occasioned by an unconditional withdrawal from Kuwait. They were among the most telling few moments I have witnessed here. It is impossible for foreigners to penetrate the surface of Iraqi society, but for a moment or two the curtain was drawn back. There was unrestrained joy among soldiers and civilians alike. There is no doubt that ordinary Iraqis want an end to the war but, for a moment, we caught a glimpse of an otherwise hidden enthusiasm for an initiative from their own side.

FAREWELL YUGOSLAVIA

Misha Glenny

BELGRADE, FEBRUARY 1991

Yugoslavia's republics became increasingly nationalistic. The ethnic disputes and political tensions encouraged the belief that the country could no longer remain united, and that civil war was not far away.

It has been a typical sort of week for Yugoslavia. It began with the country escaping, by a whisker, full-scale civil war between its two largest nations, the Serbs and the Croats. The southern republic of Macedonia then declared itself a sovereign state, while workers surrounded Serbia's parliament to denounce the government they had elected, overwhelmingly, less than two months ago. In the north-west, Slovene lorry drivers brought their republic to a standstill by blocking the borders with Italy and Austria for half a day. General strikes have been threatened in at least three of the six republics while the Serbian minority in Croatia confirmed its UDI by planning elections in defiance of the Croatian authorities. The army has accused the Croatian Defence Minister of wanting to slaughter the wives and children of Serbian Army officers, while Serbian police are making house to house searches of Albanian homes, in the province of Kosovo, to confiscate arms. As you can see, just another week in Yugoslavia.

But there will not be many more weeks like this because

Yugoslavia as we know it is coming to an end. The country can no longer bear its own labyrinthine complexity. Down in the dirty kitchens of this Gothic political edifice, a cauldron of blood simmers: chefs, deranged by the struggle for power, experiment with poisonous recipes, one of which will eventually provoke the cauldron to boil over.

The latest such attempt was cooked up by the Federal Secretariat for Defence. A week ago, when Croatia and the army were at daggers drawn, the Defence Ministry released a film purporting to show that the Croat Defence Minister, Martin Spegelj, was planning a massacre of Serbs, reminiscent of the atrocities committed by the Croatian Fascists, the Ustashas, during the Second World War. Spegelj, it must be said, is a hardliner in the Croat government, but he is no Fascist. In a normal society, the documentary would never have been allowed anywhere near a TV screen, so crude were its manipulations. But in Yugoslavia, the truth was drowned long ago in a flood of lies and baseless denunciations, and the television programme triggered the exact reaction that its makers had intended – hysteria in Serbia, a resurrection of the terrible phantom of the Ustashas – for the Serbian-dominated army nothing short of a *casus belli*. And war it would have been, were it not for the breathless, last-minute agreement of the collective state presidency.

But that agreement is temporary: newly sovereign Croats, who have always suspected that inside every Yugoslavia is a Greater Serbia waiting to get out, have said they will only be part of a restructured Yugoslav confederation – otherwise they will leave. Serbia has said it will only accept a confederation if all Serbs live in Serbia, which means a massive revision of the Balkan borders. Croatia says it will now reimpose its authority over the Serbian minority – which has declared independence – in southern Croatia. Serbia will not tolerate this.

Serbs and Croats are bracing themselves for a war. Some believe it may take the form of a series of protracted guerrilla wars, others say it may begin as a straight fight between Serbs and

Croats which will expand to embrace all the nationalities in Yugoslavia. But there are those who doggedly maintain that Yugoslavs, of whatever nationality, have no desire to resuscitate the crimes of the past. There are many such people, but the one thing they lack is a political solution to the tangled web of hostilities and antipathy which make up the legacy of Tito's Yugoslavia. For many years, Yugoslavia was a dictatorship of bureaucrats whose mediocrity was, in retrospect, quite awe-inspiring. Many of these political airheads continue to hold key positions in the republics and the federation, while great minds are excluded from the political process because of their refusal to join in the nationalist agenda. Political tourists who wish to soak in the ominous atmosphere of the mid-thirties should book now, before it is too late. As fear of war reached a fever pitch all Croat political parties agreed on a common platform to resist army aggression. Their leaders – spanning the spectrum from Communist to crypto-Fascist – stood as one in front of tens of thousands of demonstrators in Zagreb's newly named Ban Jelačić Square. To paraphrase Kaiser Wilhelm, when he received his necessary war credits in 1914: 'I could no longer see any parties, I could only see Croats.'

Nobody from outside can now help Yugoslavia. Its people are trapped by their history, from which there must exist some escape route; but, at the moment, the road looks more hazardous than it has done for fifty years, when civil war last broke out.

THE SIX-DAY COUP

Bridget Kendall

Moscow, August 1991

The world held its breath as Mikhail Gorbachev, the President of the Soviet Union, was detained by plotters as he holidayed by the Black Sea.

The events of this week sound like the plot of one of those KGB thrillers you might pick up at an international airport to read on the plane. On holiday in the Crimea, the Soviet President is betrayed by his own Head of Security. A delegation headed by his own Chief of Staff is allowed in to blackmail him. All his phones are cut off; he is made a prisoner in his own dacha, surrounded by a terrified family and at first ignorant of what is really going on. Meanwhile, conspirators across the country move to take over from elected governments and councils, using the power of the media, Tass and Soviet television to convince the masses that they are now in charge. Senior generals are dispatched to Kiev and to Tbilisi to warn the Ukrainian and Georgian presidents that the Soviet military will move in unless they keep their heads down. Judging by how slow many other republican leaders were to react defiantly, the generals paid visits to other republics too. In the Baltics, where attempts to blackmail would have been useless, the practice scenarios over the past year came into their own. The local military commanders had already found out how easy it was to seize buildings, so now they took over telephone exchanges and TV stations in earnest, to win crucial blanket control over communications.

But in Moscow the coup leaders made a fatal mistake. Boris Yeltsin, President of the Russian Federation, slipped out of his flat on Monday morning, by some accounts only minutes before they came to arrest him. The apparent plot to put him in solitary confinement, and there to try to blackmail him too, had gone disastrously wrong. By then, the coup was already doomed. The Russian parliament became a powerful centre of resistance. For some extraordinary reason, the coup leaders left the telephone system intact, and President Yeltsin's aides were able to fax his appeals and decrees, calling on Russian citizens to defy the new Kremlin orders, across the Russian Federation. Once a disorganized talking-shop, Russian democrats instantly united, and responded to the call. Miners announced they would go on strike in Siberia. The Mayor of Leningrad called on workers there to start organizing themselves to join in if need be. The Baltic governments swiftly declared their independence from the Soviet Union, and announced that they would back the strike call too. Journalists at the central television and radio station, in the newspapers, even in the official news agency Tass, refused to obey the new dictatorship. Alongside chilling draconian decrees of the new Emergency Committee, Tass journalists began to slip in other reports, hinting more and more openly of the mood of resistance across the country. A day late, but still influential, some republican leaders decided to make their support for the resistance clear. The President of Kazakhstan unambiguously condemned the coup. Rumours began to leak out that even inside the Communist Party leadership, the army and the KGB, the ringleaders were facing opposition. Unexpectedly, their attempt to call an emergency party plenum to sack Mikhail Gorbachev as party leader failed, because those who had been kept in the dark said they wanted to see their general secretary first, before they held a plenum to kick him out. But the crucial factor was the armed forces. A tank commander withdrew from the Russian parliament, after an appeal from Boris Yeltsin, saying he would not fire on other Russians. And men from two divisions defected to Boris Yeltsin's side. Ten tanks rolled up to help man the barricades outside his parliament, followed by three hundred paratroopers.

By now, the coup was in serious trouble. Military officers had grappled with maps and charts to work out how to fulfil the coup leaders' orders and bring columns of heavy tanks into the busy Moscow capital. For a whole day, taxis, trolley buses and bread vans intermingled with armoured personnel carriers on the main streets. Curious shoppers lifted their children to take a closer look at the tanks and chat to the soldiers. So when, in a dramatic climax, Moscow's new military commander announced a curfew, Muscovites simply ignored it and hastened to their Russian parliament to join in the defence.

The coup leaders' nerve failed. In the early hours of Wednesday morning, they called off an attack on the building. The people and Boris Yeltsin had won; and the dénouement began. Key ringleaders flew in haste to the Crimea, perhaps to plead with Mr Gorbachev, perhaps to try to hold him hostage, to save their skins. Two other senior Communists, one of them linked to the plotters, followed in another plane. And, in a race against time, Boris Yeltsin's vice-president and prime minister assembled a delegation and followed in a third plane, all arriving at Mr Gorbachev's front door almost at the same time.

The Soviet President refused to see his former captors. Instead, they were clapped under armed guard. In less than three days, the KGB and defence chiefs who tried to seize power were in gaol. Other arrests followed swiftly. The Prime Minister, Mr Valentin Pavlov, who had collapsed after his blood pressure soared, was put under armed guard. Only the sinister Soviet Interior Minister, Boris Pugo, escaped arrest. As he heard Boris Yeltsin's guards mount the steps to his apartment, he put his gun in his mouth and shot himself.

What followed after that is now part two of this extraordinary sequence. The hardliners are out. Mr Gorbachev, traumatized but thankful to be alive, returns to assume his role as Soviet President, and discovers the country has been transformed. His old call for caution and compromise depresses and horrifies those who had stood firm to save their country from a new Stalinist repression. Boris Yeltsin, the real hero of the moment, seizes the political initiative with both hands. No longer is President Gorbachev allowed to sit isolated and aloof in the Kremlin. He is forced to come and answer for his mistakes and bumbling intentions to the Russian President, to whom he now owes all. Almost none of his former colleagues has survived this coup. He appears isolated, defensive and unable to do anything but endorse decrees which Boris Yeltsin has already signed.

The next events, yet to unravel themselves, are already visible on the horizon. The signing of a new Union Treaty, to let the republics take over their own affairs as sovereign states. If Ukraine's decision to seek independence does not halt the process, then, in a few weeks or months, everything on Russia's territory could be under Boris Yeltsin's jurisdiction. President Gorbachev's empire then becomes a theoretical concept that has no substance any more. It seems likely he will stay on for a bit at least, a transitional figure to bridge the still painful shift from the old centralized federation to a new union of independent republics, in which the new Soviet President will be a sort of British Queen or a Pérez de Cuellar, UN Secretary-General – ceremonial international peacemaker, but not the one in charge. There is still speculation that President Gorbachev might step down as Soviet President. After all, he has already resigned from his party post as general secretary. And it could be, after what he has been through, that Mr Gorbachev would even welcome a rest from politics. Certainly, many Soviet citizens think it is time he went away to write his memoirs. And what a good plot he has to start with. No inventor of fiction could ever have devised a better one – these were six days that shook the world.

DUBROVNIK SIEGE

Allan Little

ZAGREB, NOVEMBER 1991

The historic Croatian port city came under sustained attack as Serbs fought Croatians in a battle for territory in the former Yugoslavia.

At sunset the sky above Dubrovnik's white stone walls glows smoky rose and salmon pink, and gives way slowly to encroaching night. The only sound is the lapping of the gentle Adriatic on the ancient fortified waterfront. The effect is bewitching. And that is when it starts. You see the flash first, then, seconds later, hear the boom of the barrel as it sends another artillery shell, flying in a low arc, screaming over the ancient rust-coloured roofs of the old town. The Croats lob mortars and artillery of their own from positions around town, sometimes close to the old walls, bringing the might of the Federal response to within a whisker of the city's architectural treasures.

The Federal Army's presence is visible, inescapable and menacing. They have taken commanding positions on the hills above the city. Offshore their gunboats glide silently past. You cannot get away from this overpowering sense of being trapped. It is a presence that has worn down Dubrovnik's fifty thousand people to a state of depression, inertia and exhaustion. The town seems permanently on the verge of tears.

Take Andreo Ruso. He showed me into his son's bedroom. 'Look through the hole in the wall,' he said. If you refocus your eyes, they settle on Zarkovice hilltop where the Yugoslav national

264

flag marks the spot from where they fired the shell that destroyed his second-floor flat. I have seen this hilltop, framed in this way, by broken bricks and mortar, in buildings across the city. The military rationale of much of the JNA's bombardment is bewildering. Why did they slam shell after shell into a complex of hotels housing three thousand refugees? They emerged from their underground shelter next morning bewildered and, in some cases, clearly in shock. While I was there, raking through the physical and emotional aftermath, the siren struck up again. Instantly, we were pushed underground by an official who knows only too well the cost of complacency. In the safest room in the complex, a group of young mothers were purging their own fear for the sake of their children, trying to distract attention from the pounding above by playing games, telling stories. I wondered what reserves of courage and energy they were drawing from. Some had endured this for five weeks.

Our hosts made a fuss of us, fetching candles so that we could see the faces of those we were interviewing, fetching clean plastic cups and flasks of hot coffee. We were their esteemed guests. Only afterwards did they raise, in a polite and embarrassed sort of way, the question of Europe. Why does Europe not care? I felt – I feel – humbled by the question, and by the way it is put by the ordinary, sad people here. I had no answer. My Croatian interpreter, a compassionate and courageous young woman, overheard a phone-in on Zagreb Radio. 'You have to understand,' said a caller from Hamburg, 'that we live in the rich world. It sees its catastrophes on television. When it has seen enough, it presses the button.'

I left Dubrovnik punch drunk with tales of grief. The journey out was no relief. Ours was to be, though we did not know it, the last refugee ship to be allowed to leave. Hours after we sailed, the Federal Navy imposed a total naval blockade on all Croatian ports. Even the single ferry a day, which held out the prospect of escape to a handful of people, was gone. On the quayside there was chaos. Two hundred and sixty people, mostly the elderly, pregnant women or mothers with small children, had been selected. I watched one young man kiss his wife goodbye. He hugged his little girl, and held her head in his big hands, staring for a moment into her face. No one spoke. Then he turned and left without a word.

We sailed at sunset, a new artillery exchange striking up on the hills above. On board Marko Rilovic was savouring his eightieth birthday slumped, exhausted and asleep, on a black vinyl couch in the reception area where he and his wife had been dumped. Marko had lived all his life in the house in which he was born, keeping a small vineyard, some cattle and pigs. They had fled ten days earlier. They had no idea where they would go. 'I've put our names on the list in the purser's office. I think it's the Red Cross.' She shrugged and tears dripped down her miserable face. It seemed that it was the indignity of it all that pained her most. 'We are the Kurds of Europe,' she said. Kate Boljan is twenty-two and eight months pregnant. Her husband, Ante, is still trapped in Dubrovnik. She had had to choose, effectively, between him and her unborn child. 'I don't know whether I will see him again, or whether he will see the child. My baby will need water and food and electricity. Of course it was a hard decision.'

As we sailed in the dark past coastal villages in Montenegro, the refugees saw their first electric light in five weeks. One little girl, no more than five years old, screamed at her mother that all the houses were on fire, and asked whether the army was shooting here too. Children know the vocabulary of war – the difference between artillery and mortar, sniper and machine-gun fire.

When I left Dubrovnik I thought I had seen the exercise of gratuitous cruelty by men who knew that they could do anything, from the relative safety of their hilltop bunkers, with impunity. It seemed, under the rockets, as though they were laughing at international public opinion, laughing at Europe's decision not to decide. I thought I was already witnessing an army inflicting its worst, day after day. I had sat beneath a sturdy wooden desk, during one heavy artillery raid, on the telephone to London, and heard a Serbian politician tell *The World at One* that Dubrovnik was not, as he put it, perishing, that those claims were propaganda. There were mortars and shells dropping only two hundred yards away – the sound was deafening.

In fact I had seen nothing at all compared with what has come since. Back in Zagreb, you can watch pictures from Zagreb television, shot from the very position on Zarkovice hill where the army has its closest artillery post. Now I can watch, every day, through my Zagreb television screen, the beautiful Adriatic port city from the other side of the lines; its familiar ancient alleyways, even that street from the old town to the Hotel Argentina, along which we strode quickly and nervously, hugging the wall and glancing anxiously at the Federal flag flying on the crest of hill. This has an unsettling *through the looking glass* quality about it, especially when you see an artillery piece or a machine-gun being fired, with what seems like cavalier abandon, into the very streets where the good, suffering people of Dubrovnik – the people who had shown me so much kindness, and whom I left less than a week ago – are still cowering, in daily and increasing fear for their lives.

LYNCH MOB

Carole Walker

TBILISI, JANUARY 1992

The streets of the Georgian capital became increasingly violent as supporters of the beleaguered President, Zviad Gamsakhurdia, who was holed up in the parliament building, clashed with others who backed the country's interim military government.

Tbilisi used to be one of the pleasantest cities in the old Soviet Union: sunny, with abundant fruit and vegetables in summer, its people proud of their hospitality and of the Georgian food and wine they like to consume in great quantities. Here, the usual greeting amongst casual friends is an almost passionate embrace. But the violent battle for power has made it an apprehensive and frightening place under the rule of the gunmen, and these days almost every man is armed with a Kalashnikov.

On the morning I arrived, after an overnight drive over the mountains from Armenia, the Interior Ministry, next to the Parliament, was in flames. Machine-gun fire resounded around the almost deserted city. Rather naïvely, we dodged through back streets to the Tbilisi Hotel, then the opposition headquarters. I had stayed there a few months before and had adored its crumbling grandeur and dusty chandeliers. This time, parked outside the front lobby was an armoured personnel carrier, mounted with a small cannon blasting periodically in the direction of the Parliament. Dishevelled fighters were sleeping in the ornate restaurant. A couple of days later the hotel was set on fire during a counterattack by troops loyal to the President. Today it is a blackened shell, the chandeliers a pile of broken glass.

During the conflict several people likened the network of narrow streets just above the Parliament to Beirut under the control of a patchwork of different militia groups. But here at least the gunmen from whichever faction generally welcomed and helped us. Driving through this could still be a little scary; the nervous fighters, waiting around each corner, liked to point their guns at your head. Six young men, bearing Kalashnikovs and the uniforms of the Georgian National Guard, danced in front of the car barring our way towards the rear of the Parliament, where President Gamsakhurdia was besieged. These were some of his troops, but it is often impossible to distinguish between the opposing forces. When I got out, rather gingerly, and explained that we wanted to see the President we were whisked off towards his refuge faster than I would have liked. There was a fearsome wallop of artillery shells landing a block or so away, and endless outbursts of machine-gun fire apparently all around us. I felt heavy and unbalanced in the navy blue BBC flak jacket, which weighs something like twenty pounds, but I think I achieved a personal best in the one hundred metre sprint across open ground to a sandbagged window at the rear of the Parliament itself. All this to be told Mr Gamsakhurdia was too busy to talk to us. Within days he had fled.

It is still hard to understand how a split within the President's own government led to such conflict. Certainly a key figure was Tengiz Kitovani, the head of the Georgian National Guard, who took several of his men with him when he rounded on the President. The opposition lay the blame on Mr Gamsakhurdia himself. They say he became a dictator and failed to keep any of the promises he made in the run-up to his landslide victory in the presidential elections. He says it was down to bandits and criminals hungry for power. Both sides, variously, cite the involvement of the new imperialist Russia, the old Soviet KGB, Mr Gorbachev, the CIA and James Baker. There is evidence, though, that the disintegrating Soviet Army may have played a part. Its soldiers did remain steadfastly in their barracks. The deputy commander of its forces in the Caucasus told me that this was a matter for the Georgian people to sort out amongst themselves – an attitude unthinkable a short while ago.

To some extent it is the bloody squabble that the hardliners long predicted would follow the erosion of central power, but there are strong indications, too, that what was the Soviet Army may be responsible for the flood of weapons into this area, either directly or indirectly. One young fighter, leaning against a Russian T-55 tank outside the opposition headquarters, said it was obvious.

'Have you ever bought a Red Army watch?' he asked me – something almost every foreign visitor to the former Soviet Union is offered. I admitted these made good presents for friends at home. 'Well,' he said, 'these are just a little more expensive.' He patted the rusty tank and grinned. The huge howitzer field guns almost certainly proved decisive in forcing President Gamsakhurdia to give up the fight. But the violence at demonstrations involving ordinary Georgian people may prove to be a more worrying indicator of things to come.

On Friday we were about to leave what seemed a rather low-key demonstration in support of President Gamsakhurdia when a group of masked gunmen, dressed in black and straight from the pages of a cheap thriller, opened fire. At first the rapid crack of their machine-guns was over our heads; then I heard bullets whizzing past my ears. I tried to get behind a rather small pile of concrete construction blocks. My interpreter stood in a daze until I dragged her down beside me. A man in front of us just doubled up, a great flow of blood came from his stomach. Another man who had been standing next to my cameraman was hit in the shoulder. With the attackers gone the crowd grabbed us and began dragging us from place to place, insisting we film the wounded and dying. One man had been shot in the head. But the image I cannot get out of my mind is the face of the gunman who got left behind – the one who was lynched by the hysterical mob. They had him in the back of a wrecked minibus, holding him by the scruff of the neck while they rubbed shattered glass into his face and pointed a pistol at his throat. He turned his blood-streaked face and stared straight at the camera. Those eyes were, literally, blind with terror. Rather feebly, in English, I tried to tell the people to stop. The crowd turned on us, screaming that we must tell the truth, that we had been telling lies; we just had to leave.

The animal violence that we saw there was somehow far worse than all the artillery and machine-gun fire: Georgian attacking Georgian with bare hands. It is hard to see how they can put that behind them now, how they will manage to bury their differences, and embrace one another in friendship again.

SOUTH AFRICA'S NEW DAWN

Fergal Keane

CAPE TOWN, MARCH 1992

In a referendum, South Africa's white population gave an overwhelming endorsement to President de Klerk's reforms – paving the way for an end to white minority rule.

The day is clear and sunny and the waters of Table Bay are sparkling in the distance: from the jagged shapes of the Hottentots Holland Mountains, curving around the coast to the milky white sands of Blouberg Strand, there is an extraordinary calm. It could have been on a day such as this that Jan van Riebeeck's ships loomed on the horizon, edging in from the Atlantic, to cast their long shadow across the southern half of Africa. The poet John Masefield, writing of Columbus, called the ships of the explorer 'doom burdened caravels', recognizing that what they carried with them was the beginning of a new order: the order of the white man. On the southern tip of Africa, as in the Americas, history was to roll across the plains, mountains and rivers subjugating or annihilating anything which stood in the way. For the native peoples of South Africa it amounted to a catastrophe: as the white man drove back the horizon, the tribes of the Cape were either annihilated or forced into slavery; trekking further into the wilderness, the whites defeated black tribe after tribe. Defeat and humiliation became bywords.

For whites it was a pathway to unimagined privilege, but also to fear and isolation: as the world moved forward they languished in the seventeenth century, despised and rejected; as they inflicted a code of racial supremacy on the black man so the world inflicted its moral apartheid on them. They were of Africa yet had cut themselves off from it; they yearned for the fellowship of nations yet were shut out. That was until yesterday: in one great leap the whites came back to Africa, and to the world. It was not only F. W. de Klerk's triumph, it was a victory for ordinary people, because the choice to reject racism and embrace peaceful co-existence was a deeply personal one. Implicit in the 'Yes' vote was a recognition of Anthony Trollope's wise dictum, that South Africa was a country of black people and always would be: no redrawing of borders would ever change that fact. For any one of us to reject the certainties we have grown up with is difficult: it involves a measure of risk that most people would shy away from, and that is what makes yesterday's vote so remarkable. The people who voted 'Yes' grew up with apartheid; leader after leader told them it was the only way in which to ensure the survival of the white race; racial separation marked every aspect of their lives, it was not something that could be taken or left.

In the light of that we should not be too surprised that just over thirty per cent of whites felt unable to leave the past behind: they are not all raving racists, not all bitter-enders and certainly not all potential soldiers in Mr Terre' Blanche's promised war of liberation. For the most part, I suspect, they are frightened people who have yet to complete the journey to realism. Now that the cause for which they campaigned has been well and truly lost it is difficult to believe that the right-wingers can sustain a concerted fight against the inevitable. Some will doubtless try to stain the future with blood – most though will, in some way or other, come to terms with the demands of survival, realizing that a loss of political control does not necessarily mean losing a way of life. The more pragmatic in the ranks of the right will almost certainly come to the negotiating table, whatever the taunts of 'traitor' and 'sell-out' that may come from the extremists.

A decade ago, when I first visited this country, there was a defensiveness and an arrogance about many whites that filled me with despair. After a while I learned to avoid arguments on the subject of apartheid – they invariably led nowhere. South Africa was a depressing place to be in: the heavy hand of the state was demolishing organized opposition, the border war was rumbling and liberals were wringing their hands in despair. Back then, it would have been impossible to imagine a white president standing on the steps of Parliament and congratulating his people for voting for an end to minority rule. And yet now that it has happened, there is less a sense of surprise or amazement than there is of relief. It is as if the South African nation breathed out a long sigh yesterday – and blew away the foul dust of history.

NEIGHBOURHOOD GRIM REAPERS

Alex Kirby

BRAZIL, JUNE 1992

Heads of state and government from around the globe travelled to Rio de Janeiro to discuss world poverty and ecology at the Earth Summit.

The very name Brazil is evocative. Flying down to Rio, my mind was full of the exotic associations learned in childhood: of parrots, mahogany and anacondas, overlaid with more recent imagery – of a uniquely rich environment facing an unprecedented threat. But behind all of these was another picture. Brazil is a country where they kill children. And if the same thing happens in other parts of Latin America, it happens often enough in Brazil to suggest it has the consent of a number of influential people.

Figures tell part of the story. In Pernambuco, in north-east Brazil, an average of three children a week were being killed by the death squads in early 1988. And a campaigner I met, Ivanir dos Santos, who lived on the streets himself till the age of four, says the number of children killed in the state of Rio de Janeiro alone last year was four hundred and forty-two, more than one a day.

Rio is a violent city: two friends of mine were robbed at knife-point during the Earth Summit. Most of the children who die are killed on suspicion of involvement in a crime. If they are criminals, it is not too surprising. Brazil has perhaps the greatest

275

disparity of any country between rich and poor. More than half the national income goes to the richest 10 per cent of Brazilians. The poorest 10 per cent eke out among themselves 0.6 per cent of the country's wealth. With the economy rocking on its heels – savage inflation and an immense foreign debt – the poor in Brazil are very poor, which helps to explain why seven million children have to fend for themselves on the streets.

The children are the prime targets for the death squads – though not the only ones. I met two poor but upright mothers whose children were in a group abducted by the police almost two years ago. None of the children has been seen again: to be young, poor and black in Brazil is to ask for trouble. Most of the killing is thought to be the work of serving or former police officers and of private security guards, usually paid by shopkeepers to deter crime by eliminating those thought to be either actual or potential criminals.

I wanted to meet some of the killers. Not surprisingly, I was not able to. But the distinguished Brazilian film-maker Otavio Bezerra had interviewed some of them and he let me listen to his tapes. My abiding memory is of men who not only show no trace of remorse for what they do – one remarked that he felt not a drop of pity – but who are convinced that they are doing society a favour. They see themselves, quite simply, as pest-control officers. Several believe they are in fact doing their victims a favour, too. Better die now in childhood, they argue, almost in so many words, than live to be an adult criminal ten years hence. Had I not been in Brazil for the Earth Summit, I might have found it easier to write off the killers as the psychopathic products of a horribly warped society. In fact I find it hard to condemn them. They, at least, are straightforward about what they do. And they care enough about their society to do something, even if the thing they do plumbs depths we thought were behind us.

The summit was about environment and development. But more and more it seemed to me that I was watching two summits. The one that discussed the environment, although it could have done much more, did carve out some essential toeholds for future progress. But the development summit, so far as I could see, did very little. It failed to agree on a more rapid increase in overseas aid, the most elementary step possible for reducing poverty. It certainly did not agree to reduce the poorest countries' debts, or to change the rules of international trade in a way that would give them a better chance of earning their own living. And it did not agree that the rich countries should limit their own over-consumption.

The industrial world has learned to worry about the environment, and it has also learned to live with poverty; the wretched of the earth are part of the familiar backdrop of life. They are wallpaper. They will not go away. They do not need to, because nothing they can do or be could ever threaten us. Statistics can often simply numb the mind. But every now and then you come across a formula which will not leave you, some set of digits which casts a new light on the scene. The reality of poverty is summed up, for me, in the recollection that every day forty thousand children aged under five die of preventable causes – hunger, or easily treated diseases like measles. A friend puts it a different way: the daily forty thousand he visualizes as a jumbo jet crashing every fifteen minutes, with the loss of everybody on board.

This is not news, it is the way things are – reality. And the Earth Summit failed, in any way I could discern, to decide to change reality. Perhaps it is unreasonable to have hoped otherwise. Perhaps it would be reasonable, instead, to accept the summit's promises that some time – after the recession, after we have sorted out Eastern Europe, when things pick up – we will get around to tackling poverty. George Bernard Shaw thought there was a place for unreason. He wrote: 'The reasonable man adapts himself to the world. The unreasonable man persists in trying to adapt the world to himself. Therefore all progress depends upon the unreasonable man.'

How do the Brazilian death squads fit into all this? Reasonably enough, I think, they act deliberately to achieve a result the world achieves on a far grander scale despite itself. They hardly merit condemnation for that. And in a steadily more crowded world, there will be all the more need for pest-control men, for the neighbourhood grim reapers. We should be giving them medals.

RELIGIOUS TOLERANCE

Mark Tully

As Indian fought Indian in religious clashes in various parts of the country, our correspondent attended the Shiah Muslim festival of Muharram in a small village in the north. He discovered that it was possible for all faiths to live together happily.

In Ayodhya, a town in the north Indian state of Uttar Pradesh, Hindus were squaring up for another round in their fight to build a temple on land occupied at present by a mosque. In the state capital, Lucknow, the police were on the streets preventing Shiah and Sunni Muslims clashing during Muharram. In the small town of Mustafabad, in the same state, a Hindu police officer sat peacefully under a tree watching a Shiah Muharram procession.

During the ten days of Muharram, Shiahs mourn the death of Husain, the Prophet's grandson. He was killed at the Battle of Karbala by the army of the Caliph, the ruler of the Muslim Empire. Shiahs believe that Husain's father should have succeeded the Prophet and that the line of succession should have passed on through his family, while Sunnis accept the Caliphate established after the Prophet's death.

Mustafabad, where the police officer witnessed such a peaceful Muharram, used to be dominated by the Naqvis, a Shiah Muslim family who were the local *taluqdars*. That meant they were less than nawabs or rulers, but more than mere landlords, but Indian democracy has taken away their lands and their power. The roof of the porch in the women's quarter of the Naqvi family house has fallen in, bats have occupied the rooms, the lawn in the middle of the courtyard is bald and brown. No Naqvis live in Mustafabad any longer but they do return in large numbers every year for Muharram.

Much else has changed in Mustafabad too, but one thing remains; the harmony between Shiahs, Sunnis and indeed Hindus. I went with the Naqvis to several Majlises, or meetings where Husain is mourned, and found a Brahmin singing Soz, that is a verse describing the tragedy of Karbala. At one Majlis a Naqvi from Pakistan, a country which claims Muslims and Hindus are two different nations, followed the Brahmin. The Pakistani recited a verse about the pathetic plight of Husain's family cut off from all supplies of water, Husain's son shot by an arrow while lying in his father's arms and Husain's own valiant last stand. His emotional recitation reduced the congregation to tears.

On the evening before the last day of Muharram a shallow trench about ten feet long was dug in the middle of the Naqvi lawn and filled with burning coal. Hindu village women in brightly coloured saris as well as Shiahs dressed in black crowded into the courtyard to see a young man carrying a copy of the Koran on a lectern with lighted candles on the front of it step onto the bed of fire. He wobbled, nearly dropped the Koran, somehow steadied himself and did a sort of hop, skip and jump to get out the other side with his feet badly blistered. Other young Shiahs followed him running across the glowing red coals, not walking as they should have done, and all blistering their feet too. I was told that the young men's faith should have preserved their feet but the organizer of the ceremony said the trouble was for the first time he had used coal because wood was so expensive now.

On the last day of Muharram, the most important gentlemen of the village came to pay their respects to the Naqvis. One of them was the stationmaster, a Sunni. When Naqvis leave from his station he still asks their permission before flagging off the train. Then we went to worship the Tazias, or models of Husain's tomb, many of them very elaborate constructions of bamboo and silver paper. Hindus also came to touch the Tazias reverently to pray for blessings. The grand old lady of the Naqvi family tied red and gold thread round my wrist although that is a Hindu custom. In India when religions are allowed to develop naturally they all borrow from each other.

The traditional procession carrying the Tazias through the streets of Mustafabad then started. Sunni drummers led Shiah men beating their chests so ferociously that their shirts were soon stained with blood and wailing, 'Yah Husain, Yah Husain' (O Husain, O Husain). Young boys flayed their bare backs with whips that had blades attached to their chain lashes, and some, in their frenzy of grief, even cut their heads open with knives. But to avoid angering the Sunnis who, along with everyone else, had turned out to watch the procession, the Shiahs dropped the tradition of cursing the Caliphs, and restricted themselves to mourning Husain.

Eventually the procession reached the square in the centre of Mustafabad where, right opposite a Sunni mosque, a Naqvi made an impassioned appeal for religious harmony to an audience of Shiahs, Sunnis and Hindus. He ended up by giving a Hindu one of the Tazias for safe keeping and announcing that the Shiahs would start next year's Muharram by collecting the Tazia from the Hindu's house.

Why did the police inspector in Mustafabad have such a relaxed Muharram compared to his colleagues in Lucknow and Ayodhya? One reason is that Mustafabad is comparatively remote and so rarely visited by politicians who use religion to win votes. Another is that in Mustafabad Muharram is celebrated by the laity without benefit of clergy. In Ayodhya Hindu priests are leading the agitation for the temple, and in Lucknow clergymen who fear their livelihood will be threatened if differences between Shiahs and Sunnis are blunted have taken over Muharram. That just goes to show that, left to themselves, Indians still respect each other's religions and enjoy each other's festivals. It is the priests and the politicians who are undermining that old Indian tradition.

SIBERIAN SHAMAN

Angus Roxburgh

The ambitious schemes, conceived in Soviet times, to exploit the mineral wealth of Siberia have had serious consequences for the native peoples and their environment.

Distances in Siberia are so enormous that every town and village feels like an island, each cut off from its neighbour, marooned in an ocean of ice and snow. It came as no surprise when I heard the people here referring to European Russia as 'the mainland'. Supplies to the city of Yakutsk are brought in from the mainland by air and during the three months of summer when the River Lena is navigable by ship. At the moment the huge container ships sit in solid ice. On the hushed streets, even the air seems to be frozen. At minus forty degrees the snow squeaks underfoot. One gets an impression of complete and utter desolation and isolation.

And yet, Siberia surely is the land of the future. As resources wear thin in other parts of the world one can imagine developers in the twenty-first century clamouring to get here, for beneath the permafrost the Siberian ground is incredibly rich. It has half of the world's coal reserves, and a quarter of its oil, gas and diamonds. There is gold and precious minerals. Timber stretching to every horizon. After centuries of regarding Siberia as at best a place for exiling convicts to, the Soviet Union woke up to its potential in the 1960s. To help them tap the resources, Leonid Brezhnev's

Kremlin devised what they called the construction project of the century, a new more northerly Trans-Siberian railway known as BAM – the Baikal–Amur Mainline. Its building was chronicled tunnel by tunnel, bridge by bridge in Soviet news bulletins. This was man conquering nature, Socialism bringing civilization to a dark continent.

Today, it is clear that the region's headlong industrial revolution is repeating most of the mistakes of the West's, but on a mammoth Siberian scale. Neryungri is a city of one hundred and twenty thousand which stands where seventeen years ago there were just forests and great rivers, reindeer and bears. It is the heart of the south Yakutian energy complex, consisting of enormous open-cast coalmines, coke factories and power stations. I watched lorries as big as two-storey houses trundling around the sides of the Neryungri coalmines, each carrying a hundred and eighty tons of coal, sending up clouds of choking dust. At Berkakit, the BAM station that serves the area, soot fell constantly out of the sky, slowly covering my notebook as I wrote in it. The sulphurous air caught at the back of my throat. Perhaps Brezhnev's developers imagined Siberia was so huge a little pollution here and there would do no harm. Or more likely they did not think about it at all. Nor did they think much about what it would all mean for the region's aboriginals. About half of the thirty-odd indigenous peoples of Siberia are in danger of extinction. Their languages and traditions are dying out. The first assault on their way of life came in the thirties, when agriculture was collectivized. The final blow was BAM, and the industrialization that came with it.

Until 1976 the south of Yakutia was populated almost entirely by Evenks, nomadic reindeer-herders with oriental features. The reindeer fled from the new industries, deep into the Siberian forest or *taiga*. Even families were split. The parents moved with the reindeer herds, while their children stayed in boarding schools in the village, speaking, of course, Russian, and forgetting their parents' tongue. I visited herders in the *taiga* and saw a way of life that I never imagined existed in Russia today. They live all year round in simple canvas tents in the snow. They used to build wigwams of poles and deerskin, but that tradition too has been lost. Inside the tent they burn wood in a little stove, but one herder told me, 'Sometimes I wake up and it's sixty degrees below zero. I wouldn't wish this life on my worst enemy.' The ground is unsuitable for agriculture, so the Evenks eat reindeer meat, and almost nothing else. They consume every part of its body, from the brain to the intestines, much of it raw. They spend most of their meagre income on vodka. Alcoholism rates here are among the highest in Russia. So are suicides. The average life span is just forty-five years.

The people here look like American Indians, and they suffer the same problems, of a nation under threat from the advance of a civilization they neither understand nor want. One night, deep in the *taiga*, I watched an Evenk shaman, a kind of witch-doctor, make spells and call up spirits from who he said were his forebears on the upper planet. He danced and beat a skin drum, jangling a collection of metal charms attached to the back of his tunic. His wife had no truck with this. She was drunk and sat cursing her husband for being a 'lousy shaman'.

One wonders if there can be any way of developing Siberia and introducing modern civilization without destroying the livelihoods of the natives and driving them to drink and suicide. The Communists got it wrong. But would anyone else have got it right?

HAIR FORCE ONE

Gavin Esler

WASHINGTON, MAY 1993

The President's efforts to get his budget plan through the House of Representatives were overshadowed by a series of gaffes made by White House staff.

Richard Nixon once maligned America by claiming to speak for its 'silent majority', but recently released tapes from 1972 show that the President was so out of touch with the views and basic decency of most Americans that when confronted with the Watergate abyss, he jumped right in. Four days after the Watergate burglars were discovered, Mr Nixon's voice, recorded by himself on tape for posterity, offered the following opinion: 'I do not think you are going to see great uproar in this country about the Republican Committee trying to bug the Democratic head-quarters.' How wrong can you get? Well, the Clinton White House has yet to reach the depths of consititutional crisis forced on America by Mr Nixon's inability to see what was truly important, but in the past week the Clinton team have looked so out of touch on apparently trivial matters that the 'silent majority' of ordinary Americans have been seething with rage.

Item one, the two-hundred-dollar haircut. Mr Clinton trav-elled to the west to campaign for his economic policy – with its calls for massive tax increases including an energy tax. If he fails to rally support for this shared suffering his policies, and perhaps his presidency, will come unglued in Congress. But while Air Force

286

One was parked on the tarmac of Los Angeles International Airport, one of the world's busiest, a Beverly Hills hairstylist named Christophe, who charges $200 a session, was summoned on board to trim Mr Clinton's troublesome grey hair. Two runways were closed for nearly an hour, delaying commuter flights while the clippers came out on what is now called Hair Force One.

White House spokesman George Stephanopoulos appeared incredulous that the news media treated this as an important story. 'I think he does have the right to choose who he wants to cut his hair,' Mr Stephanopoulos cried, buffeted by enquiries on how Mr Clinton's $200 tonsure helped his claim to be the President of the common man. Opposition politicians could not believe their luck. Republican Congressman Dan Burton said, 'He ought to be more concerned about trimming the deficit than his own hair.'

The second bizarre misjudgement led the *New York Times* to report WHITE HOUSE FOLLIES – THE GANG THAT CAN'T FIRE STRAIGHT. The people who were fired were seven long-time employees in the White House travel office who dealt with the arrangements of the Press. Like all White House reporters I should state a personal interest: the former travel staff have always been helpful and apparently professional in fixing even the most complicated of President Bush's trips to twenty-five countries and all fifty US states. The travel office boss had been there for thirty-one years serving both Democrats and Republicans. But according to White House spokeswoman Dee-Dee Myers, an outside audit found 'gross mismanagement' and 'shoddy accounting practices' sufficient to warrant a criminal investigation by the FBI. Oh, fair enough, you might think. But then it was revealed that the new travel co-ordinator would be Catherine Cornelius, a twenty-five-year-old distant cousin of President Clinton. Ms Cornelius had produced a report on the failings of the travel office, calling it 'overly pro-Press' – clearly a major sin – and suggesting, surprisingly, herself as a suitable person to take over.

Then it was learned that a Hollywood producer named Harry

Thomason, an FOB, or 'Friend of Bill', had complained to the White House that his friends were being frozen out of competing for White House travel business.

The next revelation was that World Wide Travel, a company from Little Rock, Arkansas, was to get the travel contract. The owner of World Wide, Betty Carney, had long-standing political ties to Mr Clinton and was also a former business associate of David Watkins. David Watkins is now a senior member of the White House staff and the man who fired the original travel office.

'Cronyism stinks,' thundered the *New York Times*, and suddenly the week of campaigning by the President on his economic programme turned into another public relations disaster. Grilled about Ms Cornelius's qualifications for the job, other than family ties, the White House reported that she handled travel arrangements for the Clinton election campaign last year. This was greeted with guffaws of laughter from reporters, many of whom (including the BBC) are still being billed thousands of dollars for travel with that campaign which, if memory serves, ended more than six months ago, without clear explanations of what the bills are for. The accounting seems, well, shoddy. In a quick recovery, World Wide Travel and Ms Cornelius are now out, five of the dismissed staff have been put on leave, not fired, pending a full investigation. And ah, um, yes, the first White House Press flight organized under the new, much more efficient arrangements was unfortunately delayed owing to technical problems.

Voters might forget some of this, but the $200 haircut is the stuff of which political legends are made. The serious point is the way in which the radar screens of a President who once seemed so in tune with ordinary folk seem to have drawn a blank on these issues. The White House even manipulated the FBI to suggest a major criminal investigation was taking place, to the great irritation of the Attorney General, Janet Reno, one of the few to emerge with any credit from the wreckage. None of this is irreversible, and the Clinton team's failure to recognize the basic morality of most Americans on such matters is not exactly in the Richard Nixon league. But the White House in the past month has forgotten two basic rules of survival in politics. Rule one: do not make unnecessary enemies; and rule two: few voters know whether $300 billion or $300 million is a lot of money to spend on defence, but everyone knows two hundred bucks is a lot to pay for a haircut.

SHEPARD'S FUNERAL

Fergal Keane

MABOPANE, AUGUST 1993

Black township violence claimed more than seventeen thousand lives in the years leading up to South Africa's historic election of 1994. Often, hundreds of people would be killed each month. Few were untouched by the violence.

Death came to my personal world this week. It took away Shepard Gopi in a matter of seconds. He was a gentle human being whom I knew mostly as a husky voice floating in the warm darkness of my backyard. Shepard was the boyfriend of Paulina, an equally gentle person, who has worked for the BBC for some ten years. He had a job in a large furniture store, had his own car and seemed to all of us to be a happy man, a man who looked to the future. He divided his time between my house and that of a friend in nearby Alexandra township. When I returned home last Friday night, I found Paulina sitting at the kitchen table weeping, my wife doing what she could to offer consolation.

The facts, as explained to me, were brutally simple: the previous night Shepard had gone to Alexandra to meet his friend. They went to a drinking club and talked for several hours. When Shepard came out, a group of gunmen surrounded him. One of the gang opened fire with an automatic rifle and shot Shepard ten times. On a street where the rubbish is piled in mounds, Shepard Gopi, Shepard of the laughing voice, died in a pool of his own blood. The following day his father arrived at my house, carrying his son's clothes and a few other personal belongings. This was how Paulina learned of her lover's death.

As she sat weeping at the kitchen table I felt at a loss as to what to say, how to console her. But Paulina knew, far better than I, that this was death without sense, without reason, without meaning. 'These are terrible times. Why are we killing each other?' she asked. The answer, of course, was one that most people wanted to shy away from, a truth that lurked in the darkness. It lay in recognizing that the humanity had drained out of a great many people, that for the young men who killed Shepard it was as easy to take his life away as it would have been to allow him to live.

The generation that produced Shepard's killers had grown up believing that violence should be their first resort. They had good teachers: policemen who shot first and asked questions later, secret police who tortured and murdered with impunity and distant political leaders who urged them to make their townships ungovernable, their schools into places of revolution. But while the grown-ups have decided it is time to talk, the generation they have spawned have begun to lose themselves in fields of blood. I have encountered such wild-eyed young men on the streets of the townships time and time again in the past month.

They are the people who place burning tyres around the necks of their victims, they make up the gangs that enforce school boycotts and strikes, they are the people who have of late taken to digging up the corpses of their enemies and setting them alight. This final act of desecration encapsulates the brutalization, the nihilism which is eating its way into the social fabric of those townships where violence has become endemic.

Before I lose myself in despair, let me return to the short life of Shepard, or more particularly to his funeral. With four of Paulina's friends packed into the car we set off early for the black homeland of Bophutatswana, to the township of Mabopane where the funeral was to take place. It was a bright, warm morning, and the journey north took us barely forty minutes. This was a township quite different from the ones I had spent so much time in recently. There was order and quiet, with no barricades and no prowling armoured vehicles. We followed a long line of buses and cars to the dusty graveyard, which rose out of the bush about a mile from the township. At the graveside, the family congregated under an awning which had been specially erected. Behind them were singers from one of the burial societies to which township residents pay a sum each month to secure a decent funeral for family members.

The wind came up from the east and sent clouds of dust from the open grave drifting over the mourners. We coughed and turned our faces away. Some women began to sing a lament, one of those old cries of pain that seem to rise out of the ground and fill every pocket of space. One by one we walked to the grave and took a handful of earth, which we cast down onto the coffin of poor dead Shepard. A notice handed around to mourners noted that he had been born in 1961, and shot dead thirty-two years later. As the diggers began to shovel earth down into the grave, I wept for Shepard and his family and for Paulina, but also for the burned and mutilated dead who had crowded my dreams after the last terrible month in the townships. As we walked away from the graveyard, the minister who had performed the burial service came up to me.

'Thank you for coming,' he said, 'thank you so much. You see,' he said, 'it is that love that is important.' Standing amid the streams of mourners, I held on to his words: I knew that in their simplicity, they spoke volumes about this country's amazing capacity for hope in the face of fear, brutality and so much loss.

A DOG'S LIFE

Stephen Jessel

PARIS, SEPTEMBER 1993

A new addition to the family brought considerable changes to the lifestyle of our correspondent.

We knew when we brought him home for the first time that January afternoon that life could never be quite the same again. The days would have to start earlier, bedtime would be later, social life would inevitably be affected. There were other considerations too: the French are famously tolerant in such cases, but would it be possible to take him out to cafés and restaurants? What about travelling, staying in hotels, preparing his food? Suppose it was necessary to go away at short notice? Getting a dog certainly complicates your existence. The circumstances under which the animal bounded into our life are too shaming to go into. After half a century of principled and acute opposition to dogs – not least because of their somewhat casual approach to personal hygiene – a deadly combination of an only child and sustained moral blackmail wore me down. Of the creature himself, the less said the better. He came from the equivalent of the Battersea Dogs' Home, where they were desperate to be rid of him for reasons instantly obvious to anyone setting eyes on him. His parentage can only be a matter of the most fantastic conjecture; I overheard at the Bois de Vincennes a mother say to a child: 'No, *chéri*, it isn't a monkey.'

Each day he has to be taken long distances across Paris to be

293

exercised, and not, you may be sure, by the moral blackmailer whose pet he is supposed to be. Fortunately our flat has a long corridor along which he can hurtle, in the course of a singularly witless game involving a pair of old socks. To anyone contemplating buying a dog in Paris, I would counsel deep thought lasting, say, half a second, followed by an unshakeable decision never to do so.

It would be much wiser to take up a simpler, less expensive pastime such as running a Formula One racing-car team or collecting Rembrandts. In France it costs between three and four times as much to go to the vet as it does to visit the doctor. The kennels where he stays from time to time provide rooms with cable television, mini-bars and a chocolate laid on the pillow each night – at least I assume from the price that they do. Anybody can acquire a dog. It takes a real fool to adopt a lame animal, but that is what has happened.

Our four-legged friend is more of a three-quarter-legged friend, his front right paw being deformed either from birth or by an accident. The estimated cost of the operation to put this right is more than my entire gross annual salary when I started earning a living in the mid-sixties. And yet this animal has provided a useful insight into life in Paris. The British may regard themselves as sentimental about animals, but they should look across the Channel. There are ten million dogs in France, more than the number of children aged under twelve. Paris alone is home to between two hundred thousand and a quarter of a million, requiring the attentions of squads of green-overalled motorcyclists with special vacuum cleaners to restore pavements to an acceptable state.

The French can be cruel to their animals, as can some other nations. I am haunted by the sad eyes of an old Labrador abandoned in the Bois de Boulogne, tied to a tree, unable to comprehend so cynical a betrayal. But in general the reverse is true. Pets are doted on, and this is what getting a dog has disclosed. All the rules are suspended, including social ones. Parisians never talk to strangers except in the presence of a dog, when long chats about pedigree – not a very long chat in our case

– or about health, temperament and age are freely permitted. As for the law, it is simply ignored. In one of the cheese shops in the local market the first thing the eye sees is a notice stating that, by decree of the local authority, animals are not allowed to enter. The second thing one sees is the owner's Yorkshire terrier seated at the cash desk.

There are regulations governing animals on public transport. Apart from guide dogs, they are tolerated only if small and carried in some kind of container or bag. No one takes much notice, especially on the Métro. Backed by an enchanting series of Ronald Searle cartoons and fines of up to £150, a campaign against the fouling of streets was launched a couple of years ago, but there have been only a handful of summonses and fines. Earlier fears about problems with hotels and restaurants were quite unfounded. Indeed, the red Michelin guide actually has a symbol for those establishments which will not let animals in, the assumption being that in the normal course of events they will. André, who runs the bistro round the corner from the cheese shop, also has a Yorkshire terrier, a giant photo of which decorates the bar, and went to Italy for his holidays this year. He returned outraged. They would not let his pet into the public rooms of hotels or onto the beach.

When I tell people about the quarantine regulations in Britain, where dogs do not have to be vaccinated and identifiable through a tattoo in the ear as is the case in France, they refuse to believe me. To get to know the people in the *quartier*, get a pet. It will reveal a dimension you did not suspect. Offhand waiters in cafés regularly nominated for European surliness awards will, unasked, bring bowls of water. And you realize, too, how many people in Paris are lonely. There may be something slightly absurd about the middle-aged businessman with his unsmiling face walking his primped and clipped poodle, but perhaps half the inhabitants of the capital live by themselves and for them Toutou may be much more than a toy. In a glittering but hard-hearted city, he may, quite literally, be a best friend.

NIGHTMARE IN RWANDA

Andy Kershaw

Kigali, May 1994

Up to a million people had been slaughtered when the United Nations Secretary General blamed the world community for standing by while Rwandan killed Rwandan.

Lieutenant Henry N'Sengiyumva blinked over the bridge into the River Nyabarongo, its swirling waters the colour of stewed tea. 'The killing is slowing down,' he muttered. 'A week ago we were getting nine hundred bodies a day in the river. Now it is down to about three hundred.' As he spoke, the rigid corpse of a boy of about eight, still wearing blue soccer shorts, twirled by – his mouth wide open. A woman was next, floating face-down in a floral dress. Her hands were tied behind her back, her pants pulled down around her thighs. 'Sometimes they are shot or hacked to death first,' said the lieutenant, 'but often they just tie their hands and throw them in alive.'

'They' are the Rwandan government forces and their drunken militias, the Interahamwe ('Those who fight together'), who have clubbed, shot and macheted so many Rwandans that the bodies are beginning to pollute the gigantic Lake Victoria.

In the ten minutes I spent with the Rwandan Patriotic Front (RPF) unit guarding the bridge in this recently captured territory, just ten kilometres south of the capital, Kigali, nine swollen and stinking corpses passed underneath us. What was, until early April, the second most densely populated country on Earth is now abandoned and empty. Even the cows and goats, wandering about the deserted villages, seem to be in a state of shock as they pick their way around the sad belongings dropped on the dirt road by terrified families. Those who ran fast enough are now sitting in muddy fields in neighbouring Burundi, Zaire and Tanzania.

I found some of those who did not make it in the village of Mayange, a cluster of mud-brick houses and a ransacked bar, silent but for birdsong and the drone of flies. Fifteen feet down, at the bottom of the village well, I saw and smelt a bloated human mush, six swollen heads and a tangle of limbs bristling with thousands of giddy bluebottles. And these were just the bodies on the surface. The RPF's priority is to stop the slaughter that the UN ran away from. The final push for Kigali, they say, will come when the army and its militias have been squashed in their stronghold in the west. They are fighting, they insist, not a tribal war but a campaign on behalf of all Rwandans – Tutsi and Hutu – to overthrow a genocidal and illegitimate government. Although predominantly Tutsi, there are many Hutus in the rebel ranks – three of my seven RPF guards were Hutu. And to feeding stations and makeshift hospitals in RPF safe areas like the town of Nyamata, the guerrillas bring refugees of both tribes. In the absence of aid agencies, the mutilated are treated by RPF doctors. In Nyamata, I watched one RPF medic examine a young woman with an appalling head-wound. The crown had been sliced off, like the top of a pineapple, by an Interahamwe machete. She was, unbelievably, sitting there smiling at me and I could see her brain.

Things were going well for the RPF until last week. Its troops, well disciplined and motivated, had secured most of the country. In RPF territory in the east refugees were beginning to return to work in their fields. Ordinary Rwandans are not relying on the return of the UN: the RPF is their security. But the RPF has got its own security problem. In areas long since liberated, Interahamwe infiltrators, posing as RPF fighters, are bogging down, by ambush, the rebel advance. And they have recently got their hands on land mines.

I know this because I walked over one last Tuesday. From the Nyabarongo bridge we drove our jeep a couple of miles down the dirt road towards Kigali. The track along the rim of a valley brought us up behind an RPF convoy of three trucks. It had stopped; I got out and walked up to the vehicle at the front to find out what was going on. To my horror, I found the truck on its side and the crater of a land mine in the road. One guerrilla was slightly injured. I scampered back to the jeep to await the commander's instructions. Absurd though it seems now, I carried on with a bit of work to take my mind off the danger so I was only half aware of the truck, twenty yards in front of us, when it started to reverse. Then there was a tremendous bang, a yellow flash and the truck flipped over like a beer mat. I felt the heat of the blast on my face. Wreckage and rocks poured down. A crater had opened where I had just crossed the road. From the banana plantation across the valley came the echoes of spiteful laughter, jeering and howls of 'We are the Interahamwe!'

Then came the shooting, I heard the bullets fizzing through the roadside vegetation a split second before the sound of the gunfire crossed the valley. It was a textbook ambush. I flung myself into the ditch. It is astonishing how rational and calculating we were under fire. At this previously unpenetrated level of fear, a curious composure came over us. For ten minutes or so in the ditch we worked out our chances. It was an awful choice: we could escape by retracing our steps, but the Interahamwe were, said the RPF lads, advancing behind us. Our other option was to carry on down a road that was clearly full of mines to an RPF base six miles away. Taking the jeep was out of the question, as the weight would surely trigger more explosions. So we left a £16,000 Mitsubishi on a remote Rwandan hillside and set off, on foot with full kit, across the sights of snipers and prayed there were no anti-personnel mines. There were. I saw two in the first fifty yards. I knew that our chances of getting through were slender, and it was getting dark. We passed through a couple of empty villages. I could smell the corpses in the darkened, shattered houses from two hundred yards away. As we tiptoed into the towns our RPF guards clicked off their safety catches. From the north we heard the boom of the big guns around Kigali. Every step towards safety was hell. Every one, I knew, might be my last. I walked, and waited for the bang.

Although I still feel drunk with the terror of that march, my own experience was trivial compared to the unrelenting nightmare thousands of Rwandans are living through every day. This afternoon, in government territory, hundreds more villagers will be pulled out of detention centres at random and butchered. Children are being hacked to pieces right now, and the world dithers. Every civilian I met in the country, mainly Tutsi but not all, said a total RPF victory was Rwanda's only hope. Only they, it is said, are capable of stopping the slaughter. But as long as the RPF's progress towards the killing fields is delayed by land mines, Interahamwe ambushes or UN intervention, the increasingly desperate government killers may rush to complete their final solution for Rwanda. And Lieutenant N'Sengiyumva on his grim vigil by the Nyabarongo River, will soon, I fear, lose count of the corpses altogether.

YEAR ONE

Humphrey Hawksley

Cambodians marked the first anniversary of their UN-sponsored elections in an atmosphere of corruption, danger and fear.

We were alerted by the squealing of a pig and pulled up in the dust along the main east–west highway. A group of children pounded gruel with a stump of wood. A lorry wobbled past overloaded with people swathed in chequered red and white scarves, squashed together with gun barrels poking out here and there between them. The landscape was flat. The weather incredibly hot, clear and beautiful with a haze which rose off the fields as they stretched away towards the mountains.

Mr Hem Seng was strapping his pig to the back of a bicycle. It was wriggling. But he was laughing, a cigarette hanging from his lips, as he fought the animal down and eventually handed it over to a new owner who pedalled off to the next village. The price was £15. Cash in hand. Insurance money in case he was made homeless. Hem Seng, who lived in a neat bamboo compound with countless relatives and children around him, said simply that when the UN had run Cambodia last year he was safe. But now there had been elections and the UN had gone it was dangerous again. The Khmer Rouge guerrillas were getting closer every day and if he had to flee his village he would have to have enough money to look after his family. So although he had never been directly threatened, the mystical, shadowy presence of the

Khmer Rouge which hangs over the whole of Cambodia had encompassed him. Instead of allowing his smallholding to flourish, he was selling it off bit by bit in anticipation of becoming a refugee.

And he was not overreacting. Further up the road around Battambang, the country's second city, we found forty thousand people camped along the roadside under plastic sheeting, the familiar blue of the United Nations. They had fled the fighting between the Royal Cambodian Army and the Khmer Rouge, a theatre of battle which stretched almost from the outskirts of Battambang to the guerrillas' headquarters in Pailin, a seedy gem-mining town on the Thai border. Government troops had captured Pailin, then lost it. The Khmer Rouge came to within ten miles of Battambang and then retreated. In between were the burnt villages.

We drove from the roadside refugee camps to the hospital at Battambang and began to piece together a horrific picture of the new democracy in this country. It started with a story about when government troops took Pailin. The senior officers rode into town and daubed the best houses with paint, claiming them as their own. They looted anything of worth − televisions, videos, whisky, cigarettes − and stockpiled it. They ordered in the best food from across the Thai border. At the same time, the soldiers who had actually fought the battle were given just one cupful of rice with a pinch of salt for their rations. That was it. So when the Khmer Rouge came to take the town back, the soldiers deserted their posts. The officers, of course, ran.

One wounded soldier in the hospital said he had to make his own way back because vehicles meant to be used for troops had been commandeered by the generals to ship out their television sets and other booty. Another soldier told how troops shot a colonel who told them to stand and fight. A young officer lay dying in the hospital. He had been hit in the head by a hand grenade. There was no doctor around. No intensive care. No air-conditioning. His wife had to buy her own medicines and she said that he had not been paid for months by the government.

In the brief period that the army held Pailin, the generals demanded several hundred thousand pounds to repair the road to Battambang – and got it. When the town was lost again, the government asked for the money back. The generals said simply that it had been spent. The war, fought with obsolete equipment by soldiers who do not receive salaries, costs £200,000 a day. It is almost certain that a large proportion of that goes straight into the foreign bank accounts of Cambodia's corrupt military leaders. In other words, if they ended the war, they would be doing themselves out of a fortune.

Really, there is nothing more to be said about peace prospects in Cambodia. Most of the people who are running the war on both sides do not want peace. The Khmer Rouge earn millions of pounds a year from gem mining and logging in areas under their control. That wealth would go to the national coffers if there was a peace agreement. The Khmer Rouge leaders would stand to win nothing. The latest appeal from the Cambodian government is for Western military aid to defeat the Khmer Rouge. That is unlikely to happen. Perhaps the main lesson learned from the $2 billion UN operation is that Cambodia has been shown how it should be run and has been given the best chance any corrupt, war-torn country is going to get from the international community. The finger of blame has shifted now. It is pointing towards the Cambodians themselves.

SATELLITE SHOPPING

Kevin Connolly

MOSCOW, JUNE 1994

Signs of Russia's new market economy were becoming visible: luxury cars on the streets, new office buildings under construction and the very latest economic status symbol, satellite television.

Even more than the extension of the right to enter the Eurovision Song Contest to countries not otherwise regarded as part of Europe, it is a rite of passage for the modern emerging market economy. At the end of a satellite television home shopping programme, a screenful of national flags is flashed up with instructions to buy whatever you have just been watching. A few years ago there were just a few familiar banners from France, Germany, Great Britain, Sweden and the like, but these days the screen is a riot of colour, testament to the number of new states which have taken their rightful place among the nations of the world. I have friends in Slovenia and Lithuania who greeted the acquisition of the other trappings of statehood, such as membership of the United Nations, with indifference and who yet swear they had tears in their eyes when they first made it onto the screen.

When your flag appears, together with a local telephone number and the price in your national currency, you can, I think, reasonably count yourself a citizen of the Free World, with all the benefits that implies. Those benefits, I can tell you from detailed first-hand study, include access to Willie Nelson compilation albums unavailable in the shops, a set of steak knives guaranteed never to go blunt and a small cooker shaped like a pork pie hat which bakes a loaf of bread in fifteen minutes.

The home shopping services, it must be said, offer only the dimmest of windows onto the rest of the world. Their stock in trade is the half-hour-long programme about a particular product, punctuated by a two-minute commercial break in which you see a commercial about the same product, made out of material you had already seen earlier in the show. You see the idea now. What you get in other words is the rhythm of ordinary television without the content. Not that the programmes are without entertainment value. My own personal favourite is the one about the set of knives, but in form and content they all follow the same basic pattern. They start off with someone having a problem caused by the fact that they do not own the product which is being advertised. In this particular case it is a chef who picks up a knife with a great theatrical flourish and then finds it is too blunt to pierce a tomato. In fact, not only is it too blunt to pierce the tomato, it is so blunt the tomato keeps rolling away when he tries to cut it. I know, it happens all the time. The chef then turns to the camera and delivers the look of bewildered frustration which is the authentic hallmark of this whole televisual genre. Delivered by better actors it might convey the impotent sense of rage at the breakdown of daily life, which is its purpose. The programme then gets to the point, and stays there. This is where you really get sold something. The basic pitch is always toward saving time and money. After all, runs the underlying message, get yourself stuck with a blunt vegetable knife and you could waste the whole weekend peeling that particular pile of potatoes.

I personally find the idea of so much time being saved faintly depressing, if only because it implies that everyone else has always got something much more interesting to do than whatever it is they are currently doing. This is a world where hour-long chores are endlessly being reduced to ten-minute tasks and where hours are being saved every day. Strange that, when of course the target audience already has so much time to kill that they are watching the home shopping channel. But I suppose the producers would argue that they have only got the time to watch it because they have already invested wisely in the sort of products advertised before. The saving money pitch is just as unpersuasive. In this particular programme the chef, still labouring along with that tiny rubber-bladed old knife that the rest of us use, produces out of a potato the size of a family car a tiny scrap of cookable vegetable. Once again we are treated to a close-up look of rage and frustration. But feel sorry for the actor too. This is not what you lie in bed and dream about on the night before your first day at drama school. There follows of course the offer, delivered by an unseen presenter speaking in a tone of rising astonishment which makes you think he is worried the company will be forced out of business by its own reckless generosity.

For the seasoned viewer there is always something faintly puzzling about the offer itself too. In this case, for example, you are given, yes given, a multi-purpose knife which, it is suggested, is good for everything from trimming your nails to fashioning ocean-going balsa rafts. It is one of a set of thirty-three, but hold on a second, if this knife really does do everything, what are the other thirty-two for? The programme closes of course with the same chef displaying a dazzling look of fulfilment. His knives are so good now that the vegetables in his kitchen peel themselves in the cupboard when they hear him opening the cutlery drawer. He is happy. On the home shopping channel the only problem in anyone's life is the one directly related to non-ownership of whatever is currently being offered for sale.

Russia's flag, I have to say, is not up there on the screen just yet, but the programmes with their innocent acquisitiveness are already wildly popular here. If that knife ever makes a visit to Moscow, it could find itself getting mobbed at the airport. This country has passed many milestones on the road to international economic integration in the last few years. When that flag finally appears on the screen, it will know it has truly acquired a market economy and everything that goes with it.

HELL ON EARTH

Roger Hearing

GOMA, JULY 1994

Goma was once just a little-known town in Zaire, close to the border with Rwanda. But the arrival there of hordes of refugees from the Rwandan civil war led to one of Africa's greatest disasters and Goma became synonymous with tragedy and suffering on a biblical scale.

Two men came into Goma Airport to die last week. They staggered to a grass verge, sectioned off by barbed wire from the journalists' tent, and lay down gasping. On the other side of the wire those who were keeping the world informed about the plight of more than a million refugees broke off from satellite telephone conversations to attempt to help. One man was already dead and the other one was taken off to hospital in an aid agency car. On one side of that barbed wire we were drinking water and eating French Army field rations: on the other side, people were dying in their thousands from exhaustion, hunger and dehydration.

It is really only in disasters of this scale that the divisions among humans become so cruelly obvious. The haves and the have-nots: those condemned to a lingering death and those with the good fortune to be mere observers are separated by only a few inches of wire. It is not that most journalists can remain uninvolved observers in conditions like these, but it is generally futile and mostly counter-productive to attempt to help aid workers who actually know what they are doing. So we are left trying to take comfort from the indirect benefit we bring by trying to stir consciences and open cheque-books in the outside world.

Any such benefit will probably be far too late for Andrew, a car mechanic I met as he walked vaguely past one of the bigger camps on the outskirts of Goma. He was one of the unfortunate, even amongst the blighted refugees of Rwanda. Born in Uganda and seen still as an outsider, he was not put on any food aid lists and so was left to starve in the camp. He did not want to be there anyway; he had only fled with the others because he would have been labelled as an enemy spy and hacked to death with a machete if he had not. His mattress, with a few dollars sewn inside, the last of his payment from working on a feature film about Rwanda's mountain gorillas, was stolen at the border by Zairean soldiers, so now he had nothing. And, since there was little else he could usefully do, he had determined to keep on walking. He did not expect to survive the night, and I do not suppose he did. He is probably now one of the many thousand corpses thrown into the giant pits dug by the side of the airport road, his body distinguishable only by the fact that he had no one to wrap him in a rush mat, the modicum of dignity in death even the poorest of Rwandans is afforded by his relatives.

I wanted to help Andrew but, with the increasingly volatile crowd around him, it would have started a riot. At least that is what I told myself, and by then he had melted back into the throng. I will remember his sad and dignified face for a long time. There is really no comfort here, and there are no lessons to be learned. If more than a million people leave their homes and flee into another country, even with the best planning in the world, no aid agency can swing neatly into action, no health programme can stop the spread of diseases like cholera. Many aid workers feel acute frustration at their apparent impotence in the face of such suffering. That, plus the scenes of horror that resemble some allegorical medieval wall-painting, may have produced the idea that, in some awful way, these people have brought all this on themselves.

It was primarily members of the Hutu ethnic group who committed the appalling massacres at the beginning of the war in which perhaps a million, mainly Tutsis, died. There is strong evidence that the murderers and their supporters are now here in the camps and dying with the rest of cholera and dehydration. I have heard normally rational and compassionate aid workers talk seriously about divine retribution. Apocalyptic scenes, perhaps, producing apocalyptic reasoning. But you only have to go into the camps to see that the innocent are suffering too: the children, the old, even the unborn and, as a collective punishment, this is harsh in the extreme.

I will remember the teacher, distraught to the point of hysteria because he had done all the doctors had told him, provided clean water and sugar solution drinks, and still his son lay dying, stretched out on the jagged lumps of volcanic rock this land provides instead of soil. I suppose that if a vengeful God were looking for a hell-like place to send these people, the lava fields outside Goma would fit the bill – right down to the choking black dust that blows all day into noses, eyes and throats and the active, glowering volcano that glows menacingly at night.

It is easy to speculate from this side of the barbed wire. But trying to read the faces, to scrutinize the agony on the other side, to know the feelings of those children at the orphanage who, almost calmly, acknowledge that they are the last surviving member of their families is certainly beyond me. I just hope that, deep inside, the horror of Goma is not being stored away to provide the fuel for the next conflagration.

SIEMPRE LISTO

Martin Dowle

The Colombian city of Medellín is known worldwide for its connections with the international drugs trade and the violence which accompanies it. But not everyone there is a gangster or a drug pusher. Some spend their days or nights trying to combat the violence in their midst. Among them, troops of Boy Scouts and Girl Guides who work in the city's most dangerous hospital.

It is one o'clock on a thundery Friday night in Medellín. At the city's biggest casualty hospital, a police pick-up truck screeches to a halt, with two dazed men in the back, soaked in blood. As soon as it stops, one attacks the other, and has to be pulled out by the police. Bewildered, he wanders aimlessly shouting, 'I'm dead. I am more dead than a son of a bitch. Look what you did to me while I was sleeping. You were my friend, and now I am going to kill you.' As he turns his attention to the other injured man, the driver jerks the pick-up forward to avert another fight, but it is so violent, that the drunk man still in the back falls with a loud thud as his head hits the metal sides. In one last futile gesture, the first man, losing blood by the minute, attempts a telephone call to his mother from a public phone by the door of the hospital. Eventually, the police officers and an eighteen-year-old Boy Scout called Freddy persuade the man that he will die if he does not go inside.

It is a pretty shocking scene, but the teenage scouts insist this is one of the quieter nights at the San Vicente de Paul, the hospital selected by the scouting movement for voluntary work because it turns nobody away and tries to treat everybody. I say tries; for on other nights, the numbers arriving for emergency surgery can be so high that the surgeons have to go down the waiting queue of stretchers to decide who stands a chance of survival and, by implication, who should be left to die.

The Boy Scouts and Girl Guides work here as paramedics because the hospital simply has not got the resources to pay staff to do the work. They do twelve-hour shifts, lifting the victims of the city's drug wars and political battles from taxis and cars onto stretchers, calming angry friends and relatives only too ready to turn their violence onto someone else. The hospital does not have conventional doors, but metal gates. Inside, security guards prevent all but the injured from entering, and added protection is provided by an armed soldier, proudly bearing a peace-keeping badge from the Middle East. Just as well: two days before, the hospital was invaded by militiamen dressed up as injured patients, attempting to free one of their injured associates immediately after his operation. The gates bear two bullet holes as witness to the failed rescue bid.

The young Scouts insist they would rather do this kind of work than spend their weekend nights partying. There is a sort of stoical acceptance that in a country where the government estimates sixty to seventy per cent of the patients who come into public hospitals are victims of violent attacks, this is exactly the kind of activity Lord Baden-Powell would have wanted them to do. The San Vicente hospital handles between fifty and sixty emergency cases on a normal night. When a man comes in on a stretcher with bare feet you know that he is the victim of battles between the drug factions left over after Pablo Escobar's death, or of fights caused by militias attempting to exercise political domination over the poor; knowing that a son is going to die from the gunshot wounds, a mother or relative will proudly take off his gym trainers to keep as a memento.

Generally the Scouts keep a stiff upper lip about their work, reflecting their motto 'Siempre Listo' – 'Always Prepared' – subtly distinct from its more famous British counterpart. Freddy Rivera, a well-built eighteen-year-old, who hauls the shot-up patients out of cars and taxis onto the stretchers, admits to only one night when he felt he could not cope, when two hundred and ten victims of a bomb attack in the city's football stadium were brought in. But on the night of my visit, the cruel reality of Medellín struck home more personally for the young volunteers. A fellow Scout had been among five teenage cyclists mown down by a runaway taxi driver. He was a close friend of seventeen-year-old Andres Macias, one of the Scouts on duty. The moment that he saw his friend wheeled in through the metal gates, said Andres afterwards, was the moment he understood that anyone you knew could be brought in, and it was then that he felt the desperation and impotence of trying to deal with Medellín's violence. They all gave blood to try to save their friend as the city's blood bank was so low, it would only hand out a litre of blood for every one donated. Friends desperately appealed for more donations but, as the hope ran out for their fellow Scout, the staff in the blood unit angrily refused to hand over any more litres. As he sat on a stool by the metal gate, pensively puffing a cigarette, Feddy recalled the night a six-year-old boy, accompanying his dying brother, asked why bad people killed good people. He had no answer.

It all seemed a world away from the Scout hall over the other side of the city with its huge drawing of Lord Baden-Powell and its proud memories of a visit to Medellín by his wife in 1934; its translations of *The Adventures of Mowgli* by Rudyard Kipling and its copies of *Roverismo en Accion*; and most redolent of all, its tables and chairs made out of tree trunks, the smell of the sap tantalizingly promising nights around the campfire – sadly suspended for the moment because of the propensity of fellow Colombians to steal the tents.

CELLPHONE STATUS

Matt Frei

ROME, OCTOBER 1994

As the use of mobile telephones spread like wildfire through Italy, the Speaker of the Lower House of Parliament banned their use in the chamber, and the Italian telephone company published a booklet about mobile telephone etiquette.

It happened to me last week. I was sitting in a restaurant with three Italian colleagues. The conversation was lively, but as so often, much of it was conducted on the cellphone, with each guest around the table talking on the *telefonino* as opposed to each other. I watched as Gianni dexterously held a glass of wine in one hand and a cigarette and the cellphone in the other. He chatted away in a boisterous tone, laughing for public consumption but without letting the smoke get into his eyes. Giorgio took the conspiratorial approach. He was crouched over, his face barely visible, whispering revelations into his slimline model. Antonio, I was convinced, was speaking to me. He muttered something into his hand, when I realized that he was not speaking to me at all, but to the tiniest, most elegant, wafer-thin, foldable, After Eight-sized *telefonino* that Italy has to offer. It dawned on me that I was being completely ignored. There was only one thing for it. I grabbed my cellphone, a bulky old model: the telephone equivalent of a blunderbuss. When it rings, which is very rarely, it emits a rattling noise as opposed to the subtle chortle of a nightingale that is now *de rigueur*. I was going to ring the office to check if there were any messages, an entirely futile task designed solely to save face. I dialled the number and waited. The others were engrossed in their own conversations. And then *it* happened. My cellphone emitted a loud bleating noise. The others all looked up. I looked down at my phone and to my horror discovered the letters BLOC TOT had appeared on the digital panel. This is short for *blocco totale*, total block. It could mean any number of things: the user has not paid his bill, or the telephone company has put a block on all calls – a disciplinary measure for unreliable payers. Whatever the reason, the *blocco totale* means rustication from the Elysium of *telefonino* users – social death. It also means spending a day at the Great Inquisition, the SIP telephone headquarters in the north-east of the capital just behind the Vatican.

It is a cruel twist of the Italian mobile phone system that serious problems cannot be ironed out on the phone. You have to turn up in person. The waiting room of the Great Inquisition was full of crestfallen sinners, cradling their *telefonini*. I had been given number 187 in the queue. After one hour the small piece of paper showing my number had been torn to shreds, so nervous was I about the impending interview. Those before me got up wearily as if dragging a ball and chain and disappeared into one of the five cubicles that lined the wall. The bell rang and number 186 flashed up on the screen. I would be next. My stomach muscles tightened. I could taste the bile of anxiety. I clutched my *telefonino* even tighter and braced myself for the hot coals of booth number four.

Without looking at me the man behind the desk barked, 'Your number!' I blurted out the seven digits. He typed them into a computer terminal. Out of the corner of my eye, I could see my personal details flash up on the screen. My date of birth, my address, my profession. What else did they know? I felt naked, vulnerable, crushed by the State's omniscient apparatus. The man, who was wearing a grey short-sleeved shirt with razor-sharp pleats, looked at me without even blinking. He said, 'I'm sorry, we must have made a mistake on the last digit. Everything seems

to be in order. We will lift the block on your phone immediately.'
I did not know whether to feel relieved or enraged by this game
of bureaucratic Russian roulette, which I had survived. I left the
headquarters of SIP a free but abused man. The letters BLOC TOT
had disappeared from my *telefonino*. I had regained my place in
society.

As you can tell, in Italy the cellphone is more than just a
handy means of communication: it is a fashion accessory, a status
symbol, a social symbol, a social ritual. Another example: yesterday
I saw a couple of newly-weds near the Colosseum. She was
wearing a white taffeta version of the Leaning Tower of Pisa. He
had squeezed into a shiny grey suit with a Day-Glo bow tie,
glistening in the fleshy folds of his multiple chin. Like millions of
other Italian newly-weds they had chosen a scenic spot after
church to continue shooting the wedding video. We are not
talking about a low-cost home-made film with a Hi-8 camera,
operated unsteadily by a patient uncle. We are talking about a
Cecil B. De Mille production with a director, two cameras, a
lighting assistant and a sound man, all costing thousands of pounds.
The couple assumed different poses: the passionate kiss in front of
the Colosseum, the swooning embrace, the tracking shot skipping
hand in hand up the Via Sacra, the main road of the Roman
Forum on which emperors and senators used to stroll. In the solo
section, the groom leant against the stump of a column like Byron
or Gibbon and, no doubt contemplating the Decline and Fall of
the Roman Empire, he pretended to talk into his *telefonino*.

The cellphone is an accessory in the most intimate and sacred
moments. A friend of mine once saw an Italian businessman enter
a church in Rome for morning mass. Clutching the cellphone in
his right hand the worshipper dunked his fingers, mid-conver-
sation, into the bowl of holy water and then crossed himself
without putting the phone down. SIP was proud to tell me that
Italy has two million *telefonini* users. An astonishing one in twenty-
seven of the population pays a minimum of almost £400 for a
cellphone plus the various premium charges on calls. Even more

astonishing is the fact that half of these phones are for private and not business use. Walk down the smart Via Condotti and you will see scores of fur-clad women chirping into slimline phones. The cellphone is not just for the rich. Like the Italian fur coat it is a great social equalizer. The chestnut seller in the Campo De Fiori market carries a cellphone in a smart leather pouch hanging from his soiled trousers. In politics the *telefonino* is a symbol of power. The terminal decline of the once omnipotent but now impoverished Christian Democrat Party became obvious when the party whips started confiscating members' cellphones. Last week Irene Pivetti, the severe and devoutly Catholic Speaker of the Lower House, banned all use of the cellphone in the chamber. The thirty-one-year-old politician, who is both the moral conscience and the ice maiden of Italian politics, reprimanded deputies about the constant ringing of phones in parliament. She said it 'violated parliament's dignity and hurt its standing among the public', as if the corruption scandal had not already seen to that.

Underpinning the new-found puritanism, Telecom Italia published a manual last week on etiquette for cellphone users. *The Polite Speaker*, as the booklet is called, reminds the reader not to use the *telefonino* in cinemas, churches or theatres. Restaurant diners should never put the gadget on the table for reasons of personal and public hygiene. What cellphone users really need is not advice on etiquette but psychological counselling when their phones stop working. Besek, the Israeli telecom company, has found the solution: it organizes weekly therapy groups for abused users.

LETTER FROM GROZNY

Malcolm Brabant

CHECHNYA, JANUARY 1995

The Russian assault on the breakaway republic of Chechnya resulted in the near-destruction of its capital, Grozny. After one air raid by President Yeltsin's warplanes, our correspondent penned this open letter to the Russian leader.

Dear Mr Yeltsin,

You must be a doubly happy man this week: the American Secretary of State, Warren Christopher, says that despite everything you are still the best man for the job of leading Russia towards even greater reform and democratization. The International Monetary Fund looks like bankrolling you again after your claims of poverty even though you are able casually to throw away a billion and a half dollars, or is it four times that figure, on suppressing this little local difficulty in the Caucasus. It must be very gratifying to know that international statesmen like Mr Christopher are pragmatic enough to look at the big picture and to assure you that Russian territorial integrity is paramount and that the war in Chechnya is an internal Russian affair.

But Mr Yeltsin, does your conscience bother you? Are you worried that history will judge you alongside pariahs of the late twentieth century like Saddam Hussein of Iraq and President Assad of Syria who are not averse to exterminating mercilessly pockets of resistance to discourage others from following suit, or is the operation in Chechnya out of your control and therefore not really your fault? But did you not say recently that you had taken charge of Russia's armed forces? What should we believe, Mr Yeltsin, and why should the West trust you?

On Monday your Prime Minister, Viktor Chernomyrdin, said, categorically, that there could be a ceasefire as soon as talks began with the Chechens. Your Foreign Minister, Andrei Kozyrev, even convinced Mr Christopher that the proffered olive branch was genuine. On Tuesday the members of the Chechen delegation which met Mr Chernomyrdin were sure they had a deal and a ceasefire, which could start at six o'clock last night. But all through yesterday your warplanes, rockets and heavy guns were pulverizing Grozny. Is that the action of a man who is genuinely interested in peace?

Have you ever wondered what the Third World War might be like? Well, the past few days in Grozny are the closest you will ever get to it without the nuclear bombs. I was taking shelter in a stairwell in a block of flats in the south of the city yesterday during one of the many raids carried out by your 'Top Gun' pilots. As two MiGs dived out of the heavy cloud at two hundred and fifty feet dead ahead, and banked left to drop their cluster bombs on a residential area a short distance away, two old men staggered into the doorway. One of them, who was sixty-eight years old and shaking uncontrollably, told me he was in Grozny during the Second World War when the German Luftwaffe was in action here. The Germans bombed the oil refineries, he said, but they did not bomb civilians. Boris Yeltsin was doing what Adolf Hitler did not dare to do, he said. The other man was on crutches after being injured in the opening days of the war. The Russians are trying out their new war games and weapons here, he said. We Chechens are being used as guinea-pigs.

As another jet screamed overhead, a seventy-year-old Russian woman, Tatyana Chouchena, walked outside refusing to take cover. She carried a small parcel of belongings wrapped up in brown paper and string. 'I can't take it any more,' she said, 'the planes are the worst; they're absolutely terrifying.' Tatyana Chouchena is a Russian, not a Chechen. A large percentage of the thousands of civilians still trapped in Grozny is Russian. Many Chechen women, children and elderly men have been able to find shelter with friends and family in the country or across the borders of neighbouring Russian republics. But the Russians have been unable to get out. The question they want answered, Mr Yeltsin, is why are you bombing your own people?

Can you imagine the terror of being caught in the open during a Russian air strike? There is only a second or two to react as the jet engines scream in the dive. There is a desperate dash for cover into a burned-out shop or better still, into a bunker, as the cluster bomb is fired and explodes about two hundred feet up releasing scores of orange-size bomblets which disintegrate into thousands of small pieces that cut through flesh like a knife. Can you imagine the certain feeling that you are going to die as the percussion waves ride over you and the flashes and blasts come ever closer? Well I can tell you, your mouth gets pretty dry when they stop twenty metres away and you suddenly discover that six people around you have been killed.

What, Mr Yeltsin, will you say to the mothers of hundreds of young, frightened, inexperienced conscripts who were incinerated in their tanks after officers from your once awesome Red Army ignored history and the military handbooks by sending them into confined spaces where ambushes are so easy to carry out? As the dogs tear at their bodies in this human abattoir, will you say that they died to defend their country? Or did they die, as soldiers so often do in war, because of politicians' vanity or insanity?

Whatever the answers, Mr Yeltsin, there is not too much to worry about. The West still thinks that you are the best man for the job.

Yours sincerely,

A cynical, war-weary correspondent. And is it any wonder?

BATTLING MANDELAS

Peter Burdin

JOHANNESBURG, MARCH 1995

The spectacular decline in the friendship between the South African President, Nelson Mandela, and his estranged wife, Winnie, looked likely to end in her departure from his government and in their divorce.

It should have been one of the great love stories of the century. The freedom fighter jailed for twenty-seven years and the wife who waited, who took up the struggle on his behalf, who became known as the Mother of the Nation and was beside him when he was released to resume his battle for justice. The fact that it all went wrong is not simply a personal tragedy for two people or a blow for those who like a little romance with their politics, it is the personification of a national wound that has left President Nelson Mandela a sad and lonely leader, and that exposes a dangerous rift in South African politics that could still bring about his government's downfall.

Nelson Mandela is still fond of speaking about how he first met Winnie. She was waiting at a bus stop and as he was driving past he was struck by her beauty. He relates how at that moment he wanted her as his wife. He invited her to lunch and proposed to her. He can still describe how he was attracted by her spirit, her passion, her youth, her courage and wilfulness. Winnie's youth has now gone, but over the years the other qualities Mandela noted have been honed to create a formidable woman. Her spirit and courage have made her the idol of the townships with a degree of popular support that makes many within Mandela's ANC fearful of acting against her. Her wilfulness: refusing to apologize for a speech attacking the government, and dismissing corruption charges against her as a vendetta, now presents an almost daily challenge to her estranged husband's authority.

Nelson Mandela's expressed desire as South Africa's first democratically elected president has been to reconcile black and white and bring a new morality to government after years of dirty tricks and government inspired violence during the old regime. Sometimes he must feel his estranged wife, although a deputy minister in his government, is following an opposite agenda. She has attacked the government for spending too much time appeasing white fears and not enough meeting black needs. And as for a 'new morality', hardly a week goes by without new allegations of corruption coming to light. The local Press are having a field-day and make much of her lavish lifestyle, living in a mansion, driving a Mercedes and consorting with a convicted criminal who has bought her a house in Cape Town.

And yet in Winnie Mandela's mind this is all a vendetta, got up by those who oppose her. There is no doubt that during the years of apartheid she came under terrible personal and political victimization as the wife of the regime's leading enemy. She was exiled to a place without toilets or running water, her home was burned and she was banned from any contact with family or friends. She herself once admitted she had been brutalized by her experiences, but today it often appears as though she believes she is still living in those apartheid days. Any criticism of her actions is not because her actions were wrong but because the state is victimizing her. It is a view of the world that fits uneasily with her responsibilities as a member of the government.

There are growing voices in the ANC advising President Mandela to sack her, but the old man resists. His patience with her has run out but it is clear that she is still the love of his life. When she won a seat on the ANC executive last year, it was touching to see the joy in his face. He embraced her warmly and as she left the stage his eyes followed her all the way back to her seat. He feels guilty about all the years in prison when he could not be a husband or a father, and the way his absence thrust her into a leadership role as Mother of the Nation. He has never publicly criticized her and stood by her in court each day when she was convicted of kidnapping, always believing her innocent. The marriage finally broke up not over political differences or corruption allegations, but only in personal acrimony after the *Sunday Times* published a letter she had written to a young lover. Many say the President cannot find it in his heart to dismiss a woman he feels he has punished enough, but there is another reason and that is political fear. The President is aware of her grass-roots support; her followers in the impoverished townships have already threatened mass action if she is sacked.

A trip to the shacks of the Winnie Mandela squatter camp in the East Rand reveals what a potent political powerbase she commands. While there is little tangible evidence of how the government is building houses or bringing water or electricity to areas like this, there is nothing but praise for Winnie Mandela and her willingness to assist the poorest families. One squatter, Peter Thebone, says only Winnie fights for black people. 'She has been a mother to us and it will remain like that for ever. Even if she is guilty,' he added, 'we will remain loyal to her.' And that is a deep loyalty that President Mandela ignores at his peril.

As he sits all alone in his presidential residence, Nelson Mandela does reflect on those twenty-seven years in gaol, and regrets that during those lost years he never saw his children growing up and was never able to enjoy a normal married life. They are sad thoughts to entertain at the end of one's life. As he listens to his favourite music, Handel's *Messiah*, and ponders how to deal with a personal tragedy that has now become his greatest political headache, he may well hark back to the wise counsel proffered by Winnie's father on his wedding day. He told Winnie she was marrying a man who is already married to the struggle, and ended his speech with the words, 'If your man is a wizard, you must be a witch.' Almost forty years on and Winnie is still bewitching the wizard in a battle of wits which has severe repercussions for the stability of South Africa.

FORGOTTEN PHOTOGRAPHER

Diana Goodman

MOSCOW, MAY 1995

As Russia celebrated the fiftieth anniversary of the end of the war in Europe, some of the veterans, who were awarded special VE Day medals, were bitter about the treatment they normally received from the State.

One of the most famous images from the Second World War is a photograph taken on top of the Reichstag in Berlin early on the morning of 2 May 1945. The Russians were on the verge of taking the city. And a young military photographer, Yevgeny Khaldei, was there to capture the moment for history. His picture shows two soldiers balancing precariously as they struggle to raise the Soviet flag. In the background, smoke rises from the ruins of what was Hitler's capital.

Yevgeny Khaldei is an elderly man now and his eyesight is fading. He has to hold his photographs close to his face to see the details. But as he pointed out the landmarks in the picture taken from the Reichstag, he could still recall the excitement of that spring morning in Berlin. Before leaving Moscow he had had the presence of mind to get hold of three old tablecloths and turn them into red Soviet flags. One was raised on the advance into Berlin, another went up over the Brandenburg Gate and the third was reserved for the Reichstag. Khaldei recalls that when he got there after a sleepless night there was still heavy fighting nearby.

But he commandeered two soldiers and took them to the roof. The famous dome of the Reichstag was burning so it was impossible to get the flag right on top, but he found a spot on a ledge at the edge of the building and the soldiers lifted the flag aloft.

I told Mr Khaldei that quite recently a group of German photographers had tried to get to the same spot to reproduce the picture but they found it was too dangerous. He said that in 1945 the exhilaration of the moment had carried him through. He had spent the whole war waiting to get to Berlin. He had followed the Red Army right across Europe and had seen the fall of six capital cities but he says that, like many Russians, he desperately wanted to fulfil Stalin's order – reach the capital of the Third Reich and hoist the banner of victory.

Yevgeny Khaldei lost most of his family during the war. His father and his three sisters lived in the Ukraine. He says they were amongst seventy-five thousand people who were thrown into mine shafts by the Germans while they were still alive and left to die. The old photographer now lives alone in a small flat in a bleak apartment building in the suburbs of Moscow. His bedroom is also his workroom. It is filled with files and negatives and, of course, reproductions of his best-known photographs. They have been used in books, on postcards, posters, even stamps but, despite the fame of his work, he has received no royalties. He lives instead on the equivalent of £13 a month. His children do their best to help out but they have not got much money either. Mr Khaldei says he lives a primitive life alone in his flat, mostly eating sausage which is all he can afford. His wife died nine years ago. She gazes out from a beautiful old print, her hair shining from the glow of photographic lamps. Despite his work during the war and after-wards, Yevgeny Khaldei was sacked by the Tass news agency in 1947. He believes it was because he had got on too well with Western photographers he met during the Nuremberg trials. And because he was Jewish.

The implications of that became terrifyingly clear when he

was only one year old. His mother was shot dead during an anti-Jewish pogrom in the Ukraine in 1918. Baby Yevgeny was in his mother's arms. The bullet went through her body and into his but somehow he survived. Seventy-seven years later he is still concerned about the dangers of being a Jew. Fascism and anti-Semitism are thriving in the new Russia, he says. 'It's an uncomfortable place to be.'

Like many people of his age, he mourns the passing of the Soviet Union, the country for which he risked his life. Yevgeny Khaldei was present on Moscow's Red Square when the start of the war with Germany was announced. He took a famous photograph of people listening to the news on the radio. He was also there to witness the grand parade when the victorious Soviet soldiers came home. But he will not be going to Red Square for the fiftieth anniversary celebration. It is an operetta, he says, designed to make Mr Yeltsin look good. Instead Mr Khaldei will celebrate victory day alone at home in his small room. He will collect up a pile of photographs of his parents, his friends, colleagues who were killed in the war and, of course, his wife. He will lay them all out in front of him. Then he will drink some vodka and for a few hours he will escape – into the past.

Mr Khaldei is immensely sceptical about the way veterans are being hailed as heroes during the victory day celebrations. Normally it is impossible for veterans to get any extra help, he says, and he believes the authorities will be happiest when they have all died off. It is easy to understand why he does not want to bother with the pomp and noise of the official celebrations and why he would prefer to spend the day alone, with his photographs and his memories.

LIST OF
CONTRIBUTORS

327